# POP SONG PIRACY

# POP SONG PIRACY

## Disobedient Music Distribution since 1929

**BARRY KERNFELD**

THE UNIVERSITY OF CHICAGO PRESS : CHICAGO AND LONDON

**BARRY KERNFELD** is on the staff of the Historical Collections and Labor Archives in the Special Collections Library of the Pennsylvania State University. He is the author of *The Story of Fake Books: Bootlegging Songs to Musicians* and *What to Listen for in Jazz*, and he is the editor of *The Grove Dictionary of Jazz*.

The University of Chicago Press, Chicago 60637
The University of Chicago Press, Ltd., London
© 2011 by The University of Chicago
All rights reserved. Published 2011
Printed in the United States of America

20  19  18  17  16  15  14  13  12  11     1  2  3  4  5

ISBN-13: 978-0-226-43182-6 (cloth)
ISBN-10: 0-226-43182-7 (cloth)
ISBN-13: 978-0-226-43183-3 (paper)
ISBN-10: 0-226-43183-5 (paper)

Library of Congress Cataloging-in-Publication Data

Kernfeld, Barry Dean, 1950–
   Pop song piracy : disobedient music distribution since 1929 / Barry Kernfeld.
      p.   cm.
   Includes bibliographical references and index.
   ISBN-13: 978-0-226-43182-6 (cloth: alk. paper)
   ISBN-10: 0-226-43182-7 (cloth: alk. paper)
   ISBN-13: 978-0-226-43183-3 (pbk.: alk. paper)
   ISBN-10: 0-226-43183-5 (pbk.: alk. paper)
1. Music trade—Corrupt practices—United States—History—20th century.
2. Popular music—Writing and publishing—Corrupt practices—United
States—History—20th century. 3. Sound recording industry—Corrupt
practices—United States—History. 4. Sound recordings—Pirated editions—
United States—History. 5. Copyright—Music—United States—History—
20th century. 6. Piracy (Copyright)—United States—History—20th century.
I. Title.
   ML3790.K448 2011
   364.16'62—dc22

                                                          2010045370

♾ The paper used in this publication meets the minimum requirements of the American National Standard for Information Sciences—Permanence of Paper for Printed Library Materials, ANSI z39.48-1992.

*This will prove a brave kingdom to me, where I shall have my music for nothing.*

Stephano, the drunken butler

Shakespeare, *The Tempest*, act 3, scene 2, lines 153–54

# CONTENTS

# FIGURES

*Illustrations of early, now forgotten, bootleg and authorized song products are essential to an understanding of this book. These images appear without permission. Their publication in the present context constitutes scholarly fair use.*

# ACKNOWLEDGMENTS

I started this project more than a decade ago, but at one point abandoned it for about four years. The defining moment—though it was quite some time before I was able to admit this to myself—was when William Warner invited me to speak on jazz fake books at the conference "Copyright and the Networked Computer" in Washington, D.C., in 2003. It was an incredibly stimulating conference, but I realized that I was intellectually out of my depth. Following that experience, I published what was effectively a case study from this project, as *The Story of Fake Books: Bootlegging Songs to Musicians*, and then put the rest away, thinking I would never return to it.

In 2008 Howard Becker and I stumbled onto each other. He asked to quote from *The Story of Fake Books*. I asked about his project and ended up commenting on it. He liked my comments. He said, "If I can ever return the favor . . . ," and I replied, "Well, actually . . ." I sent him my abandoned essay on bootlegging song sheets in the 1930s. Under his guidance, the present book emerged. Howard helped me to develop a conceptual framework and relentlessly nudged me toward thinking about the big picture, always with his great sense of humor pushing me along. "You'll revise it this way, because of course I'm right." And he was right, every time. The result is something much more ambitious than I had originally intended: an attempt at the first history of pop song piracy. Thank you, Howie.

My thanks are also due to Bill Brockman, Paterno Family Librarian at the Pennsylvania State University, for the afternoon of database searching and discovery that opened the door into the song-sheet bootlegging story. Arthur H. Zimmerman, a sheet music dealer, spent considerable time digging miscellaneous bootleg and legitimate song-lyric publications out of his collection. Rosemary Cullen at the John Hay Library, Brown University, helped me to sort out details of the appearance of authorized song-sheet magazines in the mid-1930s. A number of archivists took time to guide me toward court records in files residing at branches of the National Archives and Records Administration: Greg Plunges in New York City, Bill Doty and Randy Thompson in Laguna Niguel, California, Scott Forsythe in Chicago, and Robert Ellis in

Washington, D.C. Scott was especially enthusiastic about the project. Seven years ago, foolishly thinking that I was nearly in a position to finish this book, I promised him a copy. Finally I can honor that promise.

In an era of frenetically paced and impossibly overloaded academic publishing, my editors Doug Mitchell and Tim McGovern have been gems, seeing this book through proposal, review, and production at the University of Chicago Press, and dealing with my sometimes complex questions. Thanks, Doug and Tim, for your support.

Another book, and another dedication to my wife Sally and our sons Paul and Eric: "There Is No Greater Love"; "Embraceable You"; "Nice Work If You Can Get It"; "All the Things You Are"; "If I Were a Bell"; "Till There Was You"; and so on, and so forth. My life is a pop song.

# INTRODUCTION

Early in April 1930, in the course of several days of raids on individuals peddling bootleg song sheets on Broadway between Forty-Second and Forty-Third Street, Manhattan traffic patrolman Broger made the first arrest: a Brooklyn woman, Mrs. Sarah Yagoda, age eighty. She was brought before Magistrate Louis B. Brodsky in West Side Court by a representative of the Music Publishers Protective Association, Paul L. Fischoff, and an assistant district attorney named Weider. Said Fischoff, "Your Honor, it is not this woman whom we seek. It is the racketeer making a fortune by having copyrighted song hits printed and sold for 5¢ a copy." Fischoff explained that the song sheet held lyrics to one hundred song hits, and he claimed that songwriters and publishers were sustaining losses of several million dollars. In reporting this story, the entertainment trade paper *Variety* mentioned that the New York State Legislature had just passed a bill making it a misdemeanor to sell a copyrighted song without the consent of the owner, and Yagoda had been arrested on this charge. Fischoff and Weider interrogated her in an effort to identify the source of the "bootleg songs." They then dropped the charge, and Fischoff set off to try to find the plant where these sheets had been printed. As later events showed, he failed.[1]

This was an early shot fired by the music industry in a pop song bootlegging battle that began at some point in 1929 and continued into the early 1940s. More often than not these shots missed their mark. A decade after Mrs. Yagoda was arrested, nothing much had changed in Times Square, as the *New York Times* noted in its issue of January 5, 1939: "On any afternoon or evening, if the magistrate sitting in West Side Court is known to be lenient, the area north of Forty-second Street is a beehive for the street sale of song sheets, watches, razor blades, French pictures, flowers, neckties, toys, radio gadgets, suspenders, jewelry and wearing apparel."[2]

For that matter, has the scene in Times Square changed much another seventy years later? Vehicles are now banned in favor of pedestrians, and street vendors are everywhere. Watches, neckties, jewelry, clothes, handbags, and diverse other items, many of questionable origin, are sitting out for sale. As for music, songs sheets are long gone, but the vendors offer cheap cell phones and other modern-day equivalents to the "radio gadgets," and if at the close of the first decade of the twenty-first century pirated compact discs have disappeared from the folding tables, this is only because so many people—the vendors, their prospective buyers, and the office workers above—are using an iPod, a computer, a cell phone, or some other digital device to listen to personalized compilations of electronically shared songs, pirated or not.

The thread that ties these events together runs far deeper than this particular, if highly visible set of connections, then and now. For the past eighty years, in America, and then in Europe, and then worldwide, there has been a succession of disputes over the unauthorized mass distribution of popular songs, via song sheets, fake books, music photocopying, pirate radio, phonograph record piracy, tape piracy, album bootlegging, compact-disc piracy, and song sharing. Some of these disputes are over, having given way to assimilation or obsolescence. Some of these disputes continue today, with no resolution in sight. No doubt new disputes will emerge. As long as clever individuals continue to come up with attractive new methods of delivering songs to the general public, the disputes will seemingly continue indefinitely, in their ever-changing guises.

Underpinning these ever-changing guises is a generic situation that occurs over and over again. Famous musicians and powerful music corporations want to maintain a monopoly over the songs they control and to prevent others from distributing their songs without paying for the privilege. Other people want to use these songs without paying for them and without having to accept the package they come in, that is, to use them in ways the monopolists did not foresee or take into account. A struggle then follows between the two parties over obedience and disobedience. This struggle takes different forms, but in the end has the same result. The monopolists give in.

The specific form of the monopoly and the struggle varies in a lot of ways, especially as the technology for reproduction changes, the nature of what people want and will pay for changes, the kind of people involved in the unauthorized copying changes, and the legal framework supporting the monopolists changes. But the underlying pattern stays the same. It goes something like this:

**A repeated pattern.** Within an existing distribution system—seemingly, any such system—the creators or producers of a cultural product, or the leaders of distribution systems to whom those creators or producers assign ownership of that product (as is normally the case), attempt to provide full protection for the product. But inevitably the attempt fails. A loophole develops as someone discovers the new method of dissemination and starts to distribute the goods without paying the people who think that they are the "owners." If the existing system of distribution is exceptionally powerful, the loophole may close before fighting begins. (This has happened, for example, in commercial radio, where a station is so utterly dependent upon advertising income that its manager quickly quashes, say, a disobedient disk jockey who broadcasts just music and skips the ads.)[3] Otherwise, once the owners perceive that the value of the escaping product is sufficient to merit attempts at containment, they fight. When the fighting involves conventional business rivals, the fields of battle are in the realms of patents and copyright, organized boycotts, antitrust actions, and so forth. This is business as usual. But when the challenge comes from outside of normal business circles, the owners shout "bootlegging!" or "racket!" or "piracy!" They claim huge financial losses, based upon projections of the number of unauthorized objects being distributed and the assertion that each projected sale of an unauthorized object equals a lost sale of an authorized object. They call in the FBI and compose indignant and moralistic press releases concerning violations of the rights of songwriters, regardless of the actual contractual arrangements that might exist between songwriters and song owners regarding artistic control and financial remuneration. They file civil suits against the unauthorized participants or against legitimate participants who assist the illegitimate ones, and they lobby for modifications of transportation and trade agreements, to suppress interstate and international transportation of unauthorized goods. When these legal and legislative paths fail, they persuade the government to prosecute the unauthorized challengers as criminals.

The pattern plays itself out in one of two ways, assimilation or obsolescence. In cases of assimilation, eventually the monopolists give in and start doing what the bootleggers were doing: the song owners create a legitimate form of the new mode of distribution (legitimate at least in the sense that no one wants to pursue further prosecutions). Because the monopolists routinely control a formal distribution network that is much more stable and comprehensive than the sorts of improvised networks that might be put together by pirates and bootleggers, assimilation often puts the pirates and bootleggers out of business. It all reverts to authorized business as usual.

An alternative result is obsolescence. Sometimes a new, different, and attractive song product comes along to replace the contested product, and the original dispute quickly evaporates. Sometimes there are irreconcilable differences, and the fighting drags on. This is particularly true of song distribution systems that operate on an international basis, in which case a distributor of cultural goods from one nation might deliver his product to audiences in another nation without the approval of the "owners" operating in the country that lies at the receiving end of this distribution chain. In cases like these, not only distributors, but governments come to be at odds with one another, in their differing approaches to legislation on and interpretations of the ownership of cultural goods, and perhaps also simply in their desire to support the sale of homegrown cultural goods, with practical home-based economic considerations taking precedence over international generosity.

Either way, whether quickly or slowly, if the process of assimilation has not kicked in, then the process of obsolescence will eventually take over. Inevitably a new song product will replace the existing one. If by chance that new song product is distributed in an unauthorized manner, then fighting transfers to a new battlefield, and the pattern starts all over again. In this sense, song-sheet bootlegging, fake books, music photocopying, pirate radio, disk and tape piracy, and song sharing are all the same story, an unending and ever-mutating fight over the control of songs.

**Equivalency and transformational use.** From another vantage point, the intersection of songs, distribution, and disobedience may be parsed into two categories: *equivalency,* whereby someone is just out to make a fast buck by copying a song product without paying the owners; and *transformational use,* whereby some creative person, thinking outside of the corporate box and also operating outside of that box, comes up with a song product that in some respect offers a new way to appreciate music. Equivalency is merely illegal copying, a venal practice. Transformational use involves imagination in one or more areas of our complex relationships to songs. A creative song product might facilitate musical technology, portability, fidelity, performance, enjoyment, or understanding. If such an invention arises outside of authorized channels, it becomes just as much of a threat to control of the marketplace as any instance of merely illegal copying.

A clear-cut example of an equivalent product would be a counterfeit compact disc. A CD counterfeiter copies not only the digital signal encoded on that disc, but the packaging as well. The counterfeiter reproduces the original artwork, photographs, and text as closely as possible, shrink-wraps the jewel-box case, and then sells the item on the street or (more boldly) distributes it to legitimate retail stores. A counterfeit CD presumably costs considerably less than its authorized equivalent, the illicit manufacturer not having to pay as much in production costs and normally not paying anything to song-licensing agencies. So the album may be sold at a lower price than its authorized equivalent.

Clear-cut examples of transformational products would be song sheets (compilations of lyrics without notated music) and fake books (compilations of songs in a concise musical notation). In a new era of phonograph records, movie musicals, and AM radio, bootleg song sheets gave general listeners easy access to current popular songs without their having to trawl through piles of authorized sheet music. In a new era of cocktail lounges as social activity, bootleg fake books gave professional nightclub musicians easy access to requested popular songs, again without their having to trawl through piles of authorized sheet music.

What is most interesting in the give and take between equivalency and transformational use is that song owners would have us believe—and indeed have time and again successfully persuaded the general public, and legislative and judicial authorities—that not just blatant counterfeiting, but any and all forms of song bootlegging and song piracy exemplify equivalency. Whatever the circumstances, so their argument goes, if the song in question is the same, authorized and unauthorized, then the product in question is the same, authorized and unauthorized. If they own a song, they own any type of product that captures or conveys some aspect of that song. This is the central principle underlying copyright. Transformational use has no place in this model.

But it's not all just the same. Bootleg song sheets provided a convenient new product for general audiences in the 1930s. Fake books provided a convenient new product for musicians from the 1950s onward. From 1958 in Scandinavia, and from 1964 in the British Isles, shipboard disk jockeys broadcast pop songs onshore to offer northern European listeners an alternative to a nationalized radio fare consisting mainly of classical music, news, drama, and religious programming, with only small doses of pop songs. From the late 1960s onward, mass-produced, illegal dance mixes allowed party-givers to play compilations of favorite popular songs from a single recorded object rather than from a stack of disks or tapes; entrepreneurial fans began to sneak tape recorders into rock concerts and then to circulate the results; and choirmasters and band directors discovered that they could make customized arrangements of songs and photocopy the parts for their singers and instrumentalists. In our own day, countless songs reside in the electronic ether, divorced from their original packaging, wrested from their owners' control, and utilized in any imaginable way. Songs sheets, fake books, music photocopying, album bootlegging, and song sharing—all of these objects and activities involve transformational uses that separate these five intersections of songs, distribution, and disobedience from the more mundane acts of manufacturing and distributing an illegal copy of a legitimate disk or tape.

What happens, then, in these transformational instances, is that an unauthorized song product might come into being because someone imagines a usage that the monopolists refuse to endorse. The monopolists refuse because the new song product threatens to undercut existing price systems and profit margins (the normal situation), or because it threatens to wrest full control from the song owners (also the normal situation), or because it threatens to undercut a benevolent, government-controlled, monopolistic cultural system (exceptionally, in the case of pirate radio in northern Europe, where the issue was not ownership of popular songs, but control of their dissemination, or rather, a refusal to disseminate).

The key to an understanding of the significance of transformational use resides in the idea of nonequivalency and its problematic relationship to copyright. Ideas for transformational use blossom constantly in the world of song, but normally these proposals for transformations of existing song products are generated through authorized channels, and the owners maintain control. This is business as usual: competing formats, competing media, challenges to patents, challenges to market share. When the idea emerges outside of authorized channels, the fighting begins, as outlined above, and owners initiate attempts at suppressing the unauthorized product via an assortment of processes. One of these is to shout "Equivalency!" Copyright law provides a potentially useful tool in this battle, because it is a statutory concept constructed in such a way as to render irrelevant any distinctions between, on the one hand, an illegally copied song product created unambiguously for the sake of making money and cutting out the owners (as per mass-distributed disk and tape piracy) and, on the other, an unauthorized transformational song product that has enabled new uses (as per song sheets, fake books, and so forth). Instead, copyright addresses a different and essentially opposing concern: regardless of its nature, does a given unauthorized product in some sense reproduce a song, or some recognizable fragment of a song, controlled by an authorized owner? Time and again, the judicial and legislative answers are, yes, it does.

Despite the potential usefulness of copyright law, it is largely ineffective. Prosecution through copyright infringement repeatedly fails to suppress unauthorized distribution, not just because the equivalent unauthorized song product costs less, but because the nonequivalent, transformational, unauthorized song product enables desirable new uses. Even if, time and again, copyright wins victories in legislatures and the courts, time and again disobedient acts continue, because unauthorized distributors and the general public understand that the alleged equivalency among all song products is false. For that matter, song owners sometimes reveal in statements to the press that they too have glimpses into the potent attraction of a transformational use. But even with such understandings, song owners persistently downplay the notion of nonequivalency, or deny it, or ignore it altogether. And why not? They are just protecting their own financial interests as best as they can.

That does not matter. The cat is out of the bag. Once unauthorized distributors and their public come to recognize that a given new but illicit song product facilitates a transformational use, and that this usage is too attractive to ignore, the newly desirable song product becomes too vigorous to be suppressed. The public, having been denied through authorized channels the songs that they want in the format that they want them, then begins to operate though unauthorized channels, while largely ignoring an accompanying rhetoric of criminality, piracy, and amorality that pours forth from the song owners. New ways of enjoying songs are more important than obedience. Transformational use usually trumps copyright, and musical desire normally trumps moral argument.

The concept that I am introducing here has nothing to do with legal and intellectual discussions of "transformative use" in terms of authorship and creativity, the situation in which the accusation "You stole my song" becomes instead "No, I reconceptualized your song." I address "transformational use" as a functional rather than a creative process. My use of this term concerns distribution systems, namely, a history of a succession of new modes of delivery in which the "same" song (with authorship unquestioned) is formatted in new ways that challenge existing systems. The transformational quality of these systems concerns changing representation—piano and vocal score, shorthand index card, fake book, editable photocopy, phonograph disk, audiotape, compact disc, MP3 file—not variation, satire, parody, sampling, mash-ups, or any other process of musical modification for which ownership might be contested by the "original author" or agents thereof. In this respect, functional, distributive "transformational use" has not been a significant consideration in copyright battles, and it has been fairly well disregarded in the copyright literature cited immediately below.[4] (Exceptionally, and without using this term, an appeals court judge included an eloquent acknowledgment of the functional transformation of distribution systems, musical and otherwise, in the Grokster case; see chapter 10.)

**Disobedience and criminality.** In these situations, when song owners are being obdurate and nonowners work around them, I think that the appropriate behavioral term would be "disobedience," not criminality—that is to say, disobedience in the sense of distributing or acquiring cultural goods without permission. The type of disobedience that recurs at this intersection with songs and distribution might be characterized as "public disobedience" rather than "civil disobedience," to distinguish it from the organized political actions and moral virtue that the latter term connotes. After all, the disobedient pursuit of songs touches upon confrontations with injustice only insofar as its most sophisticated practitioners construct persuasive arguments for fair use and broader notions of the public domain, and against corporate abuses of copyright. Most people certainly don't care about these abstract issues. Most people distribute songs illegally simply because they want to make money, or because they are inspired by the vision of a transformational use, or for both reasons together. Most people procure songs illegally because they want to save money, or because they subscribe to the vision of a transformational use, or for both reasons together.[5]

If being disobedient for the sake of songs stands in stark contrast to life-threatening disobedient acts performed in the course of civil rights, civil liberties, and national independence movements, there nonetheless are real dangers: hefty fines and even, for some participants, jail terms. This is not just a matter of some sleazy guy caught selling piles of counterfeit tapes. There is also, for example, Britt Wadner, who spent months in Stockholm jails for her defiant act of repeatedly broadcasting popular songs into Sweden from an offshore ship. The unauthorized distribution of songs seems to inspire people to take substantial risks, whether as manufacturers, distributors, or consumers.

In many of these disobedient situations, the distinction between equivalency and transformational use is not clear-cut. Most interestingly, practices that may seem on superficial examination to involve merely venal copying often prove on closer examination to involve some transformational twist that to some extent justifies the action. If in 1980 someone manufactures and distributes eight-track cartridge copies of the soundtrack to *Saturday Night Fever*, that is just a straightforward, unambiguous rip-off of a recently copyrighted object, but if someone else selects one favorite track each from the Bee Gees, Barry White, Donna Summer, and a dozen other disco kings and queens, and then manufactures and distributes this compilation of tracks as a customized eight-track disco-party dance mix, is that a transformational use? Yes, surely it is. In an instance such as this, intentions and possibilities intertwine in such a way that equivalency melds into transformational use, and criminality into disobedience.

Whatever term may apply, whether disobedience or criminality or some combination thereof, the unauthorized distribution of songs always carries the connotation of someone having done something bad. Probably nothing can top the irony of the situation in the mid-1970s, when Dean Burtch of the Music Publishers Association characterized practitioners of unauthorized music photocopying as "amoral violators," just after Dennis Fitzpatrick of F.E.L. Publications had filed a suit for unauthorized music photocopying against the Catholic Archdiocese of Chicago.

Years later, surveying song sharing, film downloading, and the current state of the entertainment industry in May 2003, Lev Grossman asked a question about the moral characterization of participants in unauthorized distribution networks: "does good or bad even matter?" Grossman provided this answer: "technology has a way of sweeping aside questions of what is right or wrong and replacing them with the reality of what is possible."[6]

When I pose this same question from the historical perspective of eighty years of disputes at the intersection of songs, distribution, and disobedience, I find that technology is usually crucial, but not always so. Exceptions occur in the realm of fake books, where technological elements involve nothing more recent than the printing press, the photostatic process, scissors, and Scotch tape. Exceptions also occur in the realm of European pirate broadcasting, where technological innovation means nothing more than figuring out how best to mount an antenna on a ship's deck to withstand a force-nine gale in the English Channel or the North Sea. And so, to summarize the situation concerning musical disobedience and criminality, I would borrow Grossman's statement, tipping my hat to his insight, but tweaking it a little bit: *transformational uses* "have a way of sweeping aside questions of what is right or wrong and replacing them with the reality of what is possible."

**Copyright.** The focus of this book is the wholesale unauthorized distribution of songs, that is, activities at the intersection of songs, distribution, and disobedience. I might instead define that focus as activities at the intersection of songs, distribution, disobedience, *and copyright*. Certainly copyright is a central concern. Exceptionally, and once again in disputes over broadcasting in northern Europe, the principal area of contention in pirate radio is the regulation and control of the airwaves, rather than the control of songs via powers inherent in copyright. Everywhere else, though, in a succession of diverse battles over the control and dissemination of printed songs and recorded songs, copyright is a necessary condition for bootlegging and piracy. These battles take place only because of a circumstance that recurs under a wide variety of conditions: copyright restrains the unfettered distribution of songs by allowing songs to be owned.

The relationship between songs and copyright has been so thoroughly articulated by others with considerably more expertise than I that I see no useful purpose in attempting to write anew from that perspective. I rely heavily upon the following: Russell Sanjek's coverage of copyright in his books on the music business in the United States (1983 and 1988); overviews of the global situation as it stood roughly a half-decade before song sharing appeared, in both Simon Frith's edited collection *Music and Copyright* (1993) and Clifton Heylin's study of album bootlegging, *Bootleg: The Secret History of the Other Recording Industry* (1994); Lee Marshall's *Bootlegging: Romanticism and Copyright in the Music Industry* (2005), which situates Heylin's history within the context of cultural studies; Tarleton Gillespie's explanations of the intricacies and implications of digital copyright legislation from the Napster years onward in his book *Wired Shut: Copyright and the Shape of Digital Culture* (2007); and Ray Beckerman's ongoing comprehensive website on legal battles over song sharing, "Recording Industry vs. the People" (2004– ). All of these works are supported by an immensely complex scholarly apparatus on legal and legislative aspects of copyright, and there too I take this scholarly apparatus for granted and cite specific supporting articles only when the legal literature is of extraordinary relevance to the unauthorized distribution of songs—namely, in two essays on tape piracy (1974) and record piracy (1977) that appeared in the *Copyright Law Symposium*, and in Guy Douglas's lengthy analysis of the intricacies of the Napster court case (2004).

The entertainment industry attorney Ronald S. Rosen offers a comprehensive, sweeping, historical overview of legal issues and processes in his book *Music and Copyright* (2008). Although he is mainly concerned with claims concerning creation rather than with wholesale unauthorized distribution, Rosen presents a survey of legal concepts involved in Napster, Grokster, and other file-sharing cases in his last chapter, "Music, Copyright and the Impact of New Technology."[7]

In *The Anarchist in the Library* (2004), Siva Vaidhyanathan situates Napster and its successors within the context of wide-ranging cultural studies. Vaidhyanathan lays out an ongoing struggle between anarchy and oligarchy, with, on the one hand, a desire for freedom of access to and use of the Internet, set against, on the other, efforts at corporate control of Internet content. In this struggle, copyright and related legislation provide the hammer for those endeavoring to gain control.[8]

In *Piracy: The Intellectual Property Wars from Gutenberg to Gates*, Adrian Johns places the intersection of copyright and piracy into a sweeping historical context. Johns discusses a forgotten episode of sheet-music piracy in London in 1902–5 and arguments over home taping in the 1970s, but these forays into pop song piracy constitute somewhat of a sidebar to his main interests: the history of science and of books (or, more generally, the printed word); the emergence and never-ending modifications of conceptions of intellectual property, copyright, and patents; and the complex arguments and principles underlying these developments.[9] I share with Johns the belief that current-day battles over digital piracy have a history, and I endeavor in the present book to trace that history, for pop songs, from 1929 onward.

Seventeenth-century English book printers, Johns tells us, routinely "printed some 'supernumerary' copies to make a profit on the side." Such a practice would be "central to charges of piracy for centuries," and indeed it emerged in mid-twentieth-century practices of factories pressing phonograph records on the side (see below, chapter 6).[10] As Johns notes, the eighteenth-century compilation of complete editions of Jonathan Swift's works could only have been made by pirate publishers, because the authorized "owners" of his books would never have cooperated in that way. Two centuries later, unauthorized "mix tapes," compilations of songs cutting across record labels, served an analogous function (see chapter 7).[11] In detailing pirate wars between authorized London booksellers and unauthorized Dublin reprinters, also in the eighteenth century, Johns characterizes the situation in Dublin as "a trade of reprinting, an export market, and a lack of internal regulation"; this geographical tension, whereby an English sphere of controlled printing was undermined by an Irish sphere of uncontrolled printing, anticipated the tension that emerged in the late 1980s when compact discs for Western markets were pressed mainly in Asia, and a flood of pirated copies came into circulation (see chapter 9).[12] In recounting the first years of the BBC, Johns notes that individuals who listened without purchasing a radio license were, in effect, pirates; this situation anticipates that of song sharing over the Internet, whereby the general public has not just been passively engaged in obtaining an unauthorized song product from a "bootlegger" (as it was for song sheets and fake books; see chapters 2–4), but instead has actively participated in unauthorized song distribution (see chapter 10).[13]

**Songs.** The objects in question here, disobediently distributed songs, are almost exclusively popular songs, except in disputes over unauthorized music photocopying, which can involve any musical genre. Popular songs manifest themselves through a highly malleable set of concepts and objects. As it turns out, each and every one of these possible manifestations of songs comes into play in the intersection with distribution and disobedience. Of course this is how the cat keeps escaping from the bag. Songs are such wonderfully flexible things, so effortlessly represented in so many different ways, that full control and proprietary ownership is, in the end, impossible.

The present state of songs, and their conveyance, goes something like this: People sing songs, listen to songs sung by others, and hear songs in the imagination, without sound, as mental music. Songs may be notated and represented as music with lyrics. Songs may be notated and represented by lyrics only, without music. In either respect, even a fragmentary portion, or the title alone, may serve to convey the whole. The sounds of songs may be captured on tape, on disk, or as digital files. The sounds of songs may be accepted as is, or these sounds may be reinterpreted, altered, revised, or reconceived, whether by professionals or in the imagination of a listener. Songs may be, in and of themselves, commodities, whether distributed on paper or via a recording medium, or songs may be objects to which other commodities are attached, through advertisements and contests. Songs may exist independently, as individual objects, or songs may be packaged together, by musicians conceiving albums, by manufacturers creating anthologies, by radio presenters conceiving broadcasts, or by nonprofessionals, whether playing instruments and singing, or collecting recordings on tape or in digital forms. Finally, songs are transportable, whether on pieces of paper as printed lyrics or notated music, on disks and tapes carried into the home, via receiving and playback equipment installed into any sort of vehicle, through miniaturized electronic devices carried by individuals, or as digital files posted onto the Internet. In the future, no doubt songs will be conveyed in new bottles that we haven't even imagined yet. No doubt some of these containers will be illegal.

**Distribution systems.** Song distribution systems are complex and nonlinear, and consequently they normally afford numerous opportunities for loopholes to develop. Even the most straightforward distribution chain—songwriter, performer, producer, manufacturer, distributor, vendor, consumer—will have other entities layered across it, whether rights agencies and protective associations, or educational, religious, and governmental bodies. These entities might operate at any level, from local to international, in policing or governing copyright and commerce. They might editorialize to their constituencies and lobby on behalf of their constituencies.

Ideally, the linear segments of a distribution chain operate in accord with one another, and the diverse bodies overseeing the distribution are in agreement on operating principles. In practice, this rarely happens.

Invention and manufacture typically represent weak links in the chain, because the operators may have no vested interest in song ownership. Time and again, a new methodology for the distribution of songs originated in manufacturing processes that were developed outside of the realm of songs, when someone realized belatedly that a methodology intended for some other purpose could be applied to songs. In different eras, a machine developed for dictation, a card-catalogue developed for keeping track of radio licensing fees, and a software program developed for film and television soundtracks were subsequently reimagined as distributable song products: respectively, the musical phonograph record, the fake book, and the MP3 file.

Or a manufacturer within the music industry might not share the concerns of song owners. If a production plant is operating under capacity, an illicit order helps to pay the bills and keep employees working. This has happened countless times, for printed music and recorded music.

Or a manufacturer based outside of the music industry might become involved with the distribution of songs, but without any primary interest in this activity. When the Ford Motor Company and the Lear Jet Corporation put together a consortium to develop Bill Lear's invention, the eight-track cartridge, they had little reason to concern themselves with the songs that might be recorded on these tapes, and the implications for tape piracy. Nor did the Xerox Corporation show much interest in whether or not their machines might be used to reproduce images of copyrighted pieces, apart from once pulling a television commercial showing classical instrumentalists photocopying music, in response to a howl of protest from music publishers.

Collisions of this sort magnify on an international level, owing to conflicting laws on copyright, inconsistent trade agreements, competing national manufacturing systems, the difficulty of policing imports and exports across national boundaries, and so forth. In some cases, there may not be any agreement at all. In many Asian and eastern European nations, for example, protection did not extend to "foreign works" until very late in the twentieth century. Meanwhile, the production of compact discs initially came to be centered in

Asia. In a situation such as this, naturally the temptation to manufacture unauthorized CDs is overwhelming. In the realm of songs and distribution, globalization encourages disobedience.

Further complicating the distribution chain, technological developments might offer capabilities for individualized manufacturing or distribution that operate under the radar. As the manufacture of recorded songs progressed through the twentieth century, from the mass production of phonograph records in pressing plants, to the mass production of cartridge and cassette tapes in duplicating warehouses, to the mass production of compact discs in robotically controlled "clean rooms," each of these methodologies was initially expensive, specialized, and not accessible to individuals. The process of pressing phonograph records remained permanently so, but the private manufacture and distribution of tapes and CDs became available to individuals with the introduction of low-end tape duplicators and CD burners. Then later, when songs became digital files, the whole field shifted: point, click, distribute.

With this abstract survey of song distribution systems serving as a generic model, I turn now to a concrete and unusually clear-cut manifestation of one such system. This system emerged in the late nineteenth and early twentieth centuries under the rubric "Tin Pan Alley." And from there I proceed to tell how from 1929 onward that system and other much less perfect systems were disrupted and in some instances overturned by the unauthorized distribution of song products in the realms of printed music, broadcasting, and recording.

# PART I

# Printed Music

# 1 • Tin Pan Alley's Near-Perfect Distribution System

In early to mid-1929, when song-sheet bootlegging began, the American popular song industry—or more generally, the American music industry—or still more generally, the American entertainment industry—was operating a distribution system that was as perfectly controlled as it could possibly be, horizontally and vertically, from creation of the goods to their distribution to consumers, nationwide. It was, for a fleeting moment, the musical analogue of Standard Oil.

That moment of near complete control followed upon several decades in which the development of musical recordings, music broadcasting, and musical films challenged the preeminence of music publishing. During this period, the normal state of affairs was conflict and continuous corporate upheaval, not calm and a maintenance of control. But that upheaval was always situated on legitimate grounds and did not involve any prominent criminal or disobedient activities. The Viennese scholar Peter Tschmuck catalogues a seemingly endless succession of these legitimate industrial conflicts, stretching from the 1880s to the current day, in his international survey, published in English translation as *Creativity and Innovation in the Music Industry*. Tschmuck surveys disconnections between inventors and their products when an invention came to be used in a new unintended way; clever or questionable challenges to and adaptations of patents; the consolidation of small firms into large firms following upon some grand success; and the disintegration of firms, large or small, following upon the saturation of a market or some grand misjudgment of a new product. It is important to recognize that the story of song-sheet bootlegging is in the big picture just another one of the endless disputes and disruptions that characterize the history of the American music industry—the international entertainment industry—any modern industry?—and certainly not the largest dispute. What distinguishes song sheets and the other stories in this book, is their development outside of authorized channels.[1]

At that fleeting moment of a perfect distribution system achieved in 1929, the principal players were the Tin Pan Alley songwriting industry, comprising the song owners—variously composers, lyricists, and music publishers—and their sales representatives; the manufacturers and distributors of popular songs and song products, including vaudeville performance circuits, the recording industry, radio networks, and the movie industry; and private and public agencies overseeing distribution, including the American Society of Composers, Authors and Publishers (ASCAP), the Music Publishers Protective Association (MPPA), and the federal government. What follows is an overview of the development of their interrelationships and interdependence.

**Tin Pan Alley and the vaudeville circuits.** In the 1890s the American songwriting industry came to be tightly focused on formulaic but highly creative products emanating from composers, lyricists, publishers, and song pluggers working in "Tin Pan Alley," which was situated in the area of East Fourteenth Street in Manhattan. In the twentieth century the center of activities relocated first to West Twenty-Eighth Street and then, in 1920, to the Brill Building and other nearby buildings on or in the vicinity of Broadway at Fiftieth Street. Through these years and continuing until the advent of rock and roll in the mid-1950s, the products of Tin Pan Alley would define mainstream American popular song. Since that time, the stature of its finest writers—Irving Berlin, Jerome Kern, George and Ira Gershwin, Cole Porter, Oscar Hammerstein II, Richard Rodgers, and so forth—has only grown, as the "classic" and enduring sense of their achievement has come to be recognized and appreciated.

Tin Pan Alley controlled the paper segment of the industry. Its composers and lyricists wrote the songs. From 1914, when these individuals organized ASCAP, the potential for complete control took on a new facet, in that membership in ASCAP was not open-ended, but restricted by number and by admission procedures.

The publishers of Tin Pan Alley purchased songs outright or entered into royalty agreements with the creators, and then distributed their songs as sheet music. Sales agents for the publishers "plugged" new material not only to outlets for sheet music, but just as importantly to new media for the promotion of sheet music, first recordings, then radio, then film. These agents utilized categories of bribery both modest—giving out promotional copies of sheet music—and immodest—giving out cash payments or a share of sales revenue in exchange for endorsements and performances by well-known artists, either in their public appearances or, increasingly as the years went by, through their recordings. Many of the public appearances were coordinated and controlled through the offices of two organizations: the Vaudeville Managers Association for the eastern states and the Orpheum Circuit for the nation from Chicago westward.

To my knowledge, there is no industry-wide data on sheet-music sales for this era. Publishers were self-reporting, and reports were individualized. Articles on sheet-music sales routinely give specific figures for some specific time period or segment of the industry, but overall trends are undocumented. Only in 1954 did the Music Publishers Association (MPA) trumpet a new survey representing "the first time that an accurate estimate has been made of this end of the music business," which they placed at $30 million annually, which is presumably a substantial decline from the golden years of sheet-music sales. By this time sheet music was already completely overshadowed by recordings and broadcasting in the bid for national audiences. Consequently, it is difficult to know just how well sheet music fared before the development of these new media and in the early years of coexistence and competition with these new media (discussed below). Contextual comments and the longstanding prominence of the MPPA suggest that music publishers maintained considerable clout in the industry for many years.[2]

**Copyright, phonograph records, and song licensing.** Between 1891 and 1909, hand-in-hand with the first wave of consolidation of American popular songwriting into the offices of Tin Pan Alley, the U.S. Congress passed a series of copyright bills containing incremental changes pertaining to music. The bill of 1891 allowed music printed outside of the United States to be registered for copyright in the United States, in spite of arguments from American publishers that foreign competitors would offer cheaper labor and thus lower prices, undercutting American jobs. In 1897 "musical compositions," that is, operas, cantatas, masses, musical theater, musical comedies, and so forth, were incorporated in the categories of dramatic compositions for which an earlier law, a statute of 1856, required permission from the copyright owner in order to give a performance in public; this requirement would have an enormous impact. The act of 1897 also toughened the government's stance against music piracy, although by comparison with the impact of the licensing provision, discussed below, the stand on piracy was rather impotent: copyright infringement was only a misdemeanor, and it would remain so until a modification in 1974 of the 1909 bill opened the possibility of a felony conviction for especially egregious instances of record piracy, while leaving all other categories of infringement as misdemeanors.[3]

Concurrently, and as has been the case ever after, the capabilities of American technology in the late nineteenth to early twentieth centuries were surging ahead of attempts at controlling these capabilities through American law. Thomas Edison invented the phonograph in 1878, and in the early to mid-1880s Chichester Bell (the cousin of Alexander Graham Bell) and Charles Tainter came up with their own version, calling it a graphophone. Both machines recorded sound onto a fragile and cumbersome medium, the cylinder, and both aimed at the office-supplies marketplace. The creators conceived of their inventions primarily as new means for recording dictation in office work and for replacing stenographic machines in government and legal circles, with secondary uses in the archival preservation of speech. These aims failed. The process was far too unwieldy, especially at this early stage of development, when a separate machine was required for the making of each and every copy. In effect, there were no copies. Every recording was an original.

As the office application was failing, Edison felt that a proposed alternative use of the phonograph—for recording music—would trivialize his invention, making it nothing but a toy. So early on he was already fighting two battles, with Bell and Tainter over patents, and with the world at large, over usage. He lost both. Jesse Lippincott, who formed the Columbia Phonograph Company in 1889, agreed with Edison's focus on office applications and quickly led it into bankruptcy, from which it was rescued, ironically, by Edison. Meanwhile, the Pacific Phonograph Company found success with a five-cents-per-play forerunner of the jukebox, and in the early 1890s Columbia began to bring in unexpectedly large profits from issues of recordings of waltzes, polkas, marches, national anthems, opera excerpts, and diverse songs, as well as dramatic recitations and foreign language instruction.

From the late 1880s onward, with an eye specifically toward music recording, Emile Berliner and Eldridge Johnson made significant improvements in the recording medium, experimenting with different approaches and materials that eventually yielded a flat disk (rather than a cylinder) and a reliable crank-based motor, both of which could be mass produced. A lengthy period of development and industrial infighting led to the founding, in October 1901, of the Victor Talking Machine Company, which then entered into further patents disputes with a Graphophone-Columbia conglomerate over the question of disk versus cylinder. By the advent of World War I, following further and continuing international adjustments in the interrelationships of corporations, the major American companies were Columbia and Victor for two segments of the distribution chain: phonograph records and phonograph machines. Record sales reached a pre-Depression peak of $106 million in 1921.

Following upon the 1897 bill that linked copyright permission to public performance, the Copyright Act of 1909 included a compulsory licensing provision of immense importance for the music industry. Sanjek explains its implications in his chronicle of the music business: "For the first time in American history, the peacetime bargaining process between a supplier and a user was regulated by the federal government, and the price for use of private property fixed by national law. A royalty of 2 cents for each piano roll, phonograph record, or cylinder manufactured was to be paid to the copyright owner."[4] Later in the book, in chapters on record, tape, and compact-disc piracy, I will take up this regulatory aspect of recording in much greater detail.

**ASCAP and the MPPA.** ASCAP formed in 1914 to enforce these licensing provisions of the Copyright Act of 1909, both for the public performance of music, and for recorded music. An oft-quoted Supreme Court ruling of 1915, regarding live performance in a New York restaurant, validated the authority of ASCAP in these two realms. ASCAP was to a considerable extent a Tin Pan Alley agency, and this newfound authority extended the reach of Tin Pan Alley beyond the realm of paper, by collecting income from "external" sources— public performance and recording—and then distributing that external income to individual members in the field of sheet music, whether songwriters or publishers. It was thus perfectly natural that as one of its lesser duties during the following decades, ASCAP would take a stand against song-sheet bootlegging, an activity that threatened to cut in on its members' income. In 1929, as bootleg song sheets appeared and before the stock market crashed, record sales were $77 million. Such a figure presented a serious challenge to the preeminence of sheet music, but this was OK, because a nearly perfect distribution system was in place: authorized songwriters and music publishers had their fingers in all three slices of these distribution pies, gaining income from sheet-music sales, from live performance in commercial venues, and from licensing fees on phonograph records.

The MPPA formed in 1917, three years after ASCAP. This organization should not be confused with its contemporary, the National Music Publishers Association (NMPA), which will figure prominently later in the book, in investigations into record piracy, and it should not be confused with a later organization, the MPA, quoted above for its mid-century survey of sheet-music sales. Ostensibly the specific purpose of the MPPA was to fight Tin Pan Alley's corrupt and ubiquitous practice of song plugging, as, for example, in promoting a song by bribing vaudeville stars to perform it. But this was far too incestuous a relationship to possibly succeed, having publishers police publishers. Indeed, the MPPA's initial platform died almost immediately, and song plugging continued as a standard practice in which MPPA members participated fully. But the MPPA did not fold. Instead, its principal role became that of a business trust, endeavoring to maintain standard prices for mechanical licensing and for the sale of printed music, including sheet-music versions of pop songs. Hence, together with ASCAP, the MPPA would become concerned with bootleg song sheets, which threatened the stability of MPPA financial systems.[5]

**Radio and film.** Meanwhile, as record companies and sheet-music publishers developed a co-relationship under the watchful eye of the songwriter and publishing associations, radio emerged as a powerful force in the distribution of songs. Guglielmo Marconi invented radio in London at the turn of the twentieth century. The new medium blossomed in England before the Great War, initially in competition with and soon thereafter in collaboration with the German company Telefunken. After World War I, as an element of a negotiated settlement demanded by President Woodrow Wilson, the newly formed Radio Corporation of America (RCA) acquired European radio technology and gained control of national broadcasting. Its constituent members were AT&T, General Electric, and Westinghouse, which manufactured transmitters and radios. Six years later, in 1926, RCA organized its radio stations into a network, the National Broadcasting Company (NBC). In the course of these developments, inventions in the realm of radio led to a new technology for capturing sound through electrical means, through the use of a microphone, rather than by the existing acoustical means of performance into an inverted horn. This technology provided a huge improvement in sound quality, and it had potential applications to recording. The transmission of sound through electrical means was still a long way oz from the "high fidelity" of microgroove recording and FM broadcasting in the 1950s, but it was far superior to that of the acoustical method.

As with Edison and Lippincott three decades previously in their negative reaction to the question of using the phonograph to record music rather than to take dictation, the major American recording companies, Columbia and Victor, reacted in an adversarial manner to these developments in radio. Their executives wrongly perceived radio to be a dangerous competitor to phonograph recordings, not a vehicle for promoting phonograph recordings, and they fought the new medium in every possible way. Accordingly, Columbia and Victor initially refused to adopt the superior electrical method to recording, persisting with acoustical means while smaller companies were capturing a higher quality of sound. The two major companies also continued to build radios only, while other companies began to manufacture musical furniture that incorporated AM receivers and phonographs together in a single box. These unwise decisions were exacerbated by overly ambitious expansion into other areas. The refusal of Columbia and Victor to attempt a rescue through an alliance with radio proved to be disastrous for both of them. The British Columbia Graphophone Company acquired the American Columbia Phonograph Company early in 1925. The newly merged firm, Columbia International, Ltd., then adopted the new recording method and turned its fortunes around, becoming a multinational company through further mergers. Eventually and ironically, both Columbia and Victor were taken over by American radio corporations. RCA acquired Victor in 1928. The road for Columbia in America was more convoluted, because of its international status and because of antitrust concerns, but in 1938, following a succession of divestments and corporate transfers, the Columbia Broadcasting System (CBS) revived the iconically powerful Columbia Records label.

Despite the wrongheadedness of Columbia and Victor, AM radio blossomed as a forum for distributing popular songs, and in March 1923 ASCAP entered into negotiations with broadcasters to deal with the issue of licensing fees for music heard over the airwaves.[6] The National Association of Broadcasters formed that year in an attempt to combat this action, but ASCAP prevailed. Over the remainder of this decade, the income for ASCAP members from radio rose from tens of thousands of dollars annually to hundreds of thousands of dollars annually. With radio folded in alongside sheet music and records via this licensing agreement, the popular song distribution system had taken another step toward its moment of consolidation and near perfection.

The final new medium, film with a soundtrack, was at the appearance of bootleg song sheets in 1929 still younger than AM radio, with Al Jolson having sung in the first "talkie," *The Jazz Singer,* only two years before. But very quickly, performances of popular songs became a mainstay of moviemaking and a significant vehicle for the advertisement and dissemination of new song hits. Indeed, the immediacy with which lyrics from movie songs made their way into song sheets of the 1930s, together with reproductions of photographic stills and posters taken from those same movies, testifies to the extensive impact that film had on the hit-making machine in these years.

So, the nearly perfect distribution system: a centrally located musical "factory," Tin Pan Alley, distributed songs as a paper product, sheet music, that was created by a restricted-admission "guild" of in-house members, the ASCAP songwriters. These wares were "plugged" by in-house Tin Pan Alley salesmen

who, through various means of promotion extending to bribery, gained notice for an ever-changing list of popular songs through performances of those
songs in "live" broadcasts, vaudeville, musical theater, and musical film, and
through recordings of those songs distributed directly to the public. (In these
early years, the playing of popular song recordings in the radio studio was not
yet common.) Rights to the dissemination of these songs were supported by
provisions of American copyright law and overseen in-house by representatives of ASCAP and the MPPA. With this system in place, Tin Pan Alley songs
generated huge profits directly through sales of the paper product and indi-
rectly through licensing fees paid to ASCAP members for recordings, radio
broadcasts, and public performances.

# 2 • *Bootlegging Song Sheets*

In 1929, shortly before the stock market crashed, a prevailing cultural product, sheet music, began to be challenged by a rival commodity, the song sheet. Sheet music was created and disseminated through authorized channels by the composers, lyricists, and publishers who "owned" songs, but songs sheets of this era were distributed through unauthorized channels by bootleggers. This unauthorized distribution caused great anguish to the song owners, who did battle against song sheets not only until the appearance in the mid-1930s of an authorized version of the new commodity, in the form of legitimate, licensed, song-lyric magazines, but well beyond that point, into the early 1940s. In a cat and mouse game of moves and countermoves, song owners caused the government to charge bootleggers with vending without a license; copyright infringement; manufacturing, distributing, and vending without consent of the owners; trade violations; and even, conspiracy against the United States of America. In response, the bootleggers found their way around these charges. Or they managed never to be caught. Or they suffered prosecution, accepted fines or jail terms, and got out of the business, only to be replaced by others. Or they suffered prosecution, accepted fines or jail terms, and stayed in the business anyway.

The fighting lasted roughly a dozen years. ASCAP became involved, and then the MPPA, and then the FBI. In the end, song-sheet bootlegging ceased not through efforts at prohibition, but through assimilation. The principal figure in this outcome was John Santangelo. Having entered the field with many others as organized criminals, filling a niche in the pop song market that mainstream music publishers were unwilling to service, Santangelo was ultimately absorbed into the routine workings of American business, as he pushed his way into the midst of those same publishers. Eventually he battered down their resistance to authorizing licensing agreements for song sheets, thereby achieving social and legal legitimacy, and a decent share of the marketplace.

**Song sheets, legitimate and not.** The bootleg pop music song sheets of 1929 onward were spin-offs of legitimate compilations of lyrics called "song sheets," "songsters," or "broadsides," this last being a much more generic term extending far beyond the realm of music. Although "songster" is the preferred term in scholarly studies of American music, the bootleg items are persistently called "song sheets" in published reports and court documents. When the object in question is a pamphlet of lyrics or a song-lyric magazine rather than literally a single sheet, these magazines might be labeled in other conventional ways, for example, as "song books" or "pamphlets of song" (see below, on their appearance in the mid-1930s), but never are the single sheets or the magazines called "songsters" in the bootleg arena. (Searches for the term "songster" in 1930s newspapers yield articles on birds, not pop music.) So I use the term "song sheet" throughout, with apologies to American-music scholars who might prefer otherwise.

These compilations of lyrics have a centuries-old history in England and a long history as well in America, where they often convey a political agenda, for example, lyrics associated with the Civil War, women's rights, the labor movement, an election race, patriotism, and so forth. A large collection is held at the Library of Congress, with this introduction on the library's website: "For most of the nineteenth century . . . Americans learned the latest songs from printed song sheets. Not to be confused with sheet music, song sheets are single printed sheets . . . with lyrics but no music."[1]

The activity of bootlegging music was not entirely new. In his autobiography, the music publisher Isidore Witmark recalled a minor epidemic of bootleg song-sheet peddling in Chicago in 1892 or 1893. But Witmark explained that this activity had been quashed and had not reemerged until "recently," that is, the 1930s, when he was writing his memoir.[2] Adrian Johns details a major episode of piracy in London that led to the establishment of what he calls "the first pirate hunters," who strove in the years 1902–5 to quash unauthorized reprinting of existing sheet music; this was an instance of equivalency (i.e., illegal reprinting), which is Johns's main concern in his centuries-long survey of piracy.[3] In terms of the mass, nationwide (indeed international, given Canada's eventual involvement), wholesale distribution of an unauthorized, transformational song product, 1929 is the point of historical demarcation, and bootleg song sheets are that product.

**The advent of bootleg song sheets.** Song-sheet bootlegging was evidently going on for some months before it gained public notice. On September 23, 1929, ASCAP submitted a complaint to U.S. District Attorney Charles H. Tuttle that song sheets were being sold on the street at a price of five cents per copy, that the sheets were an infringement of copyright, and that the volume of these sales was substantial enough to interfere with the sales of legitimate copyrighted copies, that is, sheet music. The *New York Times* reported that there were already several different sheets, each selling for five cents and each containing lyrics to twenty-five or more songs. At a subsequent ASCAP meeting early in 1930, another member stated that the bootlegging had threatened legitimate music publishing for almost a year.[4]

Given the timing of this story, slightly before the stock market crash on Black Friday in October, it is impossible to argue for any sort of consequential relationship between America's fallen economy and this emergent bootlegging activity, but certainly the Great Depression that followed would have played into the bootleggers' hands. Over the course of the next decade, as the battle between bootleggers and music publishers unfolded, song-sheet printers and distributors would have no problem finding people willing to hawk a bootleg product on the streets.

**An early song sheet: The *Songland Herald*.** To lend substance to the objects under discussion, figure 2.1 shows the cover page of a bootleg song sheet from 1932, the *Songland Herald,* a double-sided sheet presenting a number of song lyrics beneath images of Bing Crosby, Kate Smith, and Rudy Vallee. Newspaper and trade-paper accounts make it clear that millions of these bootleg song sheets were printed in the 1930s, but in their original format, as newspaper-sized single or double sheets, they are virtually impossible to find today. Libraries and archives seem never to have collected bootleg song sheets, for the very reason that they are bootleg objects and thus automatically create a procedural and legal nightmare for cataloguing and circulation within a legitimate setting. Antiquarian newspaper and sheet-music dealers offer diverse and numerous copies of the bootleg song-lyric magazines that succeeded newspaper-sized double-sided bootleg song sheets in the mid-1930s, but exemplars of this initial newspaper-sized format (shown here in a greatly reduced size) are now rare. This issue of the *Songland Herald* survives in the Southern California branch of the National Archives as exhibit 2 from the conspiracy trial of *United States of America vs. Al Friedman et al.*, discussed below.[5]

Through an antiquarian newspaper dealer, I acquired a disintegrating copy of a ten-cent, newspaper-sized, single sheet entitled *Latest Songs*, the July 1933 issue, offering lyrics to "Radio-Screen Song Hits," with photographs of the actor John Boles and the actress Janet Chandler on the front side and a series of announcements and perhaps intentionally humorous disclaimers on the front and back: "read carefully before buying"; "no songs repeated"; "watch for counterfeits—money cheerfully refunded upon dissatisfaction"; "ask your dealer for back numbers, 6 for 15¢"; "for music copies of these songs go to your

FIGURE 2.1. *Songland Herald* 1, no. 6 (undated [circa March 1932]), with photos of Bing Crosby, Kate Smith, and Rudy Vallee

nearest music store." Were it not for this sheet, and were it not for Al Friedman and his song-bootlegging associates stumbling into a federal prosecution for conspiracy against the United States of America, and the district attorney consequently entering the *Songland Herald* and four other song sheets into the case as evidence, I would have failed to provide a single example of the original type of bootleg song sheet. What was once so commonplace is now such a rare artifact that it can scarcely be found.

**Initial notices, and early attempts at suppression.** As soon as the unauthorized new product came to attention, the song owners attempted to suppress it. And as soon as that happened, the bootleggers began to seek loopholes in the system. The first of these loopholes was to separate the act of vending from the act of copyright infringement. Thus began the cat and mouse game between owners and bootleggers.

In this era *Variety* was, together with *The Billboard,* the leading weekly newspaper for insiders in the entertainment industry. *Variety* took up the story in late October 1929, reporting that in the previous week federal marshals had seized fifty thousand song sheets throughout the country.[6] *Variety* had mainly devoted its pages to movies, the theater, vaudeville, nightclubs, and radio during the late 1920s, with music coverage routinely comprising no more than one page per issue. But the bootlegging story evidently sparked its readers' interests. *Variety* immediately became, and it would remain, the principal source of coverage of the nationwide battle against song-sheet bootlegging over the course of the next dozen years.

Early in November 1929 an article in *Variety* noted that street peddlers, operating surreptitiously without a license, were to be found in many locations in New York City, selling song sheets for five or ten cents each. The sheets were printed secretly, without any information to identify the source, and the addresses of the peddlers changed frequently. As the year turned to 1930, *Variety* reported that song-sheet bootlegging extended into Canada as well.[7] The new product now had an international component to it, and in whatever details Canadian copyright law, trade regulations, and rules for vending might differ from U.S. copyright law, trade regulations, and rules for vending, so the effort to suppress song sheets might take on a greater complexity. As it turned out, the two countries were in sufficient accord that there were no great discrepancies in approaches to enforcement and prosecution; in episodes of songs, distribution, and disobedience from later decades, the result would be otherwise.

At the same time that Canada entered the picture, some hawkers in the New York area began to obtain peddler's licenses. In doing so, they added a different sort of complication to the suppression of unauthorized sales, by separating the issue of vending without a license from the issue of copyright infringement. A vendor might still have his products seized by the police, but if he has a generic license to vend and does not face fines for illegal vending, then all he has to do is to go back to the source and get more copies of song sheets. He can then resume vending, until the next capture.

**Criminal copyright infringement.** Allegations of criminality and racketeering entered the picture, the obvious agenda of the song owners being an effort to associate song-sheet bootlegging with some of the much more frightening and murderous types of criminal behavior and rackets that flourished during Prohibition in the arenas of liquor, gambling, protection schemes, and so forth. At an ASCAP meeting in mid-January 1930, one member claimed that "a bunch of Chicago racketeers" were "the mob" responsible for the bootleg sheets, while another asserted that "the sheet racket" had started in Times Square. Despite these rumors and allegations, ASCAP officials admitted that all efforts had failed in the attempt to identify the people or organizations in charge of the bootlegging. The report ended: "An ironic fact is that a large part of the New York sales are made under the windows of the society's office in the Paramount building."[8]

With the effort to fine peddlers compromised, the industry tried another tack. February 1930 brought the first prosecution of bootleg song-sheet publishers and distributors for criminal copyright infringement, which was a misdemeanor. The government filed charges against Morris Shapiro, Samuel A. Cohen, and Harry Paul for marketing lyrics to forty-three pop songs on a bootleg sheet. Among these forty-three songs were the hits "Just You, Just Me" and "Lover, Come Back to Me," as well as numerous long-forgotten titles, including, ironically and amusingly, a song entitled "I Can't Remember the Words" (the perfect justification for purchasing a song sheet, if ever there was one). In the course of a lengthy investigation, U.S. District Attorney Tuttle, Police Commissioner Grover A. Whalen, and John A. Paine, chairman of the MPPA, received threatening letters. Tuttle would not reveal the contents of his letter, but the *New York Times* indicated that it involved a "reminder that a man recently was stabbed in Brooklyn for trying to interfere in the sales of the songs." The article ended with a bit more detail on the unsubstantiated rumor that had circulated at the ASCAP meeting the previous month: Nathan Burkan, counsel for ASCAP, told reporters that he believed that the "racket" had started in Chicago "and that persons close to Al Capone were back of it."[9]

Shapiro, Cohen, and Paul pleaded guilty to the misdemeanor and received suspended sentences. Federal Prosecutor Henry Gerson stated that these guilty pleas would serve as a warning to others of the copyright laws and that prison sentences would be sought for those involved in similar actions in the future.[10] Thus this case raised the question, for the first of many times in this decade, would public warnings deter bootleggers? The answer proved to be: no.

Layered across the generalized cat and mouse game—one side adapting or inventing laws to close loopholes, and the other side finding new loopholes—was a more particularized second game of bluff and bargaining, focused around criminal copyright infringement and highly reminiscent of poker. How much cost and effort should the government put into prosecuting a misdemeanor? Could the government prove criminal infringement? Might the defendants be found innocent? If so, would other unauthorized distributors take that verdict as a license to bootleg? The song owners and the government were perhaps just as apprehensive as the defendants concerning the possibility of seeing a criminal infringement case through to the end of a full-blown trial by jury. So they bargained for a guilty plea. This procedure was sensible, and it became the norm. As it turned out, it would be another thirty-six years, and in a different realm of song products—fake books rather than song sheets—before America experienced its first full-blown trial by jury for criminal copyright infringement.

It is not as if the bootleg distributors were innocent. But the difference between a commonsense notion of guilt derived from newspaper accounts of their infringing activities and the actual technical documentation required to prove criminal infringement in court is immense. Writing in 1962, Edward A. Sargoy, a lawyer specializing in representing the motion-picture industry in copyright infringement cases, explained: "United States Attorneys . . . do not want to undertake the expense of a difficult investigation and trial, the bringing in of necessary witnesses from remote parts of the country, the considerable effort and tribulation of learning new law and preparing a prosecution in this highly specialized field of statutory copyright, for what is presently merely a misdemeanor," as it still was, three decades after the trial of Shapiro, Cohen, and Paul. "The apparent tendency," wrote Sargoy, "is to consider this misdemeanor no more serious than expectorating on the sidewalk, or smoking in a prohibited area."[11] For the government, this path was a bother and a risk. Reducing charges and bargaining for a guilty plea was by far the preferred path to prosecution.

The problem for the song owners was that, for defendants like these, a plea bargain on reduced charges generally translated into a light fine and a light sentence, if any. Judges positioned song-sheet bootlegging within the context of far more heinous crimes that came into their courts on a daily basis, and they acted accordingly. Consequently, many bootleggers clearly felt that this enterprise was sufficiently profitable that the risk was worthwhile and the penalties effectively amounted to nothing more than a category of business expense—office overhead, as it were.[12] As stories from later years reveal, a number of men took Shapiro, Cohen, and Paul's strategy one step further, pleading guilty, receiving a fine or a light sentence (often suspended, pending "good behavior"), and then going right straight back into bootlegging pop songs (never mind the promised behavior). Only rarely did defendants receive substantial jail terms, and normally this would be for having the brazenness to keep at it right through a third and fourth conviction.

**A new law in New York State.** So bootlegging continued, and it proliferated. In mid-February 1930 *Variety* described song-sheet activities in Philadelphia, Pittsburgh, Milwaukee, Los Angeles, and Washington, D.C. Most entertainingly, "a gang of guerillas" (surely the reporter meant "gorillas") confronted a private detective who had been hired by the MPPA to investigate printing plants in Chicago. They told him, "There are two kinds of weather in Chicago—hot and cold. Which do you want?" Also in Chicago, music publisher Milton Weil was hijacked by three men whom the MPPA claimed were members of Al Capone's gang, and whose business had evidently been disrupted in the initial efforts to combat song-sheet bootlegging. Holding Weil at gunpoint, they told him to "make good their losses or take a ride." Weil replied that he had no money. "The gunmen forced him to sign an agreement giving them permission to use all his songs for their sheets."[13] Contract by gunpoint was, unusually in these stories, a blatantly criminal action, and certainly it helped the song owners to make their case to authorities for the need to eliminate song sheets.

Meanwhile, on the street, in relations between vendor and consumers, peddling illicit items *without* a license to vend had given way to peddling illicit items *with* a license to vend—move and countermove. Criminal copyright infringement was only a misdemeanor, effectively little more than a slap on the hand, requiring a lot of work to pursue and perhaps yielding scarcely meaningful results. So the industry tried something else. In March 1930, recognizing the difficulty of these first avenues of prosecution, ASCAP introduced, through a New York state assemblyman, a new misdemeanor, for the act of "printing, publishing, or selling copyrighted musical compositions without the consent of owner." If the song owners could push through this bill, they would not have to go through the laborious process of proving infringement in federal court. Instead they could establish in a lower court that a manufacturer, distributor, or vendor had no contractual agreement to publish copyrighted songs. The act of obtaining a license to vend had gotten peddlers off the hook, with regard to the local laws in New York City, but now, licensed or not, the vendors were at risk for the nature of the product that they were selling, and the state law extended to printers and distributors as well.

New York Governor Franklin D. Roosevelt signed this bill on March 26, 1930. It was the legislation that prompted the Times Square raid leading to the arrest of eighty-year-old Sarah Yagoda. This same raid nabbed a man who would become one of the repeating offenders in song-sheet bootlegging of the mid-1930s, Theodore Aaronson. Detective Edward Sullivan identified Aaronson as the first person to be arraigned for violation of the antipeddling provision of the bill that Roosevelt had just signed.[14]

May 1930 brought a premature announcement in the *New York Times* of the demise of song-sheet bootlegging, with published statistics citing the conviction of 188 printers and distributors, and the arrest of 1,326 peddlers. This same report noted that Al Capone had denied that he had participated in this "racket" in any way. Capone had recently written to ASCAP to express "regret that his name was used by three gunmen who held up a Chicago music publisher." Capone denied that the gunmen were members of his organization, and he promised that if their identity could be proved, he would punish them (presumably for having used his name without authorization, rather than for having published song lyrics without authorization).[15] Nothing more was heard from this fragment of the story. In browsing through various sources on Capone's activities, I found no reference to his having had any involvement with song sheets.

Despite the announcement in the *New York Times,* activities in song-sheet bootlegging flourished, and efforts at suppression expanded. Over the course of the next two years *Variety* routinely reported the arrests of peddlers, printers, and distributors nationwide, and in Canada. In March 1932, coincidentally when the *Songland Herald* sheet appeared, *Variety* announced that there had now been more than five thousand arrests in North America. Under the headline "Publishers Talk Printing Own Song Sheets to Eradicate Sheetleggers," the entertainment paper went on to explain that because of the "inability of the music industry to eradicate the bootleg song sheet evil, it is now being suggested that the publishers themselves issue a song sheet in retaliation." For the time being, however, nothing came of this proposal.[16]

**Parody sheets and trade violations.** Move, countermove, move, countermove. In 1931, the California legislature passed a bill similar to that of New York State. These laws made the act of distributing bootleg song sheets somewhat more risky than it had been, most crucially in the two centers of the entertainment business, Manhattan and Hollywood. The five thousand reported arrests testify to this level of risk, even if perhaps the overall effort, to eradicate song sheets, was fruitless.

In somewhat of a sidebar to the main story, a number of bootleg song-sheet publishers strove to reduce their risk by publishing lyrical parodies of pop songs. There had not yet been any federal ruling on the relation of song parodies to the Copyright Act of 1909, and therefore any such publisher, or the distributors and peddlers of this product, could not be charged with copyright infringement. And it had not yet been established in law whether a parodist required permission from the owner of a subject being parodied. Therefore, the newly enacted New York and California state laws, requiring the consent of the song owners, might not apply to song parodies. As it turned out, New York Federal District Court Judge Alfred Coxe would only first take up the question of parody and its relation to copyright in 1944. In the early 1930s, the government was powerless to prosecute these song products along established lines.

In an attempt at a stopgap solution, attorneys working on behalf of the music-publishing industry obtained formal stipulations from the Federal Trade Commission (FTC), to the effect that parodies of pop song lyrics represented examples of false and misleading advertising. Three stipulations, issued late in 1931 and early in 1932, made their way into FTC publications before this idea was dropped for being unwieldy and ineffective.[17]

**Conspiracy against the United States of America.** The most drastic measure taken by ASCAP and the government, with the most severe results for the bootleggers directly involved (but, as elsewhere, with no real effect on the big picture), was to treat song-sheet bootlegging as an act of conspiracy against the United States of America. The first such case occurred in California in 1932, when infringement actions taken by a group of men and a teenaged boy in violation of the Copyright Act were instead prosecuted generically, as a conspiracy. Unlike the other legal strategies, which involved misdemeanor charges, or in the case of the FTC, merely warnings of future prosecution if the commission's stipulations were not obeyed, conspiracy ranked as a serious crime, a felony. This is the case, Al Friedman et al., that led to the preservation of a copy of the *Songland Herald*, held as evidence along with several other newspaper-sized song sheets. The surviving evidence includes two other fascinating documents that provided tiny glimpses into a lost world of song-sheet bootlegging.

In June, one of the defendants in this case, Willie Zimmer, had the misfortune of receiving a letter establishing his involvement in song-sheet bootlegging. The letter had been forwarded from his home to the county jail where he was being held before trial. The authorities read it and seized it:

> Well old socks.
> enclosed find six dollars for sheets, If you have time send me two hundred
> more as I can use them, That fellow from Oakland made the can. he just
> got out, he done fifty days for selling song sheets, so look out for Oakland.
> as ever your Truely
> Leo Zickel
> Post office news stand Sacramento

Exceptionally for the defendants in this case, song-sheet bootlegging proved to be a punishing affair. Judge Harry Hollzer sentenced Friedman and Zimmer to fifteen months in prison. Two other adults received, respectively, a year in prison and four months in the Los Angeles County Jail, while a fifteen-year-old boy was released into the custody of his parents, only to violate his probation in mid-1935 on a narcotics charge. (Is this the slippery slope of song-sheet bootlegging?)

Miraculously, Zimmer somehow kept his sense of humor through all of this, and in November 1932 he wrote to Judge Hollzer from prison:

> Honorable Sir—
> some months ago I was up before you, and sentenced up here to McNeils
> Island to do 15 months. I am with out funds and I would appreciate it
> if you would send me the Six dollars money order which was held as
> evidence in my case. I need some money to buy tobacco and soap "and all
> the latest song sheets."[18]

**A path not taken.** In the autumn of 1932 an unnamed songwriter in San Francisco decided to participate directly by contributing lyrics to a song sheet. *Variety* reported that this composer had "placed a number on a royalty basis with publishers of the illegal sheets."[19] In the big picture, this also was a peripheral incident, far more so than the publication of parody song sheets. But it raised some interesting questions. Could song owners cut sheet-music publishers out of the deal and work directly with song-sheet publishers, for songs not yet published in sheet-music form? An "illegal sheet" with one authorized lyric would still remain an illegal sheet if all of the other printed lyrics were reproduced without permission, but what if a whole group of song owners became involved? Could a monopolistic distribution system be overturned through the establishment of an alternative system operating through legal channels? This is in fact what eventually happened, although not in the way that the anonymous San Francisco songwriter imagined it. The alternative system was still some years away, and it could never have developed successfully without the participation of sheet-music publishers. In the end, song sheets coexisted with sheet music; they did not replace sheet music. It would have been foolish for songwriters to publish in only one form and not the other.

**Repeat offenders.** By 1933, arrests for song-sheet bootlegging only occasionally made the news, but the epidemic was raging as vigorously as ever. In its issue of June 15, *Variety* expressed the industry's frustration and despair in a two-column editorial entitled "Helpless Society on Song Sheets."[20] Throughout the mid-1930s this form of bootlegging continued to flourish. Occasional press notices announced fleeting moments of success in the attempt at suppression, but it is more the scarcity of these notices that indicates, by comparison with detailed coverage of song-sheet bootlegging in the entertainment press from 1930 to 1932, the extent to which the participants were able to go about their business without intervention in the middle years of the decade. Those few articles that did appear underlined, by implication, the brazenness of the bootleggers, insofar as reports focused on second-, third-, or even fourth-time offenders, with the aforementioned Theodore Aaronson topping the bill. Said District Judge William Bondy at Aaronson's third trial, after he plead guilty to three counts of criminal infringement:

> I will sentence the defendant to 7 months on the first count, one year on the second count and a year on the third count, to run consecutively. I will suspend execution on the second and third counts during good behavior and place him on probation in each case for a year, to run consecutively. . . . I am treating him very easy on his third offense. There is another thing he should be told; when you get out if you do wrong, without trial you will go to jail for two years. Be sure the man should get some attention.

Judge Bondy failed to capture Aaronson's attention. He resumed bootlegging song sheets, and on October 14, 1936, Aaronson's probation officer filed a Petition for Revocation of Probation, following upon a new investigation into his activities. The following day another Federal District Court judge, John C. Knox, issued a warrant for Aaronson's arrest for criminal infringement: "He has again committed the offense for which he was placed on probation, to wit, the sale of copyrighted song sheets without the consent of the copyright owners in violation of Title 17, Section 28 United States Code." Facing seven counts of infringement brought on behalf of four music publishers for the songs "On a Coconut Island," "The Stars Weep," "A Star Fell Out of Heaven," "Take My Heart," "Follow Your Heart," "Lost in My Dreams," and "Tell Me Why," Aaronson on December 21, 1936, received, as promised, an additional two years in prison: one year for the first count, and a second year for the other six, which were to run concurrently.[21]

**Arthur Hoffman and the MPPA campaign.** The principal mandate of ASCAP was to enforce licensing provisions established by the Copyright Act for radio, recording, and public performance, not to investigate illicit competition in the realm of publishing. Accordingly, this rights organization took an initial stand against song-sheet bootlegging, but within a few years it largely dropped out of the contest. Instead, the responsibility for heading the ongoing investigations fell into the hands of the sheet-music industry's own organization, the MPPA.

Arthur Hoffman, the investigator into Aaronson's continuing activities, would become the key figure in an intensification of the battle against song-sheet bootlegging. Decades earlier, in the late 1890s, Hoffman had been an employee of New York City Chief of Police John McCullagh, who was remembered for having "waged ceaseless war on gambling and vice." Evidently Hoffman brought a similar zeal to the task of combating bootleg song sheets.

He first came to notice in this realm in May 1934 as copyright manager for the music publishing firm Leo Feist and Co. In August 1934 another news report identified Hoffman as a special investigator for the MPPA.[22] One of his earliest moves in this arena led to a seizure providing further documentary evidence of the huge quantities involved in song-sheet bootlegging. In September 1935, Sam Christie, a seventy-four-year-old printer of community newspapers, was arrested in New Brunswick, New Jersey. Ledgers seized at Christie's printing plant showed that he had produced 1,250,000 bootleg song sheets. For some unspecified period of time his plant was printing fifty thousand copies per week.[23]

**Song-sheet magazines replace song-sheet newspapers.** In March 1937, Hoffman traveled to Washington, D.C., to participate in a raid that yielded copies of two bootleg song-lyric periodicals, *Paramount* and *Prosperity*.[24] By 1936 newspaper-sized bootleg song sheets had entirely given way to bootleg song-lyric magazines. In coverage of Aaronson's third conviction, *Variety*

**FIGURE 2.2.** Front cover of *Prosperity Book No. 40* (undated [circa 1937])

called the magazines "contraband folios." At Aaronson's probation hearing that year, participants variously and interchangeably used the terms "song books," "booklets of songs," "pamphlets," "song sheets," and "the sheet." Whatever the term, these compilations of song lyrics were the size of a normal magazine, the earlier large format having disappeared. Such magazines were the objects of the continuing battles against song-sheet bootlegging. Figure 2.2 shows a typical cover from one publication, *Prosperity Book No. 40*.[25]

**John Santangelo as bootlegger.** John Santangelo, the leading figure in the final act of this story, entered the news late in December 1936, erroneously as "John Angelo," when Hoffman's raid on Santangelo's printing plant in Jermyn, Pennsylvania, netted two hundred thousand bootleg song sheets. In March 1937 Santangelo and three colleagues pleaded no defense in Federal District Court in Scranton. They each received fines, and his was the largest: $600.[26] Like Aaronson, Santangelo paid the fine and resumed printing lyrics.

The years stretching from 1937 into the early 1940s brought more local arrests of peddlers and distributors, more federal indictments for criminal infringement, and further conspiracy charges, including a prosecution of Santangelo and his colleagues. By 1939 he owned printing plants in four states, and that summer he paid another fine after pleading guilty to conspiracy charges in New Jersey. Finally, on January 16, 1940, with Assistant U.S. District Attorney Valentine J. Sacco describing him as "a kingpin in the song sheet racket since 1935," Santangelo pled guilty to criminal infringement charges in Connecticut and received an eight-month prison term.[27] Worth noting among many other such stories, as further testimony to the large quantities involved in song-sheet bootlegging, is a document in the case file for *United States of America vs. James Preziosa and Tony Costello* (1941). This document orders the destruction of approximately one hundred thousand seized song sheets and the related printing plates.[28]

**The end of bootlegging.** Then, in 1941 and seemingly out of the blue, *Variety* reported near-victory in the bootlegging battle. Walter G. Douglas, chairman of the MPPA, told his organization that following actions by the FBI and New York City police, the end of song-sheet bootlegging "was virtually in sight." Douglas said that a bootlegger in a midwestern city was the only distributor remaining in the United States and that this illegal operation would be closed shortly.[29] This was not the first time that the music industry had claimed that song-sheet bootleggers had been nearly driven out of business. Previously these statements had been far more propaganda than truth. But in this instance, the claim turned out to be true. Song-sheet bootlegging ended in the early 1940s. How did this happen?

There are conflicting and irreconcilable answers to this question. On close examination, the story given out in the entertainment press depends upon chronologies retrospectively reorganized, so as not to unbalance allegations of cause—the prosecution of bootleggers—and effect—the cessation of bootlegging—and it downplays or ignores an alternative explanation, namely, the emergence of legitimate lyric magazines. I present this story first, and then present the story in a different light, as it actually seems to have occurred, divorced from a filter of reorganization and omission.

**The campaign against retailers.** Throughout this period, extending from the late 1930s into the early 1940s, Hoffman introduced two new strategies that worked in combination with criminal prosecution. He instituted civil suits against legitimate stores whose employees were selling bootleg song sheets, and he initiated a systematic nationwide mailing campaign that was followed by blanketing raids, city-by-city and newsstand-by-newsstand, to dissuade legitimate street dealerships from selling bootleg song lyrics.

When Hoffman began to concentrate systematically on major businesses, his strategy of prohibition began to have some effect. Unlike the street peddlers, corporate enterprises were genuinely concerned by the threat of losing their license to vend. In September 1937 negotiations were underway to settle suits brought against two store chains, W. T. Grant and Walgreen Co., as well as a magazine distributor, Ginsberg News Co., that circulated "bootleg lyric folios" in Westchester County and in lower Connecticut. Casting the net further, Hoffman toured upper Connecticut later that same month. *Variety* reported that Hoffman had confiscated thousands of song sheets at newsstands and in stores selling magazines in five Connecticut cities.[30]

While continuing with this approach, Hoffman developed a new and broadly effective strategy early in 1940. Distributors of legitimate sheet music assisted the MPPA in identifying stores and newsstands where the bootleg items were for sale. The MPPA sent a warning letter to each and every vendor, and then, one week after the letters went out, MPPA investigators went to each and every vendor, looking for evidence of continuing bootleg sales. Upon finding such sheets, the investigators bought copies and handed them over to local attorneys hired by the MPPA to bring civil suits against the vendors. The organization then sought to identify the distributors of the bootleg sheets and to obtain warrants for their arrest. In January 1940 the MPPA mailed final notices to approximately ninety-one thousand magazine retailers throughout the United States.[31] In June 1941, Douglas made his pronouncement to the MPPA, that the bootlegging was ending, and in November 1941, his successor, Edwin H. Morris, in his annual report to members, "declared that the illegal song sheet racket has been practically eliminated in this country."[32]

**Legitimate song-lyric magazines.** Was this a battle won through a saturating approach to prosecution? It seems so, if the press coverage is to be believed. There had indeed been a well-coordinated legal attack, with undeniably widespread effects. But something else happened as well during this period: legitimate song-lyric magazines began to appear.

In 1934, while the publishing industry was throwing up its hands in despair at the success and audacity of the bootleggers, Engel–van Wiseman, Incorporated, established two legitimate five-cent song-sheet magazines, *Popular Song Hits* and *Song Hit Folio*. These two magazines would set the pattern for this type of publication. Figure 2.3 shows the cover of an issue of the latter magazine.

The endeavors were not immediately successful. *Popular Song Hits* and *Song Hit Folio* both failed in 1936. In April 1937 their publishers founded a new corporation, Song Lyrics, Inc. They then initiated a new magazine that would prove successful for decades, *Song Hits;* figure 2.4 shows the front cover of an issue of this publication.[33]

While vigorously covering the activities of the MPPA, *Variety* only first acknowledged the existence of alternative publications on July 20, 1938, in a report on the MPPA having circulated a letter to its members. This letter stated that "it had not given its approval to the latest of legitimate song lyric magazines, 'Flash,' and that it was up to the individual publishers to decide whether they wanted to do business with the magazine." The description of *Flash* as the "latest of legitimate song lyric magazines" constituted, by inference, the first acknowledgment of its predecessors in the Engel–van Wiseman camp at Song Lyrics, Inc., the failed *Popular Song Hits* and *Song Hit Folio,* and the ongoing *Song Hits.* This report on the MPPA and *Flash* concluded with what was, in the context of attempts at prohibition, an extraordinary statement. The circular letter explained that the promoters of *Flash* had sought permission to deal directly with music publishers, but the MPPA took the position that legitimate song-lyric magazines would have little effect on bootlegging. The unidentified publishers of *Flash* took the opposing view, that "the spread of legitimate songs sheets would serve to put the contraband element out of business."[34]

Events of the following years suggest that the MPPA had it wrong and the promoters of *Flash* were right—legitimate song sheets would eventually put the contraband products out of business—but obviously the MPPA had strong reasons for pursuing its then-current agenda, and *Flash* quickly came to be classified as a criminal enterprise. In late September 1938, just two months after the appearance of a headline that had labeled *Flash* a "legit lyric sheet," it had been reclassified as illegitimate: "detectives from the rackets bureau of the Brooklyn District Attorney's office . . . confiscated 4,200 *Flash* song-sheet magazines in a raid on a local parking lot."[35]

**FIGURE 2.3.** Front cover of *Song Hit Folio*, no. 9 (November 10, 1934)

In 1939 Song Lyrics, Inc., added a second magazine title, *400 Songs to Remember* (for an example of a typical cover, see figure 2.5). This magazine complemented *Song Hits* by focusing on old favorites rather than current songs. Priced at ten cents, it promised "a carefully selected group of Love Songs, Southern, Ballads, Cowboy, Spirituals, Patriotic Songs, etc." That same year Warner Bros. introduced a ten-cent book of lyrics under the awkward title *Sing*

Session. And in January 1940, in the aforementioned article devoted in part to the MPPA's systematic campaign of mailing letters to legitimate retailers handling bootleg song sheets, but mainly covering John Santangelo's ongoing trials, *Variety* mentioned that the MPPA's nationwide circular letter also identified three legitimate song sheets then on the market: *Song Hits, Sing Session,*

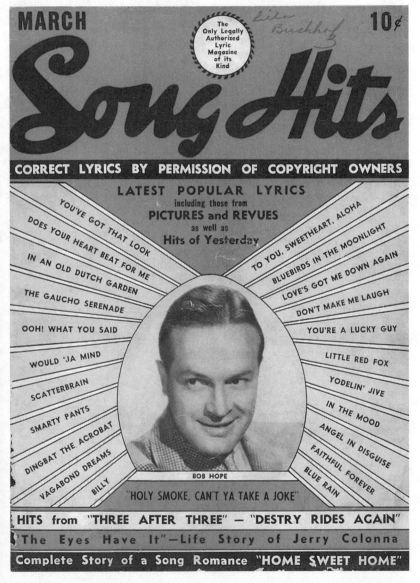

FIGURE 2.4. Front cover of *Song Hits* 3, no. 10 (March 1940)

**FIGURE 2.5.** Front cover of *400 Songs to Remember* 1, no. 3 (September 1939)

and *400 Songs to Remember*. While the MPPA was slowly "authorizing" such activity, these enterprises were flourishing. Song Lyrics, Inc., founded a third title, *Music Makers*, in May 1940. *Song Parade: America's Foremost Lyric Magazine* and *Big Song Magazine* came out early in 1941, and *Radio Hit Songs* and *Broadcast Song Hits* later that same year. Yet another such publication, *Sing*, got underway in January 1942.[36] By this point, bootleg song sheets were disappearing from circulation. Prohibition had given way to assimilation.

**Assimilation: John Santangelo's story.** On September 9, 1942, *Variety* ran an editorial entitled "Influx of Shady Characters into Song Sheet Biz Disturbs Music Publishers." The bootleggers were entering through the front door, and music publishers had misgivings about the growing business for song-lyric magazines: "What disturbs them most are the character types that have come to hold strategic if not dominant positions in this latest parasitic incubus on the music publishing industry. Many of the 'boys' have either prison records or have reputations as racketmen in other fields. . . . Not a few of the now-legitimate song-sheet operators fall within reformed classification. That is, they tried bootlegging the same product and gave that up after an encounter or two with the Federal Bureau of Investigation. . . . The music publishing industry has of late collected some evidence pointing to an alliance between the operators of a legitimate song sheet and a song-sheet bootlegging enterprise."[37]

What is to be made of a editorial like this? It was a tirade consisting of unspecified innuendo. The subject was never followed up in *Variety*. In fact, the next notice regarding song sheets, from late November 1942, offered a happy account from Lester Santly, who had succeeded Edwin Morris as president of the MPPA. In his annual report, Santly said that publishers were receiving an annual income of $275,000 through the licensing of lyrics to the three leading song-lyric magazines.[38]

Despite the vagueness of the editorial, the claim for an "influx of shady characters" might be taken seriously. By the time of this unsubstantiated editorial, John Santangelo, the aforementioned "kingpin of songlegging," had already reentered the field.

In later life, Santangelo was mainly associated with comic books. From the mid-1940s until it went out of business around 1986, his firm Charlton Publications was a significant, second-tier publisher of comic books. Charlton put out its own series devoted to various fantasy superheroes. It acquired *Flash Gordon*, *Popeye*, *Beetle Bailey*, and other titles from King Comics in the late 1960s. It produced comic-book spinoffs from famous Hanna-Barbera television animation series, including *Yogi Bear* and *The Flintstones*, as well as others like *Rocky and Bullwinkle*.[39] But Charlton started out publishing legitimate song-lyric magazines, including two of the aforementioned titles, *Big Song Magazine* and *Radio Song Hits* (for images of typical covers, see figures 2.6 and 2.7).[40]

**FIGURE 2.6.** Front cover of *Big Song Magazine* 1, no. 7 (September 1941)

In 1954 Ralph H. Manard published a biography of Santangelo and a history of Charlton Publications in the *New England Printer and Lithographer*, and in 1980 Mary Slezak updated this piece for the *Journal of American Culture*.[41] These essays present "authorized" accounts that were probably approved by Santangelo and his company. At least it seems so from their tone. But both essays have a substantial amount of detail that I have not found elsewhere, and neither interprets events in a manner that is any more fanciful than the MPPA's spin on the song-sheet story.

John Santangelo was born March 15, 1899,[42] at San Valentino in the Abruzzo region of Italy. His brother had settled in Norwalk, Connecticut, and Santangelo joined him there in the early 1920s, working in a tire factory.

**FIGURE 2.7.** Front cover of *Radio Hit Songs* 1, no. 2 (December 1941)

After suffering a severe injury, he moved to New York City and worked as a bricklayer. He became a foreman after three months, even though he did not yet speak English. Having earned a large bonus for finishing a job ahead of schedule, he became a self-employed contractor in 1926. He then spent a year working on the interior of the Roxy Theater, and he lived in the Roxy, to save money.

Santangelo next worked in White Plains, New York. In 1931 he married a Derby, Connecticut, woman and made his permanent home there, while returning to New York City for further work. According to Manard, a friend of Santangelo's wife was looking for a copy of the lyrics to "Shuffle Off to Buffalo" and asked him to pick up a printed copy of the song in Manhattan. When that friend found out that she had to pay thirty-five cents for the sheet music, when all she wanted was the words, not the music, she was outraged. On his next trip to the city, Santangelo bought fifty songs and had a printer produce all of the lyrics on a single sheet of poster-colored newspaper, which he then sold in stores and at newsstands in Manhattan for ten cents, splitting the sales income with the sellers, each party getting a nickel from each sale. Fanciful or not, and two years too late to explain the origin of bootleg song sheets, this account may explain how Santangelo got into the enterprise.

In 1933 Santangelo purportedly had nearly five hundred song-sheet dealers selling 7 million copies per month in the mid-Atlantic states and New England. By 1939 he had dealers nationwide, from Winthrop, Massachusetts, to Walla Walla, Washington. He told his biographers that he continually switched printers in the early to mid-1930s, because ASCAP was bringing pressure to bear against union firms that were printing song sheets. Then, in 1936, to get around that obstacle, he opened up his own printing plant in Waterbury, Connecticut. Santangelo also claimed that he offered to pay ASCAP royalties on the lyrics in the song sheets, but ASCAP refused, preferring to fight for suppression of the sheets.

Santangelo said that one of his normal modes of operation, in setting up new locales, was to employ boys to sell song sheets. He noted, perhaps with tongue in cheek, the coincidence that these boys tended to be related to local policemen, so that when complaints arose over vending the song sheets, the police would take his side and ignore the complaints.

After incurring several fines for his activities, Santangelo was sentenced to eight months in the New Haven County jail in 1940. A history of Charlton states that while there Santangelo met a disbarred lawyer, Edward Levy, who had gone to jail because of some unspecified involvement in a political scandal in Waterbury, Connecticut. The two became friends and agreed to take up a partnership in a publishing enterprise following their release.

Without mentioning trials, fines, or jail time beyond the phrase "legal complications," Manard asserts that in 1940 Santangelo finally persuaded ASCAP that the organization was losing money in the fight over song sheets, and he reached an agreement with ASCAP whereby hereafter the society would accept a licensing fee for the publication of lyrics. That year, in partnership with Levy, whom Manard calls "a writer with legal and banking experience," the two men enlarged the business and relocated Santangelo's printing plant from Waterbury to Derby. There they put together a staff of advertising agents, salesmen, artists, and writers in New York City. Because both Levy and Santangelo had five-year-old sons named Charles, they called the company T.W.O. Charles, but they soon changed the name to Charlton Press. *Big Song Magazine* and *Radio Song Hits*, both started in 1941, carry the name Charlton, not T.W.O. Charles.

**Santangelo's song-lyric magazines.** Like all of the bootleg song-lyric magazines, *Big Song Magazine* and *Radio Hit Songs* were printed on cheap, colored, highly acidic (and now disintegrating) paper, and neither carried advertisements to help generate income. Unlike those bootlegs, both *Big Song Magazine* and *Radio Hit Songs* had proper publication notices at the front, and both provided copyright notices for each and every lyric. *Big Song Magazine* incorporated a full-column testimony to Santangelo's newfound legitimacy: "big song magazine proudly announces to its hundreds of thousands of readers that it has consummated license agreements for big song magazine to reprint the lyrics of more than forty active music publishing houses." Following an alphabetical list of these publishers is the statement that some of these publishing houses are associated with ASCAP, some with BMI, some with SESAC, "and some are not connected with any of these three organizations."[43] Perhaps his early publishing associates were in their own ways renegades from the mainstream industry.

In November 1942 Charlton Publications established a new and serious rival to *Song Hits*, entitled *Hit Parader*. (For a sample cover page, see figure 2.8.) In its professional-looking format and in its approach to special features, *Hit Parader* showed allegedly plagiaristic tendencies to which Lyle Engel of Song Lyrics, Inc., reacted immediately by filing suit for $50,000 and seeking an injunction against further publication, on the grounds of unfair competition.

**FIGURE 2.8.** Front cover of *Hit Parader* 1, no. 3 (January 1943)

The suit charged the Charlton group, including Santangelo, Levy, and two other men, with copying the style, type, and arrangement of *Song Hits*. But nothing came of this case, and rightfully so. *Hit Parader* was no more or less a copy of *Song Hits* than were other publications emanating from less potentially threatening rivals.[44]

In addition to receiving the prison term in Connecticut for criminal infringement, Santangelo had received five years probation in Newark, New Jersey, following a conspiracy conviction. On September 5, 1944, in requesting an Order Terminating Probation, Santangelo's probation officer wrote: "Subject has made a very satisfactory adjustment for a period just short of four years; he has been regularly employed; has fulfilled probation requirements, and is felt deserving of this consideration."[45] Assimilation, indeed.

As Santangelo legitimized his activities, public notice of song sheets faded away. The last thing heard was another happy report in *Variety* in mid-March 1944: music publishers were earning approximately $600,000 annually in licensing fees from legalized song sheets.[46] In this article, all credit goes to the MPPA, and none to Engel and his enterprises. Indeed, this last report rewrites the chronology of events, placing the suppression of bootlegging before the appearance of legitimate song-lyric magazines, rather than admitting that the latter dated from as early as 1934 and probably deserved at least as much credit for the disappearance of bootleg sheets.

After World War II, Santangelo relocated Charlton to a new and larger plant on the outskirts of Derby. At some point long after song-sheet bootlegging died away, Santangelo's firm acquired *Song Hits* from the Engels. In 1954, when Manard published his essay on Santangelo and Charlton, the song-lyric business was going strong. Santangelo claimed that the company was selling six hundred thousand copies of *Hit Parader* per month. Whatever the numbers might have been, it was a success. Charlton continued to publish the two leading song-lyric magazines, *Song Hits* and *Hit Parader*, for decades, while also developing analogous titles for country-and-western music, and for rock and soul music. Santangelo headed the business into the 1970s—he died in 1979—and then handed over the leadership to family members. In the story of song sheets, John Santangelo had the last laugh.

Who won the song-sheet battle? Did the activities of the MPPA cause the demise of song-sheet bootlegging? And at what cost was this alleged victory? In terms of the immense amounts of money and number of man-hours expended in a nationwide suppression of "songleggers," how would things have worked out if, instead, those same amounts of finance and effort had been poured into the MPPA's support of legitimate song sheets? (Yes, of course that sort of free-enterprise subsidy never would have happened.)

Was this really a victory for the prosecution? Or did the legitimate lyrics magazines simply replace the bootleg products? Did individual publishers' policies of corporate assimilation, with the support of the MPPA lagging far behind, prove more sensible and more effective in combating bootlegging than all of the attempts at prohibition? And was the MPPA's claim for victory in any sense viable, with a convicted "songlegger" subsequently moving in to take over legitimate operations in this little segment of the pop song industry?[47] In the end, after roughly a dozen years of immense fussing, it was business as usual. Things ended up just as they started, except that now, in the mid-1940s, the former bootlegger John Santangelo was paying royalties to reproduce song lyrics.

# 3 • The Content and Uses of Song Sheets

There was always a piano in the house. It seems like everybody in the neighborhood had a piano. But nobody played them. They put pictures on it, doilies, and all kind of things on the piano, but it was never played.

—SAXOPHONIST BENNY GOLSON, *remembering the late 1930s in his interview for the Smithsonian Jazz Oral History Program, September 23, 2009*

In the interplay between equivalent and transformational song products, song sheets fall solidly into the latter camp. The entertainment industry itself was undergoing a process of transformation in the 1920s, and this transformation was reflected in the new product. The rising importance and attraction of songs heard via records, radio, and musical films prompted mass audiences to develop an interest in printed lyrics rather than sheet music, as these audiences came to terms with altered listening habits in a changing relationship to songs. The big development was the replacement of sheet music by mechanically and electronically driven media as the way that people learned songs.[1]

Song owners, fearful of killing their profit margins, refused to adapt to this changing environment, leaving the market initially open to bootleggers only. The new bootleg song product had its own transformational qualities that further encouraged disobedient behavior. Despite industry claims of equivalency, authorized sheet music and bootleg song sheets were not the same thing. Song sheets provided consumers with handy, organized compilations of popular songs, and these compilations were easy to transport. If lyrics only would suffice, if consumers no longer needed piano music, then why would anyone want to bother sorting through or carrying around loose piles of individual pieces of authorized sheet music, when the bootlegged alternative was so much more convenient? A bunch of songs could be bundled into a single package, printed on a newspaper-sized sheet. Later, and still more conveniently, a bunch of songs could be bound into a single magazine-sized booklet. Either bootleg package—the folded sheet or the booklet—could then be easily transported and easily shared with friends. Here the big development was conceptually diverse in its relationship to other song products, touching upon aspects of organization, functionality, portability, mobility, and interpersonal usage.

As the years went by, authorized song-lyric magazines entered the field, and new possibilities opened up, principally in the areas of advertising and subscription. If advertisers could be brought into the fold without threat of prosecution for participation in an illicit activity, and if consumers could identify themselves as subscribers without threat of prosecution for participation in an illicit activity, then the magazines would have the potential to broaden their financial base. This is something that John Santangelo had recognized long before he was accepted into the circle of legitimate music publishers, when by his own account he sought and was repeatedly refused permission to pay licensing fees for authorized usage.

The introduction of advertising into song sheets brought forth additional transformational changes, making the song-lyric product even more remote from sheet music. The big development here was a considerable strengthening of the role of song sheets in promoting the output of the American film industry.

These comments are largely inferential. Almost nothing is directly known of the audiences for song sheets, their reasons for purchasing song sheets, and the ways in which they used song sheets. A few passing references appear in the news coverage of bootlegging and in editorial comments within song-lyric magazines. These little nuggets provide clues. Otherwise, I infer meaning from the contents of the sheets themselves, on the assumption that their various components—their musical repertory, their extramusical features, and the nature of their advertisements—reveal something about their uses and audiences, or at least, their intended uses and audiences.

All song sheets emphasized connections to musical theater, radio, and musical film. All song sheets concentrated on current American popular songs, except for *400 Songs to Remember,* a publication explicitly devoted to an "old-time" repertory. While concentrating on current hits, any song sheet might venture into other areas of the popular repertory, whether "old-time" songs or cowboy songs. Many song sheets included jokes. Some bootleg song sheets also featured representations of European ethnicity in popular songs, on a limited basis, and for a limited period of time.

When legitimate song sheets came along, they continued most of these practices, while presenting additional special features, such as dance instruction, celebrity gossip columns, song-writing contests, and detailed advertisements for films. Legitimate song sheets also carried advertisements for diverse musical and nonmusical products: instrumental and vocal instruction, beauty aids, self-improvement, and so forth. Insofar as these products were oriented overwhelmingly toward women, the ads thereby suggested something about the general audience for song sheets during a period extending from the mid-1930s into the 1940s.

So, I begin with comments in published sources on general usage, on usage by choral societies, and on the convenience of song sheets. I then move on to an analysis of bootleg and legitimate song sheets, endeavoring to infer meaning from content.

**Published comments on usage and audience.** The press coverage was slim, but a few scattered sentences show that some representatives of the music industry were aware of the potential attractiveness of song sheets in response to new musical technologies. Early on, at a meeting in January 1930, a representative for ASCAP acknowledged that the landscape of popular song was changing. "Thousands now learn the popular melodies from the radio, the publishers state. With the lyrics available for five or ten cents and the strain known, impulse to buy sheet music is eliminated."[2] In March of that same year, another representative for ASCAP noted that song-sheet bootleggers had their fingers on the pulse of American popular music. Unauthorized publishers were quickly identifying new hit songs and then distributing sheets of lyrics to those hit songs throughout the United States.[3] In February 1936, while surveying the then-current and largely unchanged state of affairs in a report on thousands of arrests for bootlegging song sheets, the *New York Times* noted that "young people buy them as aids in memorizing the words which they sing to the tune as heard over the radio."[4] Collectively these statements support the big picture, the transformational opportunity that song sheets provided for mass audiences to move away from sheet music, as increasing numbers of people found that they had no need for musical notation.

**Song sheets for choral societies.** A different and perhaps somewhat peripheral usage and audience came to light in that same *New York Times* article of February 1936, which noted that choral societies were buying the sheets for use in conjunction with a single authorized copy of the sheet music. Rather than having each and every singer procure his or her own copy of the sheet music to a given song, at thirty or thirty-five cents per copy, each singer instead could have a song sheet holding a number of songs, at a nickel or a dime per sheet, and only the piano accompanist needed to buy separate copies of the sheet music for each piece. Exceptionally, this specialized usage of song sheets represented an instance of product equivalency, in contrast to the many aspects of transformational use that song sheets exemplified. Saving money by purchasing bootleg copies of lyrics was unquestionably the prime motivating factor for choral societies engaging in this practice. This peripheral, nontransformational use of bootleg song sheets anticipates a later dispute over choral societies and music photocopying, discussed in the next chapter.

**The convenience of song sheets.** An editorial comment in the first issue of *Song Hits*, from 1937, provides an insight into aspects of the portability, mobility, and functionality of song sheets: "everyone knows how useful words to the latest songs can be at parties, on picnics, camping trips and innumerable other occasions."[5] Song sheets provided consumers with a handy way to transport a substantial repertory of songs, and in that respect they stood in contrast to sheet music. Song sheets freed consumers from a reliance on fragile disks and a fixed source of electricity, and in that respect they stood in contrast to phonograph records and radios. At least in their first decade, song sheets provided the only practical means of achieving these combined goals: so long as people were willing to sing, they could take a sheet and use it anywhere.

With the widespread introduction of AM radios into automobiles, songs became mobile, and now without requiring any active participation in music making. Turn the knob; make music. With the introduction of transistor radios in the 1950s and boom boxes in the 1970s, songs gained further portability and mobility, again without requiring any active participation in music making. So, in a grand transition from general music making to general listening, this transformational aspect of song sheets, their portability, did not remain an advantage for long.

Not only could song sheets be brought along just about anywhere, but they enabled group participation too, "at parties, on picnics," and so forth. Car radios, transistor radios, and boom boxes fulfilled a similar function, but later electronic devices have taken a step away from that possibility. The Sony Walkman cassette player of the late 1970s, the Walkman CD player of the 1990s, the iPod of the new century, and other such "personal" listening devices utilize headphones and thereby isolate listeners from one another. A song sheet requires neither batteries nor headphones nor a wireless connection. Stick it into a pocket or purse; carry it anywhere; share songs with a friend (so long as there is light for reading—powered devices do have the advantage of operating in the dark). I am not so naive as to think that on the strength of this admittedly quirky argument anyone is going to throw away his or her iPod and start singing from song sheets. But the argument is worth making, if only to emphasize how very different song sheets were from sheet music, insofar as they provided, for some number of years, an attractive song package in terms of organization, functionality, portability, mobility, and interpersonal usage.[6]

**The contents of song sheets.** However slim the press coverage may have been, the sheets themselves reveal a lot through their content, and the ways in which that content changed over the years. Though they were sheets of lyrics, and later, magazines of lyrics, they were never strictly and solely concerned with delivering song lyrics to consumers. There was always something else attached. Sometimes there were many other things attached, carrying aspects of the sheets into areas in which songs played subsidiary or associative roles, to dance instruction, to radio comedy, to entertainment gossip, to self-improvement, to beauty products.

How might a song acquire value, so that it could be sold? One way of attaching value to a song would be to sell a publication or a recording of the song as a plain object in and of itself. For a song sheet, that would have entailed printing a piece of paper that presented strictly song titles and lyrics, perhaps identifying the songwriters, but offering nothing more. Perhaps some of the earliest bootleg song sheets were completely unadorned in this manner. I do not know. I doubt it. As noted earlier, I located only a few actual examples of newspaper-sized bootleg song sheets from their first half-decade of circulation, and anything else that I know about this era is secondhand, as described in news reports and court documents. All that I can say is that I am not aware that any bootleg song sheet circulated in this stark manner. The copies that I acquired included extra-musical connotations, both textual and iconographical, most normally in connecting popular songs to stars and shows of stage and screen.

Connections of this sort, the attachment to songs of additional information or images, enriched the context in which the songs appeared, thereby making a song sheet more attractive and more valuable than it would be if it were unadorned. This was a path open to any song product, legitimate or not. Perhaps the finest examples of this practice reside in the areas of long-playing jazz and rock albums of the 1960s, with notable photographs or artistic work on the covers and informative liner notes on the jackets, the latter offering descriptive or analytical essays, biographies, discographical information, lyrics, poetry, and so forth. Indeed, LP cover art became a genre in its own right, and its attraction persisted right through the era of compact discs, whose covers on reissued albums routinely offered five-square-inch miniaturized reproductions of square-foot-sized images originally conceived for LPs.

**Songs sheets, film stars, and popular shows.** Among the bootleg song sheets that I obtained, even the plainest one takes up this path, enhancing value by attaching an image of a famous entertainer to the otherwise bare bones of song titles and song lyrics, and placing this image in a prominent position, on the cover. This plainest example is a thirty-two-page booklet called *American Book 142*, with actress Eleanor Powell pictured on that cover (figure 3.1) beneath a claim for the presentation of "575 song hits." (Actually there are just short of two hundred songs in this booklet, but who was counting?) The cover proclaims that these songs derive from "radio—stage—screen." On the pages that follow, the name of a Broadway show or a movie from which a song originates is sometimes slotted in on a line between a title and its lyrics, including, for example, the song "If I Should Lose You," which *American Book 142* identifies as having come from *Rose of the Rancho*. (That movie was released in 1936; hence the provisional date of this booklet.)[7]

Every song sheet that I obtained emphasizes some sort of connection to musical theater and film in this manner, via images and attributions. The song-sheet *Prosperity Book No. 36* exemplifies a variety of possibilities available to bootleg publications. Its front cover shows the actress Claire Trevor (figure 3.2). A picture of the actor Fred MacMurray appears on the back cover. Placing a greater emphasis than *American Book 142* on the link to stage and screen, *Prosperity Book No. 36* offers lyrics selected from nearly thirty musicals of 1936. The banner below the title on the cover—"LATEST SONG HITS"— trumpets the efforts of the illicit publishers and distributors to maintain currency, disseminating lyrics as soon as possible, just as some contemporary news reports indicated. Evidently people who went to see musical theater and musical films then went out to buy bootleg sheets with lyrics from those shows.

This publication, *Prosperity Book No. 36*, includes lyrics from songs heard in twenty-one movies, mainly in the swing-dancing genre, but with cowboy films represented as well. Among the twenty-one movies are *Hats Off, Stowaway, Swing Time, Gold Diggers of 1937* (released in 1936, despite the title),[8] and *Trail Dust*. The booklet also offers lyrics selected from five Broadway productions, including *Forbidden Melody* and *White Horse Inn*, as well as the Harlem-based *Cotton Club Parade*. Lending an additional hint to the geographical and social scope of the bootleg sheets, *Prosperity Book No. 36* has song lyrics from *This*

# 10¢ AMERICAN 10¢

## THIRTY-TWO PAGES

American Book 142        Watch For American 143

# 575 SONG HITS

## RADIO ■ STAGE ■ SCREEN

### Featuring All Popular Hits

The Music Goes 'Round and 'Round

I Got Plenty O' Nuttin'

Madonna Mia

Dinner For One Please, James

Blue Illusion

Rolling In The Snow

That's You Sweetheart

A Beautiful Lady In Blue

I'll Never Forget I Love You

How'd Ya Like To Be A Little Birdie

ELEANOR POWELL

This Book Contains More Complete Songs Than Any Book Printed

MUSIC PUBLISHING COMPANY

**FIGURE 3.1.** Cover page of *American Book 142* (undated [circa 1936])

*Mad Whirl,* a show presented in 1936 at the University of Pennsylvania by its all-male Mask and Wig Club. Were the unauthorized publishers trying to reach not only the general public, but also a more "elite" or affluent audience associated with presentations on college campuses?

The next issue, *Prosperity Book No. 37,* with Mae West shown on the cover and John Mack Brown on the back, has a substantial duplication of songs found in *No. 36.* Not surprisingly, in addition to routinely exaggerating the

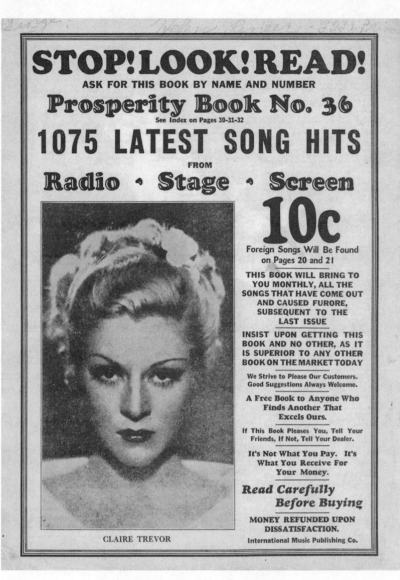

**FIGURE 3.2.** Front cover of *Prosperity Book No. 36* (undated [circa 1936])

total number of songs contained within any given issue, the publishers of bootleg song sheets had no compunction about repeating material from one issue to the next. Nonetheless, there is also a considerable amount of new material in *Prosperity Book No. 37*. The booklet incorporates songs from about ten more musicals into its contents, including the movies *Pennies from Heaven* and *The Big Broadcast of 1937* (also released in 1936, despite the title), as well as songs from another collegiate production, *Take It Away!*, presented by the Triangle Club at Princeton University.[9]

**Song sheets and broadcasting.** In a related bid to maintain currency and to call attention to the latest songs, the unauthorized distributors sometimes coordinated the sale of lyrics to new songs with opportunities to hear those same new songs on the radio. Although *American Book 142* advertises lyrics from "radio—stage—screen" without supplying any further useful information, other bootleg song sheets make the connection explicit. *Prosperity Book No. 40*, for example, has a list of radio news programs on its back cover (figure 3.3). Flanking an image of the actor James Stewart are eastern-daylight-time references to broadcasts of dance music, news, and comedy featuring, among others, the bandleader Guy Lombardo and the singers Eddie Cantor, Al Jolson, and Rudy Vallee, as well as the pop music show *Lucky Strike Hit Parade*. This was an era in which radio was still broadcasting live performances much more often than recordings. The cycling and recycling of recorded Top 40 playlists would be more than a dozen years into the future. So the bootleg publishers were in no position to identify exactly which pop songs might be heard on the radio. Still, they were doing the best that they could under the circumstances. As long as they made efforts to stay current, they had reason to believe that some of their published lyrics would be coordinated with air play on the designated radio shows.

Several years later, one of Santangelo's first legitimate song-lyric magazines, *Radio Hit Songs*, strengthened this link to broadcasting, as is explicit in its title. The unidentified editors made this statement: "RADIO HIT SONGS compiled for one week in October [1941] the number of times popular songs were heard on coast to coast network shows. All of the lyrics of the songs listed below [figure 3.4] appear in this issue of RADIO HIT SONGS and the figure after the name of each song is the combined total of performances nationally heard on more than ten programs emanating during that particular week from stations of NBC, CBS and WOR."[10] It was, in effect, an early effort to "chart" hit songs.

Unusually, this same issue of *Radio Hit Songs* also incorporated two copies of songs in sheet music for piano and voice: "Alexander the Swoose" from Paramount Pictures' film *Hedda Hopper's Hollywood*, and "There's Nothing the Matter with Me," performed by Guy Lombardo in a network radio show.[11] Generally speaking, there was not much overlap between magazines of song lyrics and publications of sheet music.

**Broadening repertory to expand audiences.** Some bootleg song sheets broadened their content beyond current popular songs in order to expand

JAMES STEWART

**FIGURE 3.3.** Back cover of *Prosperity Book No. 40* (undated [circa 1937])

their potential readership, as the unidentified editors of *Prosperity Book No. 36* explained: "In order to give you more for your money we have put into this issue Cowboy, Old Time Songs, Hobo Poems, the Snappiest Jokes and the Latest Song Hits of today. We want to inform you that the above are under their own headings except the Jokes which you will find on pages 9, 22, 23, and 24 in this book."[12] Numerous other bootleg song sheets offer pages of jokes alongside pages of lyrics, and cowboy and old-time songs are common. Poetry is less

**FIGURE 3.4.** Boxed list of current hit songs in *Radio Hit Songs* 1, no. 2 (November 1941)

usual—although of course song lyrics are themselves poetry—and *Prosperity Book No. 36* perhaps stretches the divergence from current American popular songs as far as it may be stretched, including among its "hobo poems" Rudyard Kipling's poem of 1895, "If."

Perhaps the most interesting aspect of efforts to broaden the readership for bootleg song sheets was the inclusion of foreign-language lyrics. At the risk of hyperbole, I would suggest that in this regard the bootleg song sheets stood as both microcosms and exemplars of coexisting aspects of American popular song in the first third of the twentieth century. In *Yesterdays: Popular Song in America*, Charles Hamm traces the history of popular song in great detail, showing how, on the one hand, American popular song of the song-sheet era was overwhelmingly defined by Tin Pan Alley's virtually monolithic structure (described in chapter 1) and a formulaic approach to composition practiced by its songwriters, while on the other hand, American popular song partook of the American immigrant experience. Even in the face of the dominant trends of Tin Pan Alley products, a number of hit songs of that era have as much to do with some sort of expression or evocation of European ethnicity as with Tin Pan Alley's portrayal of love and romance in America.[13]

There is no lack of precedents for the representation of this push and pull between ethnicity and absorption into the mainstream. To take one fine example, the cover page of the December 3, 1914, issue of the *United Mine Workers Journal* heralds the institution of a three-language policy with the cartoon "A Welcome Addition to the Family" (figure 3.5) and an announcement that after canvassing those segments of the union membership whose language was not English, the editors "determined that the Italian and Slavish could be read by more of our non-English-speaking brothers than any other given languages."[14] The United Mine Workers of America had been founded in 1890, and until this last portion of the *Journal*'s twenty-fifth year, its articles were exclusively in English. But then, for nearly two decades from late 1914 until 1933, the *UMW Journal* boasted on its cover of its contents "in three languages." It provided in each issue two distinct sections repeating biweekly news features under the headers ITALIAN SECTION / IL GIORNALE DELL'UNIONE DEI MINATORI AND SLOVAK SECTION / ZURNAL SPOJENYCH MAJNEROV.

The issue of March 15, 1933, was the last to carry these sections. Thereafter, without editorial comment in the months surrounding this last issue, the Italian and Slovak sections were discontinued, and the *UMW Journal* was once again published exclusively in English. Evidently some unexpressed drive toward incorporation into the American mainstream was underway. But it is not as if suddenly all of the immigrant miners were Americanized by the winter of 1933 and there was no longer any need for alternative languages. In fact, the following January, at the Thirty-Third Constitutional Convention of the UMW in Indianapolis in 1934, the Constitution Committee adopted a resolution introduced by Local Union No. 5765 of Blairsville, Pennsylvania, to have union "constitution books made out in foreign language as follows: Russian, Italian, Slovak."[15]

**Ethnic songs in song sheets.** So, when bootleg song-lyric magazines began to appear in the mid-1930s with sections devoted to songs in foreign languages, this would have been a normal idea for an American readership.

**FIGURE 3.5.** Editorial cartoon, "A Welcome Addition to the Family," *United Mine Workers Journal* 25 (December 3, 1914), 1

Indeed, for commonsense reasons of family and nostalgia, explicit connections to a European heritage would survive much longer in song than in the workplace.

The bootleg song sheet *Paramount Book No. 17* (circa late 1936 or early 1937) survives among exhibits preserved in the file from a civil equity case of 1937–38.[16] This song-sheet magazine offers, on two full pages, one or two songs for each of an array of languages/ethnicities: Bohemian, French, German, Hungarian, Irish, Italian, Jewish (i.e., Yiddish), Lithuanian, Slovak, Spanish, Swedish, and Ukrainian.

Portions of the *Prosperity Book* series give further prominence to this same feature. *Prosperity Book No. 36* (see figure 3.2), *Prosperity Book No. 37*, and *Prosperity Book No. 40* all announce prominently, at the top of a sidebar running

**FIGURES 3.6 AND 3.7.** Foreign-language lyrics in *Prosperity Book No. 37* (undated [circa 1937])

alongside their respective cover photos of Claire Trevor, Mae West, and Simone Simon, that "foreign songs will be found on pages 20 and 21."

Like the *Paramount* series, these *Prosperity* booklets offer lyrics in French, German, Greek, Hungarian, Irish, Italian, Jewish (Yiddish), Lithuanian, Polish, Russian, Slovak, Spanish, and Swedish. In *Prosperity Book No. 37* (see figures 3.6 and 3.7) and in *Prosperity Book No. 40*, Greek and Cyrillic characters

## QUAND TU CHANTES
(French)

Quand tu chantes bercée
Le soir, entre mes bras
Entendstu ma pensée
Qui te répond tout bas
Ton doux chant me rappelle
Les plus beaux de me jours
Ah! Chantez, chantez, ma belle,
chantez, chantez toujours,
Chantez, chantez, ma belle, chantez toujours,
Chantez, ma belle,
Chantez toujours!

2.

Quand tu ris, sur ta bouche
L'amour s'épanouit
Et soudain le farouche
Soupçon s'évanouit.
Ah! le rire fidèle
prouve un coeur sans détours.
Ah! Riez, riez ma belle, riez, riez toujours,
Riez, riez, ma belle, riez toujours,
Riez, ma belle,
Riez toujours!

## ΕΧΕ ΓΕΙΑ
(Greek)

Έχε γειά, καλή μου μάνα
έχε γειά γαπητικιάδα,
φεύγω πάω σταρρωνά.
γιά νά βρω τή χλεφτουριά.

## TRITT DAS MÄGDLEIN
(German)

Tritt das Mägdlein aus dem Tor:
Liegt groszer See davor.
Aj ljuli, aj ljuli,
Liegt ein groszer See davor.

2.

Schlanker Bursch sein Rösslein tränkt,
Flink es dann zum Tore lenkt—
Aj ljuli, aj ljuli,
Flink es dann zum Tore lenkt.

3.

Bindet es am Pfosten an.
Spricht zum schönen Mägdlein dann—
Aj ljuli, aj ljuli,
Spricht zum schönen Mägdlein dann:

## Щасть намъ Боже, щасть намъ щасть
(Russian)

Щасть намъ Боже, щасть намъ щасть,
Розвивати русский цвѣтъ!
Богъ намъ Вышній силы дасть,
Мы сотворимъ новый свѣтъ;
Нуже, братья, ну-жь дѣлати,
Поки еще путь предъ нами,
Дабы свѣту показати,
Шо мы еще Русинами!

Щасть намъ Боже, щасть намъ щасть,
Начинати въ добрый часъ!
Тажь надъ нами Божа власть,
Тажь и нашъ народъ не згасъ;
Славу нашу повиткаемъ,
Русскими сердцемъ, русскимъ словомъ
И весело заспѣваемъ,
Надбескидскимъ гукомъ, громомъ.

Щасть намъ Боже, щасть намъ щасть,
Русьскій неицъ, вѣрнымъ всѣмъ!
Вже загибла наша страсть,
Ну-жь ся шинъ веселъмъ;
Всюды най ся отзиває
Одинъ голосъ, одна вѣра,
Наши сердця огрѣвае,
Якъ за часовъ Владимира.

Щасть намъ Боже, щасть намъ щасть,
Устроити русский храмъ!
Богъ намъ помощь данъ и дасть,
Щобъ достойно въ свѣтѣ жити,
Щасть такъ, Боже, дальше намъ,
Якъ то наши батьки жили,
Имя русске возносити,
Щобъ го враги полюбили.

## A MAASEH
(Jewish)

Amul is gevein a Maaseh,
Die Maaseh is gar nit freilech,
Die Maaseh eibt sich un
Mit a groisen Yudischen Mellech,
Lulinke main Sinenu,
Lulinke main Kind,
Ich hob ungevoiren aza Liebe,
Wei is mir un Wind.

Amul is gevein a Mellech,
Der Mellech hot gehat a Malke,
Die Malke hot gehat a Weingurten,
Dem schonsten oif der Welt.
Lulinke main Sinenu, u. s. w.

3.

In Gurten is gewein a Beimale
Dus Beimale hot gehat a Zwaigele,
Oif'n Zwaigele is gewein a Neistele
In Neistele hot gelelbt a Feigele.
Lulinke main Sinenu, u. s. w.

4.

Der Mellech is ubgestorben,
Die Malke is gevorn fardorben,
Dus Zwaigele hot sich ubgebrochen,
Dus Feigale is fun'm Neist antlofen.
Lulinke main Sinenu, u. s. w.

## DERMOT ASTORE
(Irish)

Oh! Dermot Astore! between waking and
    sleeping,
I heard thy dear voice, and I wept to its lay;
Ev'ry pulse of my heart, the sweet measure
    was keeping,
Till Killarney's wild echoes had borne it
    away.
Oh! tell me my own love, is this our last
    meeting,
Shall we wander no more in Killarney's
    green bow'rs.
To watch the bright sun o'er the dim hills
    retreating,
And the wild stag at rest in his bed of
    spring flow'rs?
Oh! Dermot Astore! between waking
    and sleeping,
I heard thy dear voice, and I wept to
    its lay;
Ev'ry pulse of my heart the sweet measure
    was keeping,
Till Killarney's wild echoes had borne it
    away.

## LA TERRUCA
(Spanish)

Es el móvil Océano gran espejo
Donde luce, como adorno sin igual,
El terruño borincano, que es reflejo
Del perdido paraíso terrenal.
Son de fáciles pendientes sus colinas;
Y en sus valles de riquísimo verdor,
Van cantando bellas fuentes cristalinas,
Como flautas que bendicen al Creador.

2.

Primavera sus mejores atributos
Muestra siempre generosa en Borinquen:
En los campos siempre hay flores, siempre
    hay frutos
Es Borinquen la mansión de todo bien!
Aquí nace el puro ambiente que respiro,
Y se asienta la morada en que nací;
Y ese sol resplandeciente que yo admiro,
Aquí nace, aquí brilla, y muere aquí.

## UNA FURTIVA LAGRIMA
(Italian)

Una furtiva lagrima
negl' occhi suoi spuntò:
quelle festose giovani
invidiarnembro;
che più cercando io vo?
Che più cercando io vo?
M'ama, sì m'ama, lo vedo, lo vedo!
Un solo i stante i palpiti
del suo bel cor sentir!
i miei sospir confondere, per poco a' suoi
    sospir.
i palpiti, i palpiti sentir,
confondere i miei coi suoi sospir.
Cielo si può morir;
di più non chiedo, non chiedo, ah!
Cielo, si può morir, non chiedo,
di più non chiedo, non chiedo!

## DU GRØNNE GLITRENDE TRAE,
GOD DAG!
(Swedish)

Du grønne glitrende trae, god dag!
Velkommen, du som vi ser saa gjerne,
med julelys og med norske flag
og hølt i toppen den blanke stjerne!
Ja den maa skinne,
for den skal minde
os om vor gud.

2.

Den Forste jul i et fremmed land
sin store stjerne Vorherre taendte;
den skulde vise vor jord, at han
den lille Jesus til verden sendte.
I stjerneglansen
gik engledansen
om Betlehem.

3.

Om Jesusbarnet fortalte mor
saamangen aften, vi sad herhjemme;
vi kan hans bud og hans milde ord,
vi ved, at aldrig vi dem maa glemme.
Naar stjernen skinner,
om ham os minder
vort juletrae.

## MAROS VIZE FOLYIK
(Hungaran)

Maros vize folyik csendesen,
Borulj a vállamra, kedvesem.
Nem borulok, van már nékem szeretőm,
Szüret után lesz az esküvőm.

## JA DO HORY NEPÓJDEM
(Slovak)

Ja do hory nepójdem
drevo rúbať nebudem:
drevo by ma zabilo,
čo by dievča robilo?
drevo bzy ma zabilo,
čo by dievča robilo?

2.

Sekerečku tupú mám,
frajerečku bystrú mám;
frajerečka neveri,
ani otcu materi,
frajerečka neveri,
ani otcu materi.

## SALTA ŽIEMUŽĖ
(Lithuanian)

Salta žiemužė, grusčius sutraukė,
Jauna mergelė bernelio laukia.
O drylla la la o drylla la la...
Jauna mergelė bernelio laukia.
Laukiant eulaukiant piršliai atjojo,
Jauna mergelė pasidaboyo.
Teveli mano senasai mano,
Ar man' išleisi už to bernelio?
Pučia vėjelis iš ano krašto,
Nebesulaukiu nuo brolio rašto...

## O PRZYSZŁO MI PRZYSZŁO
(Polish)

O przyszło mi przyszło
Od majora pismo,
Musze maszerować, musze maszerować
Na wojenkę ista.

2.

Musze odejść ojca,
Matke miłosnice,
:Musze maszerować:|
Na pruską granicę.

3.

Na pruską granicę
Wszyscy się zjezdżaja,
:A te nasze serca:|
Bardzo się lękaja.

4.

Będzie wojna, będzie
Wele Raciborza:
|:Tam się krew przeleje:|
Jako woda z morza.

5.

Będzie wojna, będzie
W okoluško wszędzie:
|:Szczęśliwy ten wojak,:|
Co on do dom przyjdzie.

6.

Będzie wojna, będzie
W okoluško wszędzie:
|:Nie jedna matuchna:|
Syneczka pozbędzie.

appear, and lyrics in other languages, from French to Swedish, have appropriate diacritical marks. This is actually somewhat surprising, given how many corners the publishers and editors cut in other areas. In bootleg publications printed on the cheapest available acidic colored paper, in bootleg publications featuring blurred and grainy images of actors and actresses, in bootleg publications prepared so hastily and carelessly that their indexes of song titles never quite agree with their contents, the care taken with language perhaps indicates the importance that the bootleggers attributed to their potential ethnic audience.

These issues in the *Prosperity Book* series were the earliest that I obtained, and *No. 17* is all that I have seen of the *Paramount* series. It may be that foreign-language sections were introduced before 1936, but I have no evidence to that effect. This feature was perhaps neither widespread nor long-lived. Other mid-1930s bootleg issues that I obtained are English-only. I also acquired a couple of later issues in the *Prosperity* series, *Prosperity Book No. 77* and *Prosperity Book No. 78,* both of which date from around 1940, by association with the film songs featured therein. These too are also English-only. And nearly all of the legitimate song-lyric magazines that I examined, dating from 1934 onward, are English-only publications. Exceptionally, there is a nod toward ethnic heritage in the first issue of *Broadcast Song Hits* (October 1941), with English-language versions of Spanish, Italian, and Russian songs, as well as the lyrics to "Good Neighbor: Song of the 21 American Republics," which appears in three languages, English, Spanish, and Portuguese. Also, a page in Santangelo's *Big Song Magazine* (September 1941), presents "foreign songs translated into English with modern lyrics."[17]

Did the song sheets rather quickly turn away from the inclusion of foreign-language lyrics because, as with the United Mine Workers, something was in the air about Americanization? Or did the publishers perhaps simply run out of foreign-language popular songs to print? The latter explanation seems likely. Indeed, the overall proportionality in the contents of song sheets—predominantly current American popular songs with doses of nostalgia, novelty, and ethnicity sprinkled in—well represents Hamm's conception of American popular song of this era.

**Advertisements in support of the entertainment industry.** Foreign-language sections excepted, most of these features of bootleg song sheets carried over into legitimate song-lyric magazines, including the association of lyrics with images of film stars, and the identification of shows in which songs might be heard. But legitimate publishers had an additional path open to them as well. They could use advertisements to strengthen associations with a diversity of musical products.

An issue of the first authorized song-lyric magazine, *Song Hit Folio* (1934), urges readers to "learn to dance the 'Continental' . . . 'you kiss while you dance' . . . Introduced by Ginger Rogers and Fred Astaire . . . complete this issue" (see the reproduction of the cover in chapter 2, figure 2.3). Inside the magazine, side panels offer eight sequential photographs of Fred and Ginger dancing. These panels flank a step-by-step description of the principal movements of the ballroom dance, and this description in turn appears beneath promotional information for film, dance, and broadcasting. Readers learn that "the Continental was created for and danced in the new RKO-Radio picture 'The Gay Divorcée.'" It was adapted for ballroom dancing by the "New York Dancing Master" Thomas Parson, "whose Radio Dancing Lessons are heard weekly over Station WOR."[18]

In this same issue, there is also a photographic preview of another film, *The Merry Widow*, starring Maurice Chevalier and Jeanette MacDonald. A two-page spread at the back of the magazine presents nineteen stills from this movie, with captions summarizing the plot line.

Music publishers and broadcasters had their hands into this legitimate publication in other ways as well. In what was probably part of a running series of promotions of songwriters in *Song Hit Folio*, page 2 offers a photograph and biography of Arthur Schwartz, whose "latest contribution to the field is the popular 'Then I'll Be Tired of You.'" Lyrics to that song then appear on page 5. Finally, the back cover of this issue of *Song Hit Folio* promotes other areas of broadcasting via a photographic collage of well-known radio singers, comedians, actors, and actresses, including Frances Langford, Gracie Allen, and George Burns, all performing into microphones for the NBC and CBS networks.

**Gossip columns, songwriting contests, and other special features.** The first issue of *Song Hits*, introduced in mid-1937, has this note to readers: "The editorial staff is convinced that there is a big and growing need for such a publication as this—a magazine which in every issue prints the lyrics of 100 hit songs, many of them just off the press, and also keeps its readers informed as to the latest musical doings in Hollywood, Tin Pan Alley and the radio studios."[19] In the early 1940s, as song-lyric magazines gained favor in music publishing circles and the bootlegging faded away, these publications took on something more of the character of fan magazines. They included gossip columns, promotional biographies of stars in various segments of the entertainment world, and even record reviews.[20]

In a different type of bid for audience involvement, and again illustrating a path that was available to the legitimate publications but not to the bootleggers, *Song Hit Folio* urged readers to participate in a parody songwriting contest (figure 3.8). The contest was clearly an ongoing feature of the magazine, and a later issue of June 1935 had a fine offering from Henry McDonald of San

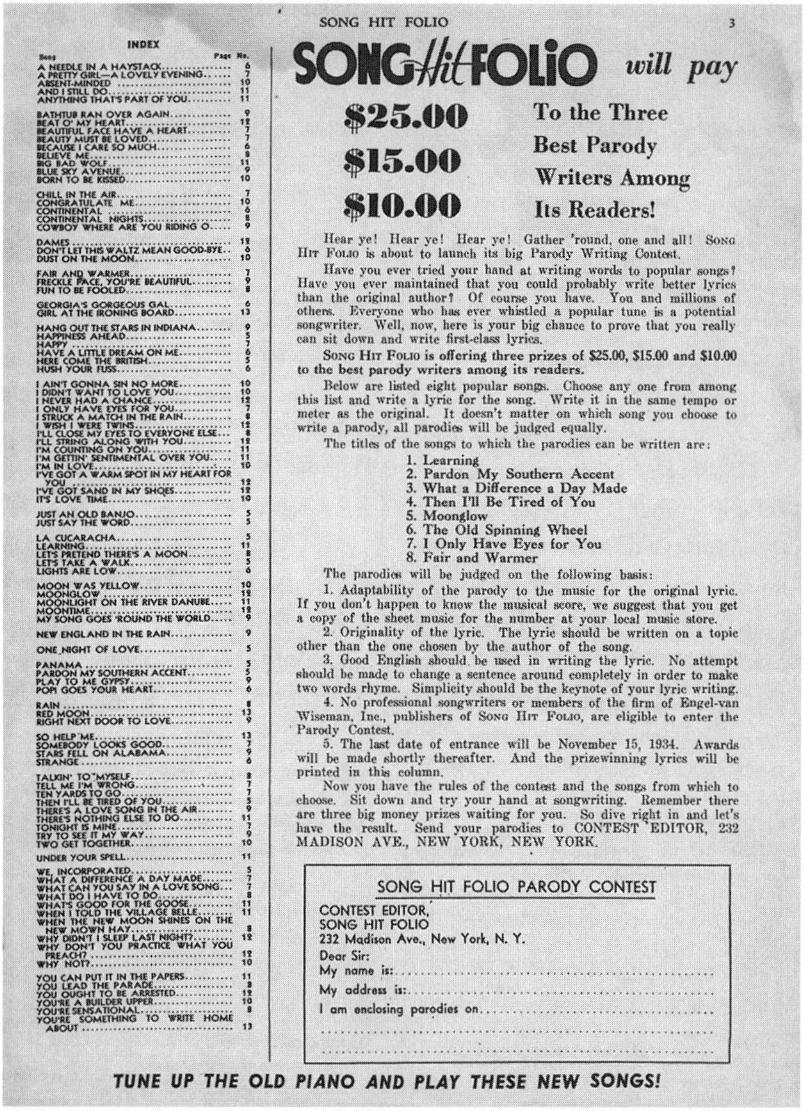

SONG HIT FOLIO 3

## INDEX



## SONG *Hit* FOLIO *will pay*

**$25.00 $15.00 $10.00**

**To the Three Best Parody Writers Among Its Readers!**

Hear ye! Hear ye! Hear ye! Gather 'round, one and all! SONG HIT FOLIO is about to launch its big Parody Writing Contest.

Have you ever tried your hand at writing words to popular songs? Have you ever maintained that you could probably write better lyrics than the original author? Of course you have. You and millions of others. Everyone who has ever whistled a popular tune is a potential songwriter. Well, now, here is your big chance to prove that you really can sit down and write first-class lyrics.

**SONG HIT FOLIO is offering three prizes of $25.00, $15.00 and $10.00 to the best parody writers among its readers.**

Below are listed eight popular songs. Choose any one from among this list and write a lyric for the song. Write it in the same tempo or meter as the original. It doesn't matter on which song you choose to write a parody, all parodies will be judged equally.

The titles of the songs to which the parodies can be written are:

1. Learning
2. Pardon My Southern Accent
3. What a Difference a Day Made
4. Then I'll Be Tired of You
5. Moonglow
6. The Old Spinning Wheel
7. I Only Have Eyes for You
8. Fair and Warmer

The parodies will be judged on the following basis:

1. Adaptability of the parody to the music for the original lyric. If you don't happen to know the musical score, we suggest that you get a copy of the sheet music for the number at your local music store.

2. Originality of the lyric. The lyric should be written on a topic other than the one chosen by the author of the song.

3. Good English should be used in writing the lyric. No attempt should be made to change a sentence around completely in order to make two words rhyme. Simplicity should be the keynote of your lyric writing.

4. No professional songwriters or members of the firm of Engel-van Wiseman, Inc., publishers of SONG HIT FOLIO, are eligible to enter the Parody Contest.

5. The last date of entrance will be November 15, 1934. Awards will be made shortly thereafter. And the prizewinning lyrics will be printed in this column.

Now you have the rules of the contest and the songs from which to choose. Sit down and try your hand at songwriting. Remember there are three big money prizes waiting for you. So dive right in and let's have the result. Send your parodies to CONTEST EDITOR, 232 MADISON AVE., NEW YORK, NEW YORK.

SONG HIT FOLIO PARODY CONTEST

CONTEST EDITOR,
SONG HIT FOLIO
232 Madison Ave., New York, N. Y.

Dear Sir:
My name is:....................
My address is:....................
I am enclosing parodies on....................
....................
....................

**TUNE UP THE OLD PIANO AND PLAY THESE NEW SONGS!**

**FIGURE 3.8.** Parody songwriting contest in *Song Hit Folio*, no. 9 (November 10, 1934), 3

Francisco, who was awarded second place for turning the song "You and the Night and the Music" into "Me and the Beer and the Pretzels."[21] Song-writing contests continued to appear, whether based on parodies of hit songs or on the straightforward creation of new lyrics, the latter contests ostensibly affording opportunities to achieve a hit song. (Was this an aspiring songwriter's prewar parallel to our modern-day *American Idol*?) Numerous examples of songwriting contests may be found in legitimate song-lyric magazines published by Engel–van Wiseman, Inc., in the late 1930s and early 1940s, in the low-budget legitimate magazines introduced by Santangelo when he was on the road to respectability in 1941, and in the publications that came to dominate the field in the 1940s, when Santangelo founded *Hit Parader* and acquired *Song Hits* from Engel.

**Aiming advertisements at women.** In addition to generating income from direct sales and from sponsored tie-ins to stage, screen, and radio, the legitimate song-lyric magazines were supported by the sale of boxed advertisements of various musical and nonmusical products. Establishing a pattern that would continue for many years, the mid-1930s magazines *Popular Song Hits* and *Song Hit Folio* mainly ran ads directed at women: "a woman proposes!"; "you want a lovely bust & form"; "the secrets of sex daringly revealed!"; "would you be interested in finding a short cut to romance?"; "beautiful eyes with Maybelline"; "your marriage forecast"; "skin eruptions"; "why be flat-chested?"; "I reduced 70 lbs."; and so on, with alleged remedies for pimples, facial hair, and other more sensitive problems.[22]

A second general category of advertisements, smaller but still substantial, were directed at amateur musicians, and occasionally, amateur dancers: "be popular! learn to play piano by ear"; "it's fun to play by ear on the guitar, tenor-guitar, banjo or uke"; "to those who think learning music is hard"; "your voice"; "learn to dance"; "compose popular songs"; "become a radio star!"; and so forth. Often these advertisements picture women playing an instrument or singing.[23]

There were also recurring advertisements for Remington portable typewriters and for cheap novels.[24] No doubt the typewriters were aimed at women in secretarial careers.

In later years of legitimate song-lyric magazines, the typewriters ads continued, as did the bids for improved musicianship. A woman's appearance clearly remained the overwhelmingly predominant concern. There were occasional appeals to men as well, most memorably in the famous advertisement for Charles Atlas's body-building program: "The 97lb. Weakling who became 'The World's Most Perfectly Developed Man.'"[25]

One obvious implication is that the principal audience for song-lyric magazines, insofar as this might be inferred from the nature of their advertisements, was women, who presumably enjoyed singing the hits of the day in all sorts of settings—public, private, family, social. Another obvious implication is that there was a secondary market consisting of amateur musicians of either sex, but again predominantly women. The cultural reasons why this was so are not obvious, and I have not discovered a suitable explanation. Men bought records. Men listened to the radio. Men sang. Men went to films and stage shows. Why wouldn't they have bought these magazines in equal numbers to women? Was there some sort of tie to an early to mid-twentieth-century conception of American domesticity that somehow reinforced a woman's interest in song lyrics? I have made inquiries to scholars in diverse areas of women's history, musicology, sociology, and theory, but none could offer any interpretive help, perhaps largely because none of these scholars had ever seen, or even heard of, a song-lyric magazine. How interesting it is that an artifact of pop culture that circulated in millions of copies in the 1930s and 1940s later utterly disappeared from our popular and historical awareness and understanding.

Here, then, is a summary of the overall development. Song sheets were transformational products, generated in response to a transformation of the entertainment industry and the consequent transformation of the way in which general audiences related to popular songs. Song sheets were conveniently suited to those new needs in ways that sheet music could not match. And so, although now completely forgotten, song sheets then poured forth, in millions of copies, bootlegged or legitimized, reaching vast general audiences (perhaps mainly consisting of women), and ultimately becoming absorbed into the mainstream of American music publications.

# 4 • *Fake Books and Music Photocopying*

For printed music, there were two notable successors to song sheets in the realm of songs, distribution, and disobedience. One was a contested product, the pop song fake book. (Jazz fake books also emerged, but without any fighting.) The other was a contested action, unauthorized music photocopying.

**Pop song fake books.** The story of pop song fake books is almost exactly a retelling of the story of song sheets, except insofar as this transformational song product was specialized, intended for musicians only, rather than for the general public. Otherwise, the outline of events should now seem familiar:

Responding to a perceived need—that professional nightclub musicians would be happy to buy anthologies of popular songs—and acting without the blessing of sheet-music publishers, bootleggers brought out a new song product, pop song fake books. They distributed these volumes through unauthorized channels. This action caused great anguish to the song owners. Once again the owners shouted "gangsters!" Once again they proclaimed equivalency to sheet music. Once again they called in the FBI, filed civil suits, and supported criminal prosecutions. Once again—this time more than two decades into the battle—they ultimately gave up on prohibition and instead successfully pursued assimilation, putting out legitimate pop song fake books that almost immediately took the market away from the bootleggers.

The two stories, song sheets and fake books, even shared the same brand of irony. Just as song-sheet peddlers were hawking their wares on the street in front of the buildings in which Tin Pan Alley songwriters, publishers, and song pluggers worked on Broadway in the 1930s, so fake-book peddlers were hawking their wares in the halls of Local 802, the New York City musicians union, in the 1950s.

**A licensing catalogue for broadcasters.** The origin of fake books resides in the realm of AM radio, in a product originally designed to aid the fulfillment of licensing agreements between performing rights agencies and broadcasters, and only belatedly marketed to nightclub musicians. In 1942 George Goodwin, a radio station program director in New York City, began to distribute, via subscription, monthly one-hundred-card packets of a personal creation that he called the Tune-Dex. By analogy with the cards found in any American library catalogue of that era, each Tune-Dex card presented an abridged summary of an American popular song, and its associated licensing information, on a three-by-five-inch index card (for an example, see figures 4.1 and 4.2). For the most part, each song took up one card, although the length of some songs required a double-sized six-by-five-inch card, folded in half to fit with the others in the card file.[1]

Goodwin's intent was to assist music professionals in identifying a song, not to convey a complete notated version of that song. On one side of any given card was the melody of the best-known portion of the song, the remainder having been omitted in the course of his abridgement. Chord symbols, providing a shorthand version of a possible harmonization of that melody, stood above the melody notes. Lyrics lay below it. On the other side of that card was information on copyright and licensing, identifying composer, lyricist, publisher, and performing rights agency.

The central idea behind the genesis of the Tune-Dex was that professionals who were responsible for maintaining licensing agreements could have a handy guide to songs. They might hear tunes and recognize them, or hear lyrics and recognize them, or just read titles on a list generated in the course of a day's work in the studio. They could then look up the appropriate Tune-Dex card to see which publisher or agency controlled the rights to a particular song. Goodwin's card catalogue was potentially useful not only in broadcasting, but in film, recording, commercial public performance, or advertising— any arena in which a promoter, producer, bandleader, agent, or other entertainment professional might become involved in licensing agreements for the use of popular songs.

The Tune-Dex was extremely successful. Subscriptions reached into every area of the industry. By the mid-1960s, when ill health forced Goodwin to abandon the project, he had issued approximately twenty-five thousand Tune-Dex cards (roughly one hundred per month for two decades) to an unknown number of subscribers.

**Transformational use: Tune-Dex cards for musicians.** More than three years after conceiving the project, and a few months after introducing it via subscription, Goodwin also began to market Tune-Dex cards to musicians performing alone or in small groups in cocktail lounges and other such venues where it was normal to receive requests for songs that an unaccompanied pianist or a group of band members might not know, or might not remember without a visual aid. In his advertisements, Goodwin pointed out that with a

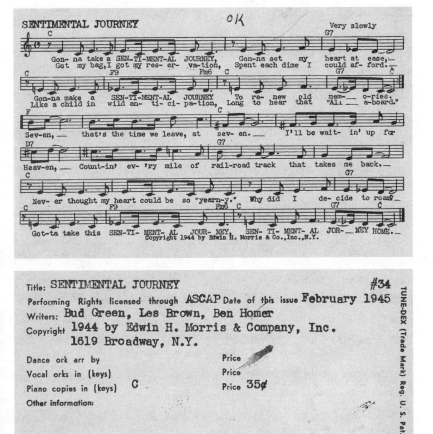

**FIGURES 4.1 AND 4.2.** Tune-Dex card for "Sentimental Journey"

concise, abridged version of the requested song in hand on a Tune-Dex card, the musician(s) could "fake" a performance, presumably well enough to satisfy the person who made the request. Failure to do so could generate complaints and possibly the loss of a job. So the Tune-Dex was a potentially valuable aid to professional performers.

But the Tune-Dex was unwieldy. The issue was portability. It was one thing for a radio station to have thousands of Tune-Dex cards sitting in permanent alphabetical order for quick and easy reference in a cabinet of wooden card-catalogue drawers situated just outside of the studio. It was quite another thing for a musician to bring shoeboxes full of Tune-Dex cards to a gig and then trawl through the loose cards, trying to find the right card for some obscure request that a customer had just made. The alternative, carrying around and sorting through heavy stacks of loose sheet music, was perhaps even more tedious and cumbersome. If instead, a stack of Tune-Dex cards might be compiled into a single bound volume, this could be something convenient, offering quick and easy access to tunes. Here, then, was an absolutely unambiguous example of transformational use: a stationary card catalogue for radio licensing became a mobile bound-volume anthology for musicians, catering to the needs of professional players in a way that separate cards or separate sheet music could not.

**Bootlegging fake books.** The battle began in 1949. Music publishers were unwilling to issue compilations of Tune-Dex cards, on the assertion that such a product would cut into profits from sheet music. So "gangsters" stepped into the void. As noted earlier, fake books offer an example of transformational use achieved entirely without technological innovation. The bootleggers paid conventional printers to use the photostatic method to assemble images of Tune-Dex cards that were organized, three cards to the page. A later generation of bootleggers would use an even cruder production method, employing the technology of scissors and Scotch tape: rather than laying out Tune-Dex cards on a page, they cut up sheet music and then taped together whatever bits they needed to convey a concise abridgement of any given tune. In either case, the printer then made copies and gathered the resulting double-sided pages into bound volumes. In the Tune-Dex volumes, the cards were laid out roughly in a generalized alphabetical order, or roughly in alphabetical order by categories, mainly of dance genres (waltzes, fox-trots, ballads, Latin dances, etc.)

In March 1949 the first unauthorized bound volume of 450 Tune-Dex cards appeared in Chicago. Beginning in 1950 and continuing through the decade, unauthorized volumes of a thousand songs each circulated nationally. The essential function of these volumes was to aid musicians in improvising ("faking") versions of American popular songs. And so, after some years, the volumes came to be known as "fake books."

It was the song-sheet battle all over again. Having published that story in considerable detail elsewhere, I think I may safely forgo the details of fake-book bootlegging here. Instead, a selection of entertainment trade-paper headlines spanning two decades ought to convey, well enough, the sense to which the attempts to prohibit unauthorized fake-book publishing unfolded along nearly identical lines to those involving song sheets:

1950: "Major Bootleg Operation Suspected in Chi[cago] Copyright Infringement Suit"
1951: "FBI Taking Action vs. Tune-Dex Bootleggers"
1951: "FBI Launches Nationwide Search to Nab Infringement Racketeers"
1962: "Chi[cago] Songleggers Change Pleas to Guilty in Fed[eral] C[our]t"
1966: "Musician Indicted over 'Fake-books'"
1966: "Musician is Fined $5,000 for his Illegal Songbook"
1969 "Jury Convicts 'Fake Book' Op[erator]s"
1969: "2 Fined $4,500 for Making 'Fake Books' of Music Hits"[2]

The attempt to suppress fake-book publications was even less successful than the attempt to suppress bootleg song sheets. One reason for this was that the audience for the new cultural product was specialized. Fake books were not for everyone. They were for musicians only. Initially the consumer demographic consisted of those professional musicians who "faked" songs as a part of their nightly duties. In later years the market expanded to take in aspiring student musicians, who began to use fake books as an aid in learning how to interpret American popular songs in live performance.

Because of this focused consumer demographic, sales of fake books could generally be made on the fly, the books pulled out of boxes in someone's car trunk, or shelved in small quantities, out of sight, hidden under the counter in a music store. Therefore it was much more difficult to justify the expense of FBI investigations and federal trials, particularly given that criminal copyright infringement was at this time, before the mid-1970s, still a misdemeanor, not a felony.

Another reason for the failure at prohibition was that musicians constituted, in and among themselves, a community. They were protective of one another, and they were tight-lipped in their testimony to FBI agents, who failed in all of their efforts to identify individuals at the head of pop song fake-book distribution systems. Some medium-sized fish were fried, but no one of John Santangelo's stature ever emerged from these investigations.

In the 1970s, after an effort spanning more than two decades, music publishers gave up the fight and began to produce authorized versions of pop song fake books. These publications were immediately successful. Unlike all of the attempts at prohibition, the rival legitimate publications quickly put the authorized bootleg publications out of business, simply by taking away their market share.

**The decline of sheet music.** The story of pop song fake books provides an example that is as clear-cut as it could possibly be, of a pattern of contested distribution, followed by the assimilation of a new song product into a legitimate sphere, and the obsolescence of the old. The transformation wrought upon pop song music publishing by song sheets and pop song fake books continued well beyond the lifetimes of the original bootleg objects. Both products may have contributed to the decline of sheet music, as music publishers feared, but neither product may be held fully responsible for that decline. Larger forces were at play: the ascendance of recording and broadcasting, the corresponding decline of music making at home, and the consequent transformation of the general pop song audience from music makers to listeners. Exact figures are lacking, but record sales had overtaken sheet-music sales early on, and certainly by the 1940s recordings were predominant. In the first industry-wide survey of music publishers, conducted in 1953, the publishers claimed $30 million in retail sales. Record sales from six years earlier, in 1947, were more than ten times that figure, and advertising income from radio operations was roughly the same as that for record sales, ten times the income from sheet-music sales.

Soon ten to one became one hundred to one. In the early 1950s, while popular artists and their companies were aiming for a recording that sold a million copies—"solid gold," in industry parlance—a million-selling sheet-music title was entirely a thing of the past. Half that amount, five hundred thousand paper copies of any single title, was a huge hit. The market for sheet music crashed further during the mid-1950s. By the spring of 1957 Elvis Presley's recording of "Love Me Tender" had sold 2 million copies, while sheet-music sales of this title reached a tenth of that, at two hundred thousand copies.[3] For hit songs less exceptional than "Love Me Tender," publishers feared "that if they print up some 75,000 copies for the rack, they might be swamped by the returns."[4] Total sales for printed hits declined still further as this decade progressed, to fifteen thousand or even ten thousand copies.

Meanwhile the new transformational products held their own. Lyric magazines satisfied general listeners, most of whom did not play the piano at home and therefore did not need sheet music. Fake books satisfied working musicians who did not want to bother with organizing and transporting sheet music or Tune-Dex cards. The old and the new were on opposing trajectories. Sheet-music sales were entering their decade of severe decline while Santangelo's Charlton Press was expanding the market for legitimate pop song lyric magazines, and bootleg pop song fake books were beginning to take hold.

In the 1960s it became commonplace for lyrics to be printed not only in magazines, but also as liner notes on LPs, a practice that the jazz singer and lyricist Jon Hendricks claimed to have originated for the Lambert, Hendricks, and Ross album *Sing a Song of Basie*, recorded in 1957.[5] For folk music and rock music and combinations thereof, the inclusion of printed lyrics became integral to an album's design. Nonetheless, lyric magazines held their own for quite some time, retaining a healthy circulation alongside the newer mass means for disseminating the words to pop songs. Despite this competition from lyrics printed on albums, Charlton added publications of country-and-western lyrics, rock lyrics, and soul lyrics to their mainstream pop song titles, *Song Hits* and *Hit Parader,* in this decade.

By the 1970s, when legitimate pop song fake books replaced their bootleg predecessors, sheet music was well on its way to becoming an antiquarian item found in archives and flea markets rather than on display racks at music stores. By the 1980s the market for lyrics was tipping away from Charlton, which went out of business in mid-decade. The dissemination of popular song lyrics had transferred overwhelmingly from paper publications to the disks themselves, with LP liner notes becoming CD inserts as the new format emerged. In recent years, lyrics have also circulated extensively on the Internet, often in unauthorized postings that might be conceived as modern-day descendants of the 1930s bootleg sheets. Meanwhile, fake books continue to be a successful song product, not only for popular songs, but in other contexts, whether bluegrass tunes or Christmas songs.

**Jazz fake books.** Unlike song sheets and pop song fake books, jazz fake books offer an instance in which typical patterns of contested distribution failed to engage, because the unauthorized product was never perceived to be valuable enough to threaten existing distribution systems and cultural goods. In 1975, as pop song fake books were gaining widespread legitimate status, a jazz fake book called *The Real Book* was created by two students at the Berklee College of Music in Boston, with some assistance from faculty members, and with compositions donated by several of the leading young jazz composers of the day, including Pat Metheny, Chick Corea, Gary Burton, Steve Swallow, and Mike Gibbs, all of whom were then working at Berklee. This being a low-budget operation, designed to help fellow students learn how to play jazz, the student creators had no intention of paying royalties for the reproduction of either the donated songs or their jazz-oriented revisions of classic American popular songs.

*The Real Book* turned out to be a wonderful resource, capturing in notation a snapshot of the conventions of jazz performance in a manner far superior to any other fake book of that era. To the surprise of everyone involved in its creation, it became popular worldwide. Nonetheless, it did not set in motion a pattern of attempted containment. While bootleg pop song fake books elicited a severe reaction immediately upon their appearance late in 1949, *The Real Book* was more or less ignored for thirty years, in part because aspiring student jazz musicians were perhaps too impoverished for the song owners to bother with pursuing remuneration, and perhaps more importantly because this product appeared during an explosion of activity in record and video bootlegging that overwhelmed the attentions of the powers that be. To be sure, *The Real Book* maintained its status as an unauthorized song product. The creators, despite their marvelous achievement, never owned up to it (let alone being celebrated for it, as they should be), and copies of *The Real Book* were sold, and continued to be sold into the twenty-first century, out of car trunks or under the counter in music stores.

Other unauthorized jazz fake books have circulated since the 1980s in paper form. These have been joined since the 1990s by digital copies circulating on CD-ROM, and more recently by postings on the Internet. All of these successors to *The Real Book* have operated under the radar, discouraged by the song owners, but not explicitly prosecuted. Clearly song owners have deemed these books not worth fighting. Consequently the pattern for jazz fake books has entailed not attempts at suppression, as with their pop song predecessors, but rather decades of disregard and an ongoing, quietly veiled mode of distribution.

The little twist on this story is that the year 2006 brought a significant step toward assimilation, without any fighting having preceded it, when the music publisher Hal Leonard issued a legitimate but somewhat altered version of *The Real Book*. Because this authorized version of *The Real Book* is not identical to the bootleg product, it remains to be seen whether the unauthorized original will fade away. In any event, now there is even less reason to fight.

**Music photocopying.** The story of music photocopying is very different from and far less tidy than the stories of song sheets and fake books, in its compass, origins, approaches to prosecution, and outcome. As far as music was concerned, there was no distinction between genres; any music might be copied, and in fact, disobedient behavior came to be concentrated in the realms of educational and religious music, rather than popular song (although of course there were many intersections between popular song and school ensembles). For this reason, although song owners did not hesitate to denounce the act of unauthorized photocopying as criminal or amoral, they were extremely hesitant to call in the FBI and pursue criminal investigations. The idea of putting a beloved band director or a local pastor on trial was a public relations nightmare. Indeed, with only one especially significant exception, song owners avoided civil suits as well as criminal prosecutions, concentrating instead on conducting a moral campaign against photocopying. This campaign was of questionable success.

Another difference is that while song sheets and fake books involved largely self-enclosed stories, the musical component of disputes over photocopying was little more than a footnote to a much more wide-ranging story. The act of photocopying music without permission arose from the development of a technology designed for business uses and having nothing to do with music per se. The prosecution of unauthorized photocopying centered around the distribution of customized college and university course packets that were cutting deeply into the national market for textbooks. Ultimately, this was the arena for a meaningful legal battle, and a succession of court rulings brought major victories to textbook publishers. Those engaged in music photocopying were obliged to follow suit, at least in theory, but because music photocopying was by comparison with course packets an ad hoc, scattered practice, it was extremely difficult to pin down. So the musical question has remained largely unresolved, with continuing disobedience, no viable prospect for assimilation, and no reasonable expectation of imminent obsolescence.

With regard to the question of equivalency versus transformational use, the act of music photocopying was also much more complicated and ambiguous than either of the earlier actions, bootlegging song sheets or bootlegging fake books. On first glance, unauthorized copying, simply to avoid having to pay for authorized publications, is a straightforward rip-off of music publishers. But on closer examination, its practitioners offer many explanations for their use of the photocopier. Although some of these explanations are just rationalizations for bad behavior, other explanations constitute justifications for music photocopying that contribute, in one way or another, toward tipping the balance from equivalency at least some portion of the way toward transformational use.

**The prehistory of music photocopying.** The seeds of this contest were planted in the use of technologies such as the mimeographed sheet, the projection of transparencies, or photographic reproduction for unauthorized copying. A few complaints along these lines surfaced in the 1940s and 1950s. In 1941, at the behest of the MPPA, the National Music Council initiated a campaign to discourage faculty at schools, colleges, and music conservatories from engaging in "illegal reproductive practices," creating and distributing musical arrangements within their institutions without permission of, and without purchasing from, the song owners. The practice continued, and a decade later, in January 1951, the MPPA sent letters to music dealers nationwide, complaining of "a growing practice among music teachers, schools and musicians of copying and arranging music for their own use without permission." Dealers were urged to speak to the appropriate members of their communities, lobbying against this practice.[6]

In 1953 the Music Publishers Association (MPA), whose members concentrated on educational, church, and concert music, accused educational institutions of systematically avoiding purchases of musical scores, folios, and pedagogical materials through the practice of the unauthorized transfer of scores and parts to microfilm, slides, or film strips. These images would then be used in classrooms and at conferences in lieu of the purchase and dissemination of multiple copies of authorized printings of the music. For example, the MPA noted, a piece of choral music might be filmed and then shown on a large screen, for group singing. The organization recognized that it would have to tread carefully. Fighting a commercial violation of copyright was both politically and legally much more straightforward than fighting an educational violation, and "it was not considered advisable to attempt to halt the trend toward audio-visual techniques becoming more popular in educational circles."[7]

A survey conducted by the MPA that same year, 1953, and reported early in 1954, revealed that roughly a quarter of annual sales of published music went to schools, churches, and other institutions, at a retail value of approximately $7.5 million.[8] So, as with pop song sheet music, the stakes were small by comparison with records and radio, but still large enough to fight over.

In 1957, while sheet-music sales were crashing, educational music sales were in the midst of a long-term increase. "Without that market, we couldn't survive," reported one distributor. In response, publishers of pop song sheet music began to move "into the educational field with choral and band arrangements of their standards."[9] That same year, Charles Hanson, a publisher who later became deeply involved in the authorized production of fake books, reported that "the appetite of music educators for good pop songs is very strong."[10] In 1959, the Music Dealers Service, a distributor based in New York, shifted its orientation from sheet music to educational music, but not without first going into bankruptcy in an attempt to unburden itself from losses in sheet-music sales.[11]

**The invention of the photocopier.** That same year, 1959, the Haloid Xerox Corporation introduced the first plain-paper photocopier. Chester Carlson had invented the concept and then developed it into a practical commercial machine over the course of two decades, beginning on his own in 1938, and from 1947 working for the Haloid Corporation in Rochester, New York. Carlson and his fellow workers came up with a name for the process, Xerography. Their devices would be Xerox machines, the first of which came onto the market in 1949. The machine became so popular that Haloid changed its name to Haloid Xerox in 1958, to strengthen its identification with the product. In 1961, two years after the introduction of a model that used plain paper, Haloid dropped its own name, becoming the Xerox Corporation. The process was faster, cheaper, and of a higher quality than such earlier technologies as mimeographing and the thermofax process. By the end of the 1960s, Xerox machines were everywhere in American offices, and the company actually engaged in efforts to maintain its trademark identity by discouraging the use of the lowercase word "xerox" in any generic sense, both within industrial circles and in American lexicography. A photocopier made by another company should not be called a "xerox machine," they said, and would standard dictionaries please not include "xeroxing" as a synonym for photocopying?[12]

**Music for educators.** Meanwhile, educational sales were becoming crucial to the music publishing industry. In 1969, under the headline "Sheet Music Sales Making Dramatic Comeback after Decades of Drought," *Variety* reported that publishers had "depended upon educational product to stay afloat," until the advent of rock music and guitar playing brought an upsurge in interest in popular songs, packaged less often in the old style, as individual pieces of sheet music, and more often as songbooks and instructional books, which were referred to in the trade as "folios." Big sellers at that moment were sheet music for the theme song from *Romeo and Juliet,* folios for the Beatles, Glen Campbell, and the films *Mary Poppins* and *Born Free,* and instructional tutorials on electric guitar playing. Choral sales were also strong, and publishers noted that both choral sales and educational sales brought in a significantly larger margin of profit than pop song sheet music and pop music folios, because royalty fees on popular songs tended to be high.[13]

The two fields, educational music and popular songs, were to some degree converging, as reflected, for example, in a report on a Youth Music Institute held at the University of Wisconsin in the summer of 1969. The report concluded that "'youth music' had to be included in the school curriculum." High school students "would rather play 'Aquarius' or 'Spinning Wheel' than one of Sousa's marches."[14] An article from 1971 reported that the key to maintaining the newly revived success of music publishing was to select appropriate pop songs that could be arranged for use in marching bands, choirs, school orchestras, and school concert bands.[15] A survey by the American Music Conference (AMC), a trade organization based in Chicago and representing musical instrument manufacturers, noted in that same year, 1971, that there were one or more instruments in 24 million American homes. In 1972, the AMC listed the leading sellers by dollar value: guitars and amplifiers first, pianos second, and band instruments third.[16] Guitars of course were much cheaper than pianos, and unit volume rather than dollar value told the tale of the instrument's popularity: in the AMC survey for 1974, guitars outsold pianos by a factor of ten to one.[17]

In 1973, the Charles Hansen music publishing firm offered such arrangements for marching band as "I Am Woman," "Duelin' Banjos," "Also Sprach Zarathustra" (popularized by Stanley Kubrick's film *2001: A Space Odyssey*), and "Love Theme from *The Godfather*."[18] That same year, Ed Silvers, president of the print division of Warner Bros. music publishing, announced that half of their gross income came from educational sales.

**Illicit music photocopying.** With the announcement from Silvers came a warning of conflict, when an ASCAP member who had been working part-time in the music department at an unidentified university in the Los Angeles area stated that the department was repeatedly duplicating as many as one hundred copies of printed music, rather than buying multiple copies of the publications.[19] The following year, Arnold P. Broido, president of the Theodore Presser Co., specializing in classical music, complained that unauthorized music photocopying was rampant, and "the ones doing the 'stealing' are two bastions of morality—the church and the school."[20] These institutions had become the core market for publishers, who were therefore reluctant to take harsh steps, knowing that they were standing on dangerous ground in terms of public relations.

In March 1975 the U.S. Supreme Court delivered a blow to publishers when it let stand, on a tie vote of 4–4 with Justice Harry A. Blackmun abstaining, a 1973 Court of Claims decision allowing—under the concept "fair use"—the library of the National Institute of Health and the National Library of Medicine to undertake large-scale photocopying of published medical journals. In June 1975, as the House Judiciary Subcommittee held hearings that would lead to the first overhaul of the Copyright Act since 1909, opposing representatives lined up. Publishers of music and textbooks were on one side, seeking to limit the photocopying of their materials to a strict interpretation of the fair use and library photocopying provisions of the pending bills. Educational institutions, church organizations, and libraries were on the other side, seeking a wide-ranging interpretation of the right to make photocopies under the fair use provision, and with that provision trumping restrictions on library photocopying. No resolution was in sight.[21]

Whereas ASCAP and then the MPPA had led the investigations into bootleg song sheets, the principal organizations involved in efforts to suppress music photocopying were the MPA and the National Music Publishers Association (NMPA), a trade association mainly for publishers of popular music. These two were supported by the Music Educators National Conference, Music Teachers National Association, National Association of Schools of Music, National Catholic Music Educators Association, numerous other educational, musical, and religious organizations, and numerous journals in these fields.

The MPA gave photocopying a central position on the agenda at its annual convention in June 1975. Following the congressional hearings, the print committee of the NMPA convened in late summer 1975 to draw up guidelines defining fair use in the field of music. Would it be possible to survey the extent of unauthorized music photocopying? Should exemptions be granted for music that was out of print? Should a reduced fee schedule apply for instances of mass copying, as, for example, when a marching band performed a special arrangement at the halftime of a football game? The NMPA understood that cooperation within the field would be crucial in dealing with actions that were tricky to enforce by legal means.[22]

In 1976 various of these educational and church organizations passed resolutions that photocopies of copyrighted music would not be used at state, regional, and national gatherings.[23] Two years later, in an editorial headlined "Dracula Would Be Proud of Us," Donn Mills of the National School Orchestra Association complained about a group performing from photocopied parts "not more than 100 feet from a booth dispensing information on the seriousness of copyright violation."

**Equivalency versus transformational use.** In the course of his complaint, Mills laid out a number of reasons why photocopying had become so attractive. Some of these reasons were venal. Photocopying was cheap. Whatever money was spent went to Xerox and its rivals, and to paper and ink manufacturers, not to publishers and songwriters. Also, certain categories of music, including instrumental and vocal books for musical theater and many works of classical music, have always been rented for sharply defined periods of time, rather than being sold outright. Photocopying undermined the system, allowing copies of rented parts to be kept permanently, and thus presenting future opportunities for the public performance of a show without the payment of royalties that would have been incorporated into a rental fee.

Ironically, other components of Mills's objections perhaps undermined his argument, or at least provided practical explanations why even well-intentioned musicians might be willing to be disobedient and make photocopies. Taken together, these reasons constituted an argument for transformational use. What if, on a given day, more musicians than expected showed up? Should the director turn them away or photocopy extra parts? What if—as is absolutely commonplace in music, particularly in theater and opera—the director has revised the published music, adapting a composer's intentions to the realities of the available talent? Should the director buy another copy, just to destroy it by scrawling revisions and instructions all over the original? Or should the director make a photocopy, cut and paste in the emendations, and then make a clean copy, using the photocopier? What if an ensemble librarian comes upon an orchestral part that has become torn or worn out? To replace the damaged item, should the librarian photocopy the part, which would normally not be sold separately? Or must the librarian be obliged to cut into the ensemble's budget, purchasing an entirely new copy of the score and parts, strictly in order to replace a single damaged page? More broadly speaking, what if a school simply does not have enough money in its budget to buy music? In later decades, as the property tax reform in California during the 1970s pointed toward the eventual long-term bankrupting of school systems and elimination of educational music programs, the practice of photocopying music as it became available perhaps took on less of a venal meaning and acquired a sort of third-world quality, whereby music education operated outside of the authorized purchasing system simply to survive.[24]

A decade later, Walter Kujala, president of the National Flutists Association, echoed some of Mills's concerns over illegal photocopying, albeit in a more compassionate manner, without likening the participants to vampires. Kujala focused on the question of rental music and explained somewhat more of why photocopying had become an advantageous process. If orchestral parts for some work of, say, Béla Bartók, Paul Hindemith, Maurice Ravel, or Igor Stravinsky, were only available as a complete set, on a rental basis; if a student needed to prepare for an audition, and the only flute parts available outside of the complete rental system were partial and possibly error-ridden selections in a book of excerpts; then the bootlegging of photocopied parts was inevitable. "Ironically, the aspiring conductor can purchase a study score for any published contemporary piece, but the hapless instrumentalist is left to fend for himself." Kujala also noted that many rentals had circulated beyond their useful shelf life. First-generation rental parts were damaged, most often from layers of written-in revisions and erasures. Second-generation rental parts were harmed by the carelessness of their copyists, introducing errors into the original version. "Too often, valuable rehearsal time is wasted in correcting or clarifying the parts." Although much of the fight against unauthorized music photocopying would consist of efforts to educate religious and educational institutions against the practice, Kujala noted that in this area the shoe was on the other foot. There was a need to educate the publishers.[25]

**The moral campaign.** The new Copyright Act, H.R. 2223, took effect on January 1, 1978. Educational institutions, libraries, and churches put out statements summarizing guidelines for fair use, and the Music Library Association (among many others in the various realms affected) incorporated these guidelines into its own statement, "MLA: Copyright for Music Librarians." All such documents emphasized that these were guidelines, not reports on judicial decisions. Actions defined therein, in some detail under the categories "single copying for teachers," "multiple copies for classroom use," and "prohibitions," were deemed to define areas in which individuals could safely make copies without danger of litigation. But, they noted, the courts might well decide to approve broader conceptions of fair use.[26]

In anticipation of the new Copyright Act, the NMPA and the MPA embarked in 1976 on a three-year, nationwide educational campaign to introduce teachers, administrators, choir directors, and clergymen to its provisions, the idea being that by the time the bill passed and became law, there would be little opportunity to claim ignorance of its provisions. Publishers and their agencies put a hard line into their public relations statements. Later violators would be "deliberate infringers, if not amoral violators who rip-off the property of America's creators and their publisher partners," said Dean Burtch, head of the MPA. Illegal photocopying was "deliberate larceny." Its "willful and deliberate offenders" were practicing "wanton defiance of the law of the land," while seeking "to wrap themselves in the mantle of so-called non-profit activity," and this would not be tolerated.[27]

**Prosecution for music photocopying.** As it turned out, this campaign was far more of a threat than a manifest for action. Suits for illegal photocopying were extremely rare by comparison with investigations and prosecutions either in the aforementioned realms of songs sheets and fake books, or in the stories of pirate radio and unauthorized recordings that follow in later chapters. I came upon only two mentions of suits filed in an educational arena. Not long after the widely circulated announcement of the conclusion of the publishers' three-year educational campaign and their forthcoming institution of a new "Get Tough" policy, *Billboard* and the *New York Times* reported the first civil action by music publishers against a college, with an ironic component attached to the complaint, in that the object of the photocopying was Christmas music. Louard E. Egbert, Jr., a professor in the music department at Longwood College in Farmville, Virginia, had made and distributed unauthorized copies of five Christmas pieces without permission from the publishers.[28] I failed to find the outcome of this suit. It seems not to have been newsworthy. Five years later, in 1985, the NMPA and the music department of the University of Texas, Austin, reached a out-of-court-settlement to end a suit over music photocopying.[29]

The only significant case regarding music photocopying occurred in the field of religion rather than in an educational setting. Dennis Fitzpatrick was the composer of such songs as "They'll Know We Are Christians by Our Love," "I Am the Resurrection," and "Til All My People Are One." He was also the president of F.E.L. Publications, Ltd., in Los Angeles. Since the 1960s, 238 Catholic parishes within the Chicago Archdiocese had been using hymnals and song sheets published by F.E.L. The publications included Fitzpatrick's songs, as well as songs by other religious composers. For quite a while this music was licensed by F.E.L. under the usual cents-per-copy royalty agreement applicable to any such publication under the Copyright Act, but in 1972, as widespread photocopying came to Fitzpatrick's attention, he instituted a new policy. F.E.L. offered a general license for copying any music from its catalogue, this licensing fee to be renewed on an annual basis in lieu of a permanent, single-payment royalty for each individual copy. The renewable license was paired with a fee for prior copying, whereby each of the 238 parishes would, for $500 per parish, be released from the threat of legal action for having previously made photocopies without permission.

Most of the parishes balked at the new policy. In September 1976, while Burtch and his fellows were casting aspersions of crime and amorality for those involved in music photocopying, Fitzpatrick and F.E.L. filed suit against the Catholic Archdiocese of Chicago. At month's end, the District Court in Chicago gave the Catholic bishop permission to collect all F.E.L. hymnals and songs, licensed and unlicensed. Monsignor Francis A. Brackin, vicar general of the archdiocese, sent out two letters to the Chicago parishes, instructing them that F.E.L. hymnals and songs were to be returned to the publisher, and music from F.E.L. was not to be used in any way until the litigation was settled. In response to widespread inquiries, Monsignor Brackin also copied his letters to bishops and archbishops nationwide, appraising them of the situation. This action later became a central point of contention, as to whether or not the church's response had effectively put F.E.L. out of business. The suit dragged on for nearly fifteen years.

A lower court initially dismissed the case, but in 1982 the U.S. Court of Appeals for the Seventh Circuit overturned that decision and reinstated the charges. The court noted that F.E.L. had collected 1.5 million copies of its religious publications from Catholic churches in the Chicago metropolitan area, including the songs "They'll Know We Are Christians by Our Love," "What a Great Thing It Is," and "Sons of God." "Neither the religious element nor the non-profit element of a performance will protect illegal copying," said the court.[30] Two years later, at a new trial in 1984 in Federal District Court in Chicago, a jury awarded Fitzpatrick more than $3 million, in three categories: $190,400 for the annual and forgiveness licenses, $2 million for lost business, and $1 million for punitive damages.[31]

Back it went to the U.S. Court of Appeals for the Seventh Circuit. The archdiocese did not contest the $190,400 award, but Fitzpatrick had earlier sought an additional $1.5 million in statutory damages for copyright infringement, on the grounds that the church had put him out of business. The Court of Appeals judges denied that request, upholding the Federal District Court's decision and stating that the rationale for the $190,400 fine had been meticulously constructed to fulfill the situation. Rather than granting an additional $1.5 million, the judges then went on to vacate the $3 million award, remanding it for further proceedings, because, they said, the inferred value of nationwide business was improperly based on the strict relationship between the Chicago Archdiocese and its parishes—a relationship whose value, $190,400, had already been ascertained. The judges argued that the trial had not established how the Chicago Archdiocese had damaged the business relationship between

F.E.L. and other Catholic dioceses in the United States, each of which was an independent entity. Therefore the extent to which the Chicago Archdiocese might be held responsible for the cessation of nationwide sales remained in question.[32]

On June 5, 1990, with F.E.L. no longer in business, Fitzpatrick returned to the Court of Appeals under his own name. These three judges—one from the previous appeal, and two others—affirmed the earlier decision, ruling that there was no evidence to support a causal relationship between the actions of the Chicago Archdiocese and the failure of F.E.L.[33] It was, in the end, a fruitless battle: Fitzpatrick was put out of business, and all for $190,400, minus fifteen years of legal fees.

**Public relations campaigns.** Apart from this single drawn-out contest, the fight against unauthorized music photocopying consisted almost entirely of an alternation of public relations efforts and public relations complaints, without resort to legal filings. In 1983, for example, Leonard Feist, then president of the NMPA, was a guest speaker at the annual meeting of the Church Music Publishers Association (CMPA), where he laid out his organization's platform on illegal copying, likening his plan to a "relatively successful" earlier effort to identify jukebox owners who had not been paying song royalties. Later that same year, the NMPA, MPA, and CMPA met in New York to discuss the topic.[34]

In 1989, Edward P. Murphy, Feist's successor as president of the NMPA, presented a biannual survey of earnings and blamed a disappointingly modest increase in printed-music sales "on illegal copying and bootlegging of music, constituting copyright infringement." Murphy said that "the most avid printed music consumers—church groups, schools and music societies—are often the most active copyright infringers, through illegal photocopying."[35]

In 1991 the Xerox Corporation ran a television commercial showing orchestra members gathered around a Xerox machine, copying music. Denny Senseney, former president of the Retail Sheet Music Dealers Association (RPMDA), organized a letter-writing campaign to complain, and Xerox pulled the ad.[36] In 1992 the RPMDA and the CMPA distributed ten thousand posters against music photocopying, and the MPA circulated an explanation of "do's and don'ts" to music clubs. At decade's end, the MPA initiated another effort via ads and posters nationwide.[37]

**Rulings on course packets.** By this time a number of significant legal battles over unauthorized photocopying and definitions of "fair use" had taken place. All of these were outside of the realm of music. Most important were the decisions in *Basic Books, Inc., v. Kinko's Graphics Corp.* (1991) and *Princeton University Press v. Michigan Document Services, Inc.* (1996), in both of which cases the photocopying businesses were ruled to have violated an allowable conception of "fair use" in producing, at the behest of university faculty, custom-designed course packets. These course packets consisted of anthologies of excerpts from publications. They were circulating independent of the rights holders of those publications, as, for example, in having the copy centers distribute just one chapter from a college textbook, in lieu of having undergraduates buy the whole book. There were large stakes at play here, by comparison with the world of printed music. In the end, a fee schedule for course packets was established, and wholesale, mass-distributed educational photocopying was thereby assimilated into business as usual.[38]

**Illicit music photocopying continues.** In 1996, *The Music Trades* raised concerns about the rise of digital copying, under this headline: "The Internet . . . Xerox Machine of the '90s?"[39] Certainly unauthorized digital images of printed music have circulated worldwide in the ensuing years. In offering hugely expanded opportunities for choice in the areas of musical acquisition, browsing, and knowledge, the circulation of printed music over the Internet has provided a boon to individuals and a new bane to publishers, as the trade magazine predicted. But in the area of performance, the printer remains crucial, and in this one area (unlike that of song sharing) the Internet really is not much more than a fancy printer. In the twenty-first century, until such time as manufacturers incorporate functioning electronic digital displays into music stands for instrumentalists and handheld devices for singers (and who will be able to afford that, anyway?), printed music will remain at the heart of performances, and disputes over music photocopying are likely to remain unresolved and probably unresolvable.

**PART II**

# Broadcasting

# 5 • *Pirate Radio in Northwestern Europe*

Like song sheets, like fake books, pirate radio in northwestern Europe is the story of prohibition and assimilation: a monopoly of song owners, the emergence of a unauthorized song product, and a long, drawn-out battle ultimately giving way to absorption of that new product into business as usual. But the particular circumstances were significantly different, principally for two reasons: copyright was not at the center of the dispute, and in several regards, governments were at odds with one another, and not necessarily in accord with the song owners.

The unauthorized distribution of printed songs was national in scope, not international, except insofar as bootleg song sheets made their way into Canada—which was a concern for the song owners, as noted earlier—and photocopies of *The Real Book* made their way worldwide—which was not of great concern, this project having operated mainly below the radar. Publishers, educators, and clergymen in western Europe shared the same concerns as their colleagues in the United States with regard to music photocopying, and in particular a number of editorials against unauthorized photocopying appeared in British music journals. But if the principles at stake crossed borders, the physical objects did not. Nobody was importing massive quantities of photocopies of concert-band parts or religious hymns from one country and distributing them in another. What would be the point of that?

Radio is different. Radio waves flow through the political construction of national borders, except in those wartime or "cold war" situations where one country actively jams the portion of the bandwidth corresponding to its opponents' broadcasts. Otherwise, the only boundaries to radio are technological and topographical, depending upon (a) the power of a station's transmitter, (b) the site of that transmitter in relation to its intended audience, (c) the method of transmission—AM signals follow the curvature of the earth and thus remain viable at much further distances than FM signals, which travel outward without bending—and (d) the nature and conditions of the terrain across which the radio waves carry. Thus the flatness of the Great Plains could allow a powerful Chicago-based AM station to be heard in Denver, but the

Rocky Mountains would obliterate any attempt to broadcast eastward from Salt Lake City to Denver via a land-based transmitter, no matter how powerful the equipment.

Because of this potential to disregard borders, the unauthorized distribution of songs via broadcasting—or pirate radio, as it was dubbed when Radio Mercur began broadcasting into Denmark from off the Danish coast in 1958—has an international component to it, and this factor put a twist on the typical patterns of distribution laid out in previous chapters. The involvement of a government in an episode of pirate radio may not necessarily entail governmental entities whose interests and resources are aligned with those of the song owners. To be sure, these interests and resources would be very much the same for any country whose nationalized radio feels threatened by pirate stations, but the unauthorized broadcasting of songs also brings into play other governments that either might not care about the pirate station, or alternatively might actively support that pirate station, for financial considerations.

In the United States, the unauthorized broadcasting of songs has been almost exclusively an annoying hobbyists' activity—annoying, that is, to song owners and the government, not to the hobbyists themselves, who love it. In 2002 Andrew Yoder published the third edition of his book *Pirate Radio Stations*, a fact that in and of itself indicates the extent of interest among the American hobbyists demographic. Yoder relates a number of stories of governmental crackdowns reminiscent of accounts of song-sheet bootlegging: disobedient broadcasting activities resulted in legal threats from the Federal Communications Commission (FCC), in raids staged by the FBI and other authorities against broadcasting facilities, and then in legal injunctions, fines, and sentences aimed at suppressing those activities. Unlike the story of song sheets, this preemptive activity seems to have worked. Or to put it another way, nearly everyone involved at the broadcasting end seemed to have been motivated by the joy of controlling a personalized radio station, rather than by efforts to make inroads into commercial radio markets. Apart from the story of RKXR radio in Southern California in 1933, mentioned below, there is no evidence that unauthorized broadcasting threatened systems for distributing popular songs via legitimate local stations or national networks in the United States. So I have chosen to acknowledge the existence of this whole area of unauthorized activity, and then more or less to ignore it.[1]

Northwestern Europe is different. A disobedient Radio Luxembourg challenged the British Broadcasting Corporation (BBC) during the mid- to late 1930s and again, after a period of German occupation and the end of the war, from 1946 to 1991. From the late 1950s onward in this region of the world, a succession of unauthorized offshore broadcasters not only challenged Radio Luxembourg in turn, but more importantly posed major threats to nationalized radio that ultimately altered existing broadcasting institutions in Scandinavia, the Netherlands, and the United Kingdom.

Reasons for the distinction between the development of popular song broadcasting in the United States and in northwestern Europe have to do with complex cultural and political agendas. In the United States, radio broadcasting began as an unfettered, chaotic endeavor in which joyful and uncontrolled amateur activities very quickly gave way to commercially motivated uncontrolled activities, once the potential of the market began to reveal itself. Chronological boundaries for this transition are not sharply defined, but the changeover from hobbyists to broadcasters is generally attributed to an event at an AM radio station in Pittsburgh owned by the Westinghouse Corporation, KDKA, which in November 1920 broadcast election returns from the presidential race between Warren G. Harding and James M. Cox.

By 1922 there were more than two hundred stations registered in the United States. Some of these stations had begun to carry advertisements, and Herbert Hoover, then secretary of the Department of Commerce, began to devise legislation to gain some minimum form of control over usage of the frequency spectrum and the content of broadcasts. It was probably more than a symbolic distinction that in the United States the task of supervising the airwaves would fall into the hands of commerce, while in Europe it would be largely a matter for postal and telegraph authorities.

In 1923 ASCAP hammered out a royalties licensing deal with the newly formed National Association of Broadcasters, with the result that song owners gained a piece of the income that advertisers were pouring into sponsored radio programs involving popular music. This agreement codified popular song distribution via American radio as a commercial endeavor.

Chaos on the frequency spectrum remained a problem for a few more years, until 1927, when the newly created FCC began to issue licenses for individual segments of the radio bandwidth. Governmental control and supervision of the spectrum led to the demise of many independent local stations, with powerful new organizations such as CBS and NBC instead gaining licenses for networks of stations. In stark contrast to developments in Europe, the system remained privately owned, and it catered to whatever content would bring in the greatest amount of advertising revenue.[2]

The defiant Radio Luxembourg was organized along similar lines, as detailed below, but this approach to broadcasting was exceptional in Europe. Early on—before ASCAP and the FCC stepped into the picture, and regardless of what their actions would be—European cultural and political authorities saw what was happening in the United States. They didn't like it. So not only in those countries where offshore pirate radio would have its greatest impact—Denmark, Sweden, the Netherlands, and Great Britain—but in most other European countries as well, broadcasting became not private, commercial, and popular, but public, benevolent, and high-brow. This was achieved through the formal creation of legitimate monopolies. Whereas the "Tin Pan Alley" system at the moment of the emergence of bootleg song sheets was effectively an improvised vertical monopoly, controlling popular songs from their creation through their distribution in the United States and Canada, and susceptible to whatever market forces might undermine that monolithic structure, much of European radio was controlled by long-term, authorized horizontal monopolies. National broadcasting institutions built transmitters and studios, hired engineers, presenters, and studio musicians, and supervised the content of all programming on the airwaves throughout their respective countries. Market forces, at least in theory, had no power to challenge these legitimate monopolies.

**A broadcasting monopoly in Great Britain.** Britain led the way. The Wireless Telegraphy Act of 1904 granted full authority to the Post Office. In the autumn of 1920, following a period of experimentation, the postmaster general banned radio broadcasts, ostensibly because these were interfering with military and naval communications, although there actually was no evidence of this. The real reasons are unknown, but they may have had something to do with an emerging political and cultural desire to control content on the airwaves. In any event, attempts to negotiate permission to broadcast remained fruitless for nearly a year and a half, with a licensed program of weekly transmissions of speech and music beginning only in mid-February 1922.

Standing up against this desire to exercise control was a growing awareness that radio was catching on like wildfire in the United States, there was possibly a great deal of money to be made, and England might get left behind. Negotiations through the course of the year led to the creation of the first BBC, the British Broadcasting Company, on December 15, 1922, as a monopoly controlled exclusively by British radio manufacturers. Only they would be allowed to broadcast. Advertising was forbidden. Instead, support for the endeavor would come from an annual licensing fee of ten shillings assessed to any and all individuals who owned a receiver. Broadcasts actually began a month earlier, in advance of the conclusion of the agreement.

Two additional provisions stood out among other aspects of this agreement. News broadcasts were tightly limited, so that the powerful British daily press, which depended upon advertising support for its survival, would not be undercut by news reports made via the new medium, which did not rely on advertising. Also, the agreement required that all licensed receiver sets were to be manufactured in the UK. That requirement generated all sorts of licensing headaches over the course of the next few years, owing to homemade and foreign-made sets. This portion of the story is tangential to the present book, and I have disregarded it, except to note here that notwithstanding the ban on advertising, a powerful set of commercial considerations was initially at work alongside the political and cultural agenda that ultimately won out in defining the BBC.

The victory of high-minded goals came later. J. C. W. (John Charles Waltham) Reith was hired as general manager of the BBC in December 1922. The following year he became its managing director. In a memorandum of December 1925, Reith outlined his position: "Broadcasting must be conducted . . . as a Public Service with definite standards. The Service must not be used for entertainment purposes alone. . . . To exploit so great and universal an agent in the pursuit of entertainment alone would have been not only an abdication of responsibility and a prostitution of its power, but also an insult to the intelligence of the public it serves. The Broadcasting Service should bring into the greatest possible number of homes in the fullest degree all that is best in every department of human knowledge, endeavour and achievement."

Reith went on to argue for a broadcasting monopoly from an ethical standpoint: only in this manner could the goals of the BBC—to inform, to educate, and to entertain—be maintained to a proper standard. Eventually, some decades later, this policy became frayed around the edges, when some increasingly popular musical genres were perceived to be beyond the pale, unqualified for BBC airtime. The institution simply could not be all things to all people, and that is the subject of the present chapter. But before those years of confrontation, Reith and his successors carried through on his intended plan, creating not only classical and dramatic programs of the highest order, but also—once the strictures on reporting were lifted—a news service that came to be regarded as the best in the world and that offered a lifeline of hope to continental Europe during the Second World War. These achievements ought not to be disparaged, whatever one's feelings about pop songs.

Reith's agenda was codified by the transformation of the manufacturer-owned British Broadcasting Company into the public-owned British Broadcasting Corporation on January 1, 1927, by which time the ownership of radio receivers was so widespread among the British population that the manufacturers had much less motivation to remain involved in broadcasting efforts aimed at stimulating sales. Reith was named director-general, and he held that position until 1938.[3]

**Broadcasting monopolies in Scandinavia.** Although unambiguously shaped by British policies and procedures, the full nationalization of broadcasting in Scandinavia actually occurred before the transformation of the British Broadcasting Company into the British Broadcasting Corporation. The Swedish government founded Sveriges Radio (SR) on January 1, 1925, as one of three monopolies in the area of media, respectively, for broadcasting, for telecommunications, and for postal delivery. As in Britain, the Swedish daily press was a powerful institution, and it succeeded in its lobbying effort to restrict advertising income only to newspapers. As with the BBC, SR operated on a strictly noncommercial basis, funded by licensing. And as the BBC would soon become, SR was a private corporation. In this instance, Swedish law mandated a proportionate institutional ownership, with no individual shareholders allowed: 20 percent of the shares went to the press, 20 percent to business and industrial firms, and 60 percent to national organizations and popular movements.[4]

By the time that radio emerged in Denmark, the country had had a long history of state-controlled systems for the distribution of communications. The state of Denmark controlled postal delivery from 1711 onward, and the late nineteenth and early twentieth centuries brought the incorporation of telegraph and telephone services into the domain of the national post office. Radio started out on a different footing, when private clubs began broadcasting in Copenhagen in 1922, but that independence did not last long. Just as Sweden was inspired by the model of the BBC, so too the Danish government took over radio broadcasting in 1925 and on March 12, 1926, formalized the takeover with the establishment of Statsradiofonien. Once again, as in Britain, annual licensing fees financed the endeavor. In its early years, the technical facilities of Statsradiofonien came under the authority of the post and telegraph ministry, while the ministry of public works oversaw programming. The latter duties transferred to the Ministry of Education in 1940, thus underscoring the power of the cultural agenda that was operating in Europe. (Imagine a department of education controlling radio programming in America!) In 1959

Statsradiofonien took a new name, Danmarks Radio. The institution was by law a monopoly throughout these decades, and it remained so until the early 1980s, when broadcasting was deregulated and local radio and television stations came into being.[5]

**A broadcasting monopoly in Holland.** In the Netherlands the situation was somewhat more complicated. As elsewhere, early activities pertaining to radio came under the regulatory jurisdiction of the postal, telegraph, and telephone ministry. But in contrast to the structures that developed in Great Britain and Scandinavia, radio in the Netherlands took shape from 1923 onward as a confederation of five national business, public, and religious associations to which the government granted a single, combined broadcasting concession. These five entities consisted of a foundation representing both the listening audience and manufacturers of broadcasting equipment and radio sets; an association of broadcasting hobbyists who would soon thereafter acquire a professional bent as they took charge of programming duties; an organization representing orthodox Protestants; another such organization, for Catholics; and another, for liberal Protestants. In 1930 the Dutch Parliament allotted weekly hours to each group, giving 5 percent of the available broadcasting time to the liberal Protestants, dividing 80 percent of the available time equally among the other four associations (whose memberships, variously commercial, professional, and religious, were significantly larger than that of the liberal Protestants), and allocating the remaining 15 percent of available weekly broadcasting hours to smaller constituencies, including educational services and other religious groups. Financial underwriting for all of these programs came variously from government grants, from licensing fees on radio sets, from subscription fees for membership in one or another of the associations, and from the sale of programming schedules.

Dutch broadcasting was dormant during the years of German occupation. Later, some of the cooperative business of the five associations came to be consolidated under new national regulations passed in 1947, but their essential structure and interrelationships remained intact into the 1960s, when pirate radio appeared offshore. At that time, roughly two-thirds of the combined hours of AM and FM programming were devoted to music, principally classical music rather than popular music. The remaining time was filled out by programs devoted to religion, news, and education.[6]

**A broadcasting monopoly in Luxembourg.** Radio also developed as a state monopoly in Luxembourg, but there the resemblance to practices in other European nations ended. Advocates of Luxembourg broadcasting, necessarily aware of the country's lack of physical resources, recognized the seemingly permanent potential for income from a commercially based system freely transmitting across borders to the immediately surrounding countries of Belgium, France, and Germany. With a high-powered transmitter, the Netherlands and England would also be well within range.

In the late 1920s, a consortium of French financial and industrial companies formed the Compagnie Luxembourgeoise de Radiodiffusion (CLR), specifically for the purpose of circumventing the nationalization of broadcasting that was then taking place in France, as in so many other European nations during this decade. Under a law of December 19, 1929, the Luxembourg postal, telephone, and telegraph ministry granted CLR a monopolistic broadcasting concession that went into operation on May 30, 1931, with the stipulation that the company be headed by Luxembourg citizens.

Radio Luxembourg made its debut in 1933. With a succession of renewals and a name change to Compagnie Luxembourgeoise de Télédiffusion (CLT), reflecting the later dominance of television over radio, continuing authorizations for and renewals of CLR/CLT extended into the twenty-first century under a succession of Luxembourg directors, with the dominant ownership transferring from France (until 1973) to Belgium (until 1996) and then to Germany. Unlike its fellow entities in the realm of European state broadcasting monopolies, CLR/CLT was a private, commercially driven institution that, as some complained and probably rightly so, paid little attention to the listening interests of the Luxembourg public, which numbered around three hundred thousand, and instead directed its full attention toward competing for tens of millions of listeners residing in the other nations of northwestern Europe.[7]

**The control of European airwaves.** So the prehistory of offshore pirate radio in northwestern Europe was the story of Radio Luxembourg and several other stations broadcasting commercial radio into state-controlled areas before World War II, and Radio Luxembourg continuing this alone after the war, its rivals either having been destroyed by Axis and Allied activities, or having been suppressed by a postwar tightening of controls on nationalized broadcasting. From the summer of 1933, Radio Luxembourg broadcast commercially sponsored programs of music, comedy, children's stories, and so forth, separately for British, French, German, and Dutch audiences. In Britain these programs were particular successful in attracting large audiences on Sundays, when Reith's conservative agenda demanded a full day of religious programming on the BBC. Not everyone shared his devout viewpoint on the function and purpose of Sunday broadcasting.[8]

Attempts to rein in Radio Luxembourg were of no avail. A Swiss-based organization, the International Telegraph Union (ITU), had been established in 1865. The organization held its first conference on radio in Berlin in 1906, and at its third such conference, in Madrid in 1932, it took a new name, the International Telecommunication Union (also ITU). The Madrid conference yielded an attempt to achieve universal agreement on usage of the radio spectrum, but Luxembourg would not accept the terms offered. Another attempt followed at the ITU conference in Copenhagen in 1948, and again Luxembourg refused to sign. The ITU would have had Luxembourg stations transmitting with a weakly powered signal proportionate to the country's small area (less than one thousand square miles) and population. But CLR was not about to discontinue broadcasting commercial programs in French, Dutch, German, and English throughout the region, and toward that purpose it built and utilized transmitters approximately one hundred times more powerful that those necessary for broadcasting strictly within the country.[9]

Not long thereafter, the only country operating in Europe as a nonsignatory in a manner even more disobedient of the ITU than Luxembourg was, ironically, the United States, which from 1953 to 1964 sent out its "Voice of America" (VOA) programs from Munich on the same wavelength that the ITU had assigned to Moscow and at twice the power that the ITU had assigned to Moscow: one thousand kilowatts rather than five hundred. By way of comparison, Luxembourg's standard radio broadcasting transmitter was then putting out 350 kilowatts, while prominent AM radio stations in the United States were typically less powerful, transmitting at fifty kilowatts of power. Some readers of this book may recall Top 40 deejays in America boasting of their stations' powerful fifty-thousand-watt signals. Consider, then, that Radio Luxembourg was seven times more powerful than that, and the VOA in Munich, twenty times more powerful, aiming to reach Soviet territory.[10]

**Needletime: Broadcasting recordings.** Of special importance to postwar broadcasting from Radio Luxembourg into Britain, and a driving force behind the later sustained success of unauthorized offshore broadcasting into Britain, was the concept of "needletime," the number of weekly hours allotted to the broadcasting of recordings on the BBC. Following two years upon equivalent provisions in the Copyright Act of 1909 in the United States, the Copyright Act of 1911 in the United Kingdom provided protection for public performances of songs, including the dissemination of songs to the public via recordings. Over the course of the next two decades, individual companies in Britain issued licenses for their phonograph records, but eventually this system became unwieldy. In the 1930s the then-major record corporations operating in the UK formed Phonographic Performance Limited (PPL) to coordinate the issuance of licenses for both public performance and broadcasting, taking up tasks that had their parallels in the United States in functions negotiated and overseen variously by ASCAP, the MPPA, the Harry Fox Agency (discussed in later chapters), and other agencies. At this point, on both sides of the water, broadcasts of live performances were still predominant. The broadcasting of recordings was only beginning to catch on as a great attraction, perhaps most famously in Martin Block's show *Make Believe Ballroom*, which began on WNEW in New York City in 1935 and ran with increasing success into the 1940s, with Block playing, for example, a recording of Benny Goodman and pretending that he was right there in the audience, talking to Benny.[11] At this point, the view still held sway that if a record were broadcast too often over the air, record sales would suffer.

A decade later, beginning at station KOWH in Omaha, Nebraska, in 1951, Todd Storz invented the Top 40 AM radio format, featuring local news and a continuously cycling limited playlist. Through his success, Storz turned conventional wisdom on its head: a huge segment of the audience wanted to hear pop songs over and over again, and the cycling of Top 40 playlists greatly stimulated record sales, rather than damaging record sales.[12]

Long before that happened, musicians unions—again, on both sides of the water—saw the writing on the wall and did what they could to assure that performing jobs would not be lost to disc jockeys. The United States witnessed two periods, from 1942 to 1944 and again from 1947 into 1948, during which the American Federation of Musicians (AFM) attempted to flex its muscle by institutional bans on the making of new recordings, but in the following decade the overwhelming reception afforded Top 40 radio washed away any footholds that the AFM had secured. Their fears that broadcasts of live music would give way to broadcasts of recorded music proved to be entirely correct.[13]

The situation in Britain was different. Not only was broadcasting institutionalized as a public service monopoly, but members of the British musicians union were disproportionately powerful within that institution. In 1946, despite the fact that only 560 of its thirty-three thousand members were actually employed by the BBC, the musicians union reached an agreement with PPL that the broadcasting of recordings would be severely restricted. The result was "needletime." Needletime agreements were negotiated in five-year contracts. In the first such agreement, which was then carried forth from the late

1940s until a renegotiated agreement took effect in mid-1964 (as an initial response to pirate radio), the entire BBC network was allowed twenty-eight weekly hours of needletime, with exceptions granted only for the playing of soundtracks (dramatic broadcasts with music being part and parcel of BBC programming) and for a presenter's review of any new recordings.

At that time, the BBC network consisted of the Light Programme, which later became Radio 2, featuring comedy, quiz shows, and "light" music, including a dose of popular recordings; the Third Programme, later Radio 3, emphasizing classical music; and the Home Service, later Radio 4, emphasizing news and drama. However the twenty-eight hours were doled out among the three networks, there could scarcely have been even two hours of recorded music per day before the weekly allotment was eaten up. A Top 40 format would have been an impossibility. Anyway, according to the government corporation's published policy, the BBC did not want its stations to function as "amplified juke boxes of the kind familiar to people who have traveled to some overseas countries."[14]

So, even before offshore pirate radio appeared in northwestern Europe, the unrestrained broadcasting of Radio Luxembourg into Britain was fulfilling a role that punctured a huge loophole into the benevolent monopolistic distribution system while placing British recording interests into somewhat of a public relations minefield within which they would tread carefully for many years. On the one hand, the recording companies needed to respect British law and at least give the appearance of supporting the needletime agreement. On the other hand, they wanted to sell records.

Although it was unlawful to broadcast in Britain in competition with the BBC, it was not unlawful to prepare recorded programs for export, even if these programs were then broadcast into Britain. In its first decades of operation, the advertising firm in charge of the British branch of Radio Luxembourg secured support from the usual sorts of products—shampoo, cigarettes, herbal creams, laxatives, and so forth—and formed a particularly longstanding association with Ovaltine. In 1948 Radio Luxembourg introduced a successful new show, the Top 20, which was not quite what Storz would soon imagine in Omaha, in presenting the best-selling records of the day, but which proceeded from a similar premise, presenting a countdown of the best-selling pop song sheet music of the day, illustrated by phonograph records of the chosen songs.

A decade later, in 1959, the agency representing Radio Luxembourg began to sell large blocks of time directly to recording companies, each of which found this an effective way to showcase their wares. The companies would then individually sell cosponsorship time to commercial advertisers. More than fifty hours of weekly broadcasting utilized this approach, and much of that involved the British recording industry, which was keen to circumvent the BBC's needletime rules. In 1964, for example, when pirate radio first came to Britain, EMI (the Beatles' label) was purchasing ten hours of Radio Luxembourg airtime per week; Decca, seven hours per week; Pye, four hours; and Philips, three hours, all of these being prerecorded in a London office and then shipped out for rebroadcast into the country via the Radio Luxembourg transmitter situated in Ardennes. Reportedly, that transmitter could reach the north of England. Radio Luxembourg remained a rival to the pirate radio stations throughout the era of offshore broadcasting in northwestern Europe, and it would send out its last English language broadcast on December 30, 1991, a month after the last British offshore pirate station closed down.[15]

During this era, the BBC did not ignore pop music altogether. All sorts of popular groups received sporadic airplay of their recordings, and—the positive side of the "needletime" agreement—many were afforded opportunities to broadcast "live," although this perhaps meant recording on tape in the studio in advance of a broadcast. Most notably, the Beatles performed on fifty-two BBC radio programs between 1962 and 1965, even as British pirate radio was getting underway.[16] Among mitigating factors operating against the BBC and in favor of the emergence of those radio pirates, probably the most important one was the fact that most pop music fans did not want to hear a stark "live" recording made specifically for a broadcast. In this regard, the same aesthetic that launched the Top 40 format in America was at play in Europe. Most fans of pop music wanted to hear hit records that took advantage of the sonic possibilities of elaborate, layered studio production. Many hits could not be adequately reproduced "live." (Hence the advent of miming on television, but that's another story.)

**Pirate radio.** In this setting of state monopolies and one disobedient little nation, pirate radio began. These events have been covered very well, most notably by Mike Leonard in *From International Waters: 60 Years of Offshore Broadcasting* and by Robert Chapman in *Selling the Sixties: The Pirates and Pop Music Radio*. Leonard offers an immensely detailed, soup-to-nuts account, including not only the history of every known station, but also scores of reproductions of relevant photographs, promotional flyers, program schedules, and the like, and concise, practical explanations of agreements concerning territorial waters, piracy, and freedom of the seas. Chapman focuses on two British stations,

Radio Caroline and Radio London, situating these stations within a sophisticated sociocultural analysis that addresses, among other things, political and financial actions and motivations of the participants, the nature of popular music in the UK, and the relationship of pirate radio to a peculiar manifestation of upper-class counterculture in London in the mid-1960s. In the pages that follow, I have drawn upon their work, selecting episodes that exemplify threats to national sovereignty over the airwaves, and ignoring any and all hobbyist activities and failed commercial ventures.

**Broadcasting and extortion in Southern California.** Exceptionally, the first such incident occurred in the United States. In 1932 a group of businessmen based at an office in Los Angeles registered the SS *City of Panama* with the Panamanian government, outfitted the ship with a transmitter, and gained a license from Panama ostensibly for the broadcast of low-power, experimental, noncommercial programs from an anchorage outside American territorial waters. This last bit was a ruse. In May 1933, with the businessmen having sold ad time, RKXR began sending commercials and popular music into the Los Angeles area at a signal strength that interfered with legitimate Southern California radio stations operating in the vicinity of 810 and 820 on the AM dial. "Reception of RKXR was also reported from places as far afield as the east coast of the United States, Hawaii and even northeastern Canada." Here was a threat not to a nationalized broadcasting system and its control of content, but rather to both American commerce and to a nationalized agreement on the right of the FCC to license uses of the radio spectrum.

Complaints to the government initially had no effect, but when individual stations attempted to enter into negotiations on their own, the owners of RKXR attempted extortion, stating that they would transfer their broadcasts to a different frequency only in return for large payments. This maneuver, and the implied threat that the RKXR methodology might be taken up by others, brought forth international governmental cooperation and assistance. Panama cancelled the station's license and the ship's registration. Notwithstanding common agreements on freedom of the seas—more on that in a moment— representatives of the U.S. Department of State then seized the ship in international waters in August 1933, and the Coast Guard towed it into Los Angeles harbor. The situation did not recur.[17]

**The first European pirate station.** The notion of commercial offshore broadcasting in northeastern Europe was floated, so to speak, in Britain in January 1945, when the Newspaper Proprietors' Association gave out this statement: "It is said that there is a plan for broadcasting from ships outside the three-mile limit."[18] Nothing came of the idea in the UK for another two decades. Instead, the first manifestation came to Denmark in 1958 as Radio Mercur. Imitating the BBC in terms of mission as well as structure, the national network, Danmarks Radio, aimed for enlightenment and high culture in its programming. DR operated a single channel until 1951. At that time it added a second channel, but without altering its cultural directive, which incorporated an emphasis on classical music at the expense of popular styles.[19] So two Danish businessmen, Ib Fogh and Peter Jansen, took up the aforementioned idea: could songs be broadcast into the country from outside of its physical boundaries?

**Territorial waters, freedom of the seas, and "piracy."** Coincidentally, at the same time that Pogh, Jansen, and other associates brought Radio Mercur into service, international meetings in Geneva yielded the Convention on the Territorial Sea and the Contiguous Zone, which came into effect on April 29, 1958. By the terms of this treaty, a nation's territorial waters extended three miles from the coast. An additional twelve miles were also available as a "contiguous zone," but most nations maintained the three-mile limit. For example, only four decades later, at the end of 1988, did President Ronald Reagan extend U.S. territorial waters from three miles to twelve, following upon a 1982 United Nations Convention on the Law of the Sea, which offered this right to all nations.[20] In northwestern Europe, this meant that a vessel could drop anchor three miles off the coast and broadcast into an adjacent nation more or less as an untouchable international entity, at least at the start, before the affected nations formulated new policies and legislation.

Leonard notes that the term "pirate radio" came into play not only because of the obvious water-based operation, but because the stations "pirated" the broadcasting spectrum, operating on a given bandwidth without licensing authorization and often changing bandwidth, for various reasons, again without authorization. It should be noted, though, that quite in opposition to the approach on board RKXR and at its offices in Los Angeles, the European offshore stations and their onshore business offices routinely sought to avoid interfering with nationalized stations. Indeed, one of the routine reasons for changes in an offshore station's call number, extending even to jumps among the AM, FM, and shortwave bandwidths, was to stay out of the way of licensed bandwidth when a conflict occurred. In this regard, there was far more accommodation than conflict.

Another and perhaps lesser reason for the label "pirate radio" was that a number of the offshore stations, not being subject to the supervision of a national recording rights agency, failed to pay requisite licensing fees for the public broadcasting of recorded songs. In this respect, pirate radio was a cousin of song-sheet bootlegging, on the issue of the unlicensed reproduction of lyrics, and it was a cousin of recurring practices in the realm of record piracy, discussed in detail later in this book. But strictly as an aspect of offshore broadcasting, the licensing issue was peripheral. It counted for something in terms of public relations, insofar as it provided onshore authorities with moral ammunition in their arguments for a suppression of the offshore operations. It also provided a delicious bit of irony, insofar as record companies expressed public outrage at the pirate stations, to appease the song owners, while privately supplying those same stations with free records to broadcast.[21]

None of this sort of piracy had anything to do with real piracy, a heinous crime. If I may jump into another portion of the book for a moment: in his essay "Hackers, Users, and Suits: Napster and Representations of Identity," Griffin Mead Woodworth presents a brilliant analysis of the rhetoric of criminality in arguments over song sharing, whereby opponents of Napster used labels such as "pirates" and "thieves" as markers for identity and thereby suggested that individuals who used Napster were not genuine music lovers, but deviants intent on destroying music.[22] Here in Europe, exactly four decades earlier, was the beginning of a "piracy" contest that actually involved water-based operations and thereby underscored the severe contrast between metaphorical piracy and actual piracy. In fact, one of the reasons that some of the offshore stations lasted as long as they did was that European national authorities were highly unwilling to violate the new international agreement on freedom of the seas. These authorities knew full well that the broadcasting operations did not constitute actual piracy or any other egregious act justifying boarding and seizure, and none of the European stations tried the tactics of extortion that had resulted in the crackdown on RKXR in Southern California a quarter-century earlier. In the first years of unauthorized offshore broadcasting in northeastern Europe, none of the affected nations had legislation in place that would provide alternative grounds for boarding and seizure. That would come later. Each nation recognized that an unjustified boarding and seizure outside of territorial waters might jeopardize the Geneva agreement, potentially with consequences far more dire than the mere annoyance of allowing unauthorized offshore broadcasting. So initially they held back.

**Danish and Swedish pirate radio.** In the same year that this Geneva treaty took effect, 1958, Fogh and his colleagues used a Swiss-based company to purchase a ship that was then leased to a company in Liechtenstein and registered with Panama as the *Cheeta*. This sort of transnational ownership, leasing, and registration would become typical for subsequent offshore endeavors. It made suppression a more difficult task for the affected national broadcasting monopolies, because their governmental authorities would somehow have to bring pressure to bear upon other nations, in order to persuade their authorities not to accept income from the act of hosting these ships.

Outfitted with a transmitter, the *Cheeta* lay at anchor in the North Sea, and onboard in August 1958 Radio Mercur began broadcasting popular music and commercials into Denmark. The public reaction was so enthusiastic that the station soon garnered a Swedish affiliate that broadcast as Skanes Radio Mercur from the same shipboard studio and transmitter, at different hours.

In the first year these endeavors operated at a loss, but by late 1960 the business was flourishing to an extent that the owners were able to outfit a much larger ship, *Cheeta 2*. By the end of 1961 Radio Mercur was broadcasting prerecorded programs simultaneously from one ship based near Copenhagen and the other, near Funen. As the year turned to 1962, Radio Mercur absorbed a lesser, rival offshore station, Danmarks Commercielle Radio, and its broadcasting ship, the *Lucky Star*. For a brief time all three ships hosted the simultaneous programs. The owners then sold the *Cheeta* to Britt Wadner, who started her own offshore station strictly for Swedish audiences (see below), and the *Lucky Star* took up its place.

Like DR and the BBC, Sveriges Radio operated under a legal mandate that programming in Sweden be "impartial, objective, and designed to satisfy a broad range of interests and tastes."[23] Popular music was not felt to fall within the mission statement. Impressed with the Danish venture and keen to head an analogous challenge to the national broadcasting monopoly, a Swedish businessman, Jack Kotschack, founded an offshore station, Radio Nord, aimed at Stockholm. Kotschack entered into a partnership with two Americans and acquired a schooner. One of the Americans was Gordon McLendon, who had immediately followed Todd Storz in the creation of the typical characteristics of an AM Top 40 radio format as head of the Dallas station KLIF in the mid-1950s.[24] Now, half a decade later, McLendon was unable to be a financial participant in Radio Nord, owing to an American regulation prohibiting his individual ownership of more than seven radio stations—he had already achieved that maximum—but he did serve as a programming consultant for Radio Nord, devising a variation on American Top 40 radio, with the selection of songs and news bulletins adapted to a Swedish audience.

It was not a simple matter to build a ship that could carry a transmitter in a gale without being damaged. Throughout his book, Leonard traces details of many such instances. In March 1961, after a long and difficult period involving technical problems in design and damage incurred from severe weather, the schooner settled into its anchorage and began to host regular broadcasts of Radio Nord. Immediate resistance from Swedish authorities brought about the cancellation of a Nicaraguan license, but the owners acquired a Panamanian registration and simply renamed the ship.

Disobedient broadcasting had began in Denmark, but it was the Swedish broadcasting monopoly that reacted first. Radio Nord was so well received that on May 5, 1961, only six weeks after that debut, SR introduced an "easy listening" service, Melodi Radio. This action had little impact on the appeal of the offshore station. Meanwhile, Britt Wadner had acquired the *Cheeta,* and her offshore station, Radio Syd, began transmitting pop music to Sweden only two weeks after Radio Nord got underway.

In 1962, in a nod toward the acceptance of a Top 40 format and a further recognition of the success of the offshore broadcasters, SR added a playlist of hit songs to its Melodi Radio service. That same year, all four Scandinavian countries—Denmark, Sweden, Norway, and Finland—passed legislation making it illegal to supply, to broadcast from, to advertise on, or in any way to assist an offshore station, short, of course, of assisting in a rescue, in those repeated instances when a ship was floundering in a storm. (The government was trying to stop the operation, not to kill the operators.) The Norwegian and Finnish laws were preemptive, neither country having offshore stations.

In response, Radio Nord went off the air in June 1962, and Radio Mercur, the following month. In January 1963 Kotschack sold the Radio Nord ship to British investors. By way of compensation, DR, the nationalized monopoly, introduced a third Danish channel, for "light music," without commercials. The new channel 3 aimed to reach young people, and some former employees of Radio Mercur were brought into the fold as deejays. SR followed suit in 1964, adding a third national channel for popular music in Sweden. So, unlike the monopolists in many of the other stories in this book, the Scandinavian broadcasting monopolists were reasonably practical and sensible, combining prohibition with accommodation and substantial gestures toward assimilation, years in advance of allowing commercial radio stations into their nations.

In the course of these events, Danish authorities discovered that the *Lucky Star* had lost its registration and was a stateless ship. They boarded and seized it. In Sweden, Wadner had already acquired *Cheeta.* Now she bought *Cheeta 2.* For nearly four years, extending into 1966, her Radio Syd defied Swedish law.

Wadner incurred a series of fines and three terms in jail, during the first of which she took advantage of a rule allowing a convicted individual to continue occupational work. She recorded new programs from her cell in Hinseberg Prison. Several groups of Swedish advertisers were also fined for doing business with her, by placing commercials on Radio Syd. Evidently, like Santangelo and others involved in incurring repeated fines and sentences for song-sheet bootlegging in the 1930s, Wadner and her colleagues regarded these penalties as a component of the cost of doing business.

Severe damage from a storm in October 1964 led to the *Cheeta* being scrapped. Wadner transferred Radio Syd's operations entirely to *Cheeta 2*. At another ITU conference held in Montreux in 1965, a new agreement prohibited stations "on board ships, aircraft or any other floating or airborne objects outside national territories."[25] Wadner persisted nonetheless until January 1966, when extensive pack ice in the Baltic Sea obliged the crew to sail for warmer waters. That was the end of the story of disobedient pop song broadcasts into Sweden. It was not the end of the story for *Cheeta 2*, which subsequently hosted British pirate stations.[26]

**Dutch pirate radio.** Parallel developments occurred in the Netherlands, but with longstanding success. Beginning in 1960, a consortium of Dutch businessmen sponsored the development of an offshore commercial popular music station, Radio Veronica, whose name derived from the consortium's acronym, VRON (Vrije Radio Omroep Nederland). They acquired a German-made lightship and eventually arranged for Guatemalan registration. Broadcasts on a regular basis commenced that summer.

Radio Veronica catered to popular music for young people, which, as elsewhere, was a demographic that the nationalized radio programs did not address. The end of 1960 brought a new set of owners, re-registration in East Germany, and—interestingly in the context of potential charges of record-licensing violations as a component of pirate radio—a scrupulous attention to business duties, including the payment of licensing fees to the standard Dutch authorities in charge of monitoring recordings used on national broadcasts.

From 1961 Radio Veronica had a quasi-legitimacy that enabled it to conduct its business from a studio in Hilversum, where the authorized Dutch stations operated. Radio Veronica became immensely popular, and its advertising base was strong. Meanwhile, the Dutch government, permissive in many cultural areas and responsive to the general public, initially took no legislative action against offshore broadcasting. In 1964 the station introduced a Top 40 format, and in reluctant response to the enthusiastic reception of this approach, the legitimate national broadcasting company introduced a pop music channel, Hilversum 3, in September 1965.

Radio Veronica remained a viable competitor to authorized national radio into the 1970s. As that decade turned, the station became embroiled in an ugly rivalry with Radio Northsea International, and eventually five men from Radio Veronica received year-long prison sentences for having fire-bombed their rivals. But Radio Veronica survived this public relations disaster. It continued to provide the dominant national voice for popular music until Parliament passed a Dutch Marine Offenses Act, which came into law on August 31, 1974. The offshore stations then closed down, and a legitimate show operated under the name Radio Veronica on the national channel, Hilversum 3, for another two decades. Although a new broadcasting act had come into law in the Netherlands in 1966, permitting the use of advertising as a source of income, it would be many years before this option took effect. Later, in the decade stretching from 1987 to 1997, approximately twenty-five commercial radio stations started up in the Netherlands, and fifteen of these survived, the majority devoted to pop music.[27] Here was another variation on the main theme, not prohibition and assimilation, but tolerance and assimilation.

**British pirate radio.** Functional pirate radio got underway later in the United Kingdom than in Scandinavia and the Netherlands, in part because early efforts failed. But from 1964, pirate radio in Britain spread far through time and locale, as a succession of variously competitive or interdependent enterprises strove to take on the BBC. One failed project, Project Atlanta, headed by Allen Crawford, was important for acquiring and renovating the Radio Nord ship. Renamed the *Mi Amigo*, it would become, like *Cheeta 2*, a fixture in offshore British broadcasting. After all, it wasn't as if there were a lot of ships outfitted with studios, transmitters, and an antenna array.

The most important British stations were Radio Caroline and Radio London. Radio Caroline was founded by Ronan O'Rahilly, who kept it going on and off from 1964 into 1990, in the face of hostile legislation and damaged ships. His first ship, the *Caroline*, was a former Danish passenger ferry. Outfitted for broadcasting, it dropped anchor three and a half miles off the Essex coast, near Harwich, in late March 1964, and initiated a 6 a.m. to 6 p.m. daily all-music show, beginning with a very cleverly chosen title, the Rolling Stones' "Not Fade Away."

The British Parliament and the postmaster general reacted with great hostility, but failed to arrive at an agreement on legislative action. There was, as of yet, no general international ban on offshore broadcasting, and there was little evidence that Radio Caroline was interfering with authorized transmissions and could be suppressed on those grounds. In May 1964, the HMS *Venturous* requested permission to board, but the crew of the *Caroline* refused, asserting that it was a foreign-registered ship in international waters. Following established patterns, O'Rahilly had registered the *Caroline* with Panama, through a Swiss agency. While this drama played out, the deejay, Simon Dee, gave out continuous news updates on the attempted boarding. Under the circumstances, the Royal Navy dared not take action, the *Venturous* sailed away, and Radio Caroline continued its broadcasts.

When the PPL (the British agency for the recording industry) threatened prosecution for nonpayment of recording licensing fees, Radio Caroline offered to pay not only licensing fees to the PPL, but also copyright fees to the British songwriters' agency, the Performing Rights Society (PRS). This offer, genuine or not, stymied that strategy for closing down the station.

**The early repertory of Radio Caroline.** Although it is somewhat tangential to a functional survey of the intersection of songs, distribution, and disobedience in European offshore broadcasting, the repertory of the first Radio Caroline presents a point of interest that an American readership might find somewhat difficult to fathom, illustrating perhaps fundamental differences in popular-music listening sensibilities in the United States and in Europe. Certainly I have never heard—and I can scarcely imagine hearing—a commercially successful radio station in the United States that would mix genres and styles together as Radio Caroline did, with the Rolling Stones playing alongside Mantovani's easy-listening orchestra.

Chapman provides programming lists from several Radio Caroline shows of April and May 1964, and the stylistic juxtapositions are remarkable. One half-hour show included Ray Conniff's orchestra playing "Blueberry Hill," Jim Reeves's rendition of the country-and-western ballad "I Love You Because," Etta James singing the rhythm-and-blues song "Pushover," the Searchers doing their pop hit "Needles and Pins," Paul Anka singing the ballad "Young and Foolish," and, from the soundtrack to *My Fair Lady*, a rendition of the song "With a Little Bit of Luck." Another half-hour show brought Tony Bennett and Ella Fitzgerald together with Peter and Gordon, and the New Christy Minstrels. Another half-hour show presented, in succession, Ray Charles on "Any Time Is the Right Time," Dusty Springfield singing "Something Special," the Puppets' version of "Baby Don't Cry," Andy Williams singing "A Summer Place," and Trini Lopez doing "America" from *West Side Story*. These five tracks were immediately followed by light orchestral music from the Mike Sammes Singers (who are they?), a continental ballad from the singer Ellenka Balluska, a Hawaiian-style instrumental performed by the Stringalongs, American jazz singer Mark Murphy doing "My Favorite Things," and a version of "Little Egypt" sung by the Marauders.

For Americans listening to commercial radio, there have always been categories, for the sake of marketing, or music, or both: swing, easy listening, folk, rock and roll, rock, and so forth. For Europeans, at least in that era, evidently there was "popular music," a catch-all that stood in sufficient contrast to the prevailing national broadcasts of high art music that further categorization was perhaps unnecessary. In later years, stylistic lines hardened.

**Radio Caroline and Radio London.** Following a brief period of rivalry, O'Rahilly absorbed Radio Atlanta into Radio Caroline, took in Crawford as an employee, and acquired Crawford's ship, the *Mi Amigo* (formerly of Radio Nord). In July 1964 the *Mi Amigo* dropped anchor off the Essex coast and commenced broadcasting as Radio Caroline South, while the *Caroline* hosted Radio Caroline North after sailing to an anchorage in the Irish Sea off the northern coast of the Isle of Man, where its signal reached portions of northern England, Wales, Scotland, and Ireland. Over the ensuing years, Radio Caroline North faced little competition in its region and consequently was more successful and stable than its Essex-based companion. Naturally, most of the competitors for a position in British offshore broadcasting aimed at London and the south of England, rather than at audiences in the north. Leonard notes also that the northern crew of deejays were under O'Rahilly's direction and had a greater degree of freedom to select repertory than their companions on Radio Caroline South, who came under Crawford's more conservative supervision. Leonard suggests that, because of their proximity to Liverpool and northwest England, the northern deejays may have been more in touch with the emerging style that came to be known as rock music. In any event, Crawford resigned in December 1965, and O'Rahilly took charge of both operations, regularizing their musical approaches.

British and Scandinavian threads of the story came together yet again the following month, when the *Mi Amigo* lost its anchor rope and ran aground in a storm just as *Cheeta 2* was fleeing from ice packs in the Baltic. O'Rahilly rented Britt Wadner's ship to host Radio Caroline South. He then reoutfitted the *Mi Amigo* with more powerful equipment, and that ship resumed broadcasting in the spring.

The greatest competition to Radio Caroline South came from Radio London, which got underway aboard a converted U.S. Navy minesweeper. A consortium of American businessmen founded the venture, using the typical transnational arrangement: registration in the Grand Bahamas, outfitting in Miami, a lease from a Panamanian owner, and an advertising sales office in London. Once again, McLendon, the Top 40 expert, became involved as a consultant on programming.

Radio London first broadcast from an anchorage in the Thames Estuary in November 1964. A month later, on O'Rahilly's advice that broadcasting from within territorial waters could jeopardize all offshore operations, the station relocated near Radio Caroline South, off the Essex coast. Under McLendon's guidance, Radio London launched a "Fab 40" format, the success of which cut sharply into Radio Caroline's advertising revenue. In May 1965, Caroline responded with a Top 50 chart show, but this show coexisted on the Caroline stations with numerous fifteen- and thirty-minute sponsored programs reminiscent of Radio Luxembourg's approach to broadcasting, an approach that was beginning to seem outmoded.

As Radio Caroline had done earlier, or at least gestured toward, Radio London made an attempt to defuse charges of licensing piracy in February 1966 when it signed a long-term agreement with the songwriters' agency to pay broadcast licensing fees as a percentage of its ad revenue. But the British recording licensing agency refused to negotiate with Radio London or any other pirate stations. When asked where his station got its discs, Mike Stone, press officer for Radio London, replied, "Officially the record companies don't cooperate. Unofficially, they do." Vehement denials followed his statement.

**The proliferation of offshore stations.** Early in 1965, member states of the Council of Europe signed the Strasbourg Convention, an agreement aimed at preventing transmissions from stations situated outside of national territories. The convention provided that each nation would then enact its own legislation on the matter. Denmark and Sweden had followed through, and offshore broadcasting would soon come to an end there, but the UK did not immediately respond with a new law. Consequently, new offshore stations proliferated, aiming at various niches.

Some were already underway. Perhaps partially in response to the stylistic eclecticism of Radio Caroline in its first months, David Sutch founded what he called "Britain's first teenage radio station," Radio Sutch, which began broadcasting in late May 1964 from Shivering Sands Fort, a complex of towers rising from the sea bed in the Thames Estuary. The towers were been built as part of the nation's coastal defense system during World War II, and they had been abandoned in 1956.

At its strongest, Radio Sutch reached the outskirts of London, but it mainly served a small audience in Essex. It was not important in and of itself, but its existence established a recurring practice of broadcasting from a fixed position in the estuary, rather than from a ship, and possibly within British territorial waters. The government protested, but initially took no action. Sutch's employee Reg Calvert took over the operation in September 1964, upgrading the equipment and broadcasting under a new station name, as Radio City.[28]

In September 1965, Radio 390 promised "programmes . . . for housewives . . . of the more melodious type of music." Headed by Ted Allbeury, the station signed on with Glenn Miller's "Moonlight Serenade." Late that year Radio Scotland got underway, aiming to reach first Edinburgh and then Glasgow, which offered a larger audience for pop music.

In 1966, Radio 270, situated off the north coast of Yorkshire, introduced a Top 40 format delivered by English and Australian deejays. Reportedly their imitations of New York City AM radio personalities were embarrassing. That same month, Ted Allbeury, the creator of Radio 390's easy-listening format, started up two new stations off the coast of Essex, one for Top 40 music and including some experienced American deejays, and the other presenting easy-listening music.

**Prohibition and partial assimilation.** In 1964, the year that stations first appeared offshore, annual record sales in Britain rose from 61 million units to 72 million units. Album sales rose steadily from 1964 through 1967, a period when the unauthorized stations, both offshore and from Luxembourg, had the field to themselves. Surely there must have been some sort of meaningful connection here between pop song broadcasting and gross income from record sales. Were this America, surely commerce would have triumphed. But in the UK, authorities instead dug in.

From the fall of 1966 into 1967 the government took a series of steps toward closing down the pirate stations. Their first move was to pursue a legal interpretation of the definition of a bay that brought the fort-based stations in the Thames Estuary into British territorial waters, even if these stations were situated more than three miles from the coast. Radio Scotland, after being prosecuted on the same charge of broadcasting from within a British bay, struggled unsuccessfully to find a suitable alternative anchorage for its ship.

Then, on August 15, 1967, the government enacted the Marine etc. Broadcasting (Offenses) Bill, finally affording Britain with a legal framework in support of the provisions of the Strasbourg Convention. It would now be illegal for British citizens and firms to operate, outfit, supply, broadcast from, or advertise on, an offshore station. Five more stations closed.

Prohibition was coupled to assimilation, or at least a gesture toward assimilation. Most importantly, beyond the technical reinterpretations of the boundaries of territorial waters and the introduction of the Marine Offenses Bill (as it came to be known), the BBC announced the creation of a new station devoted to popular music, Radio 1, which would make its debut on September 30, 1967. As previously in Denmark and Sweden, now there would be a British "light music" channel, which would greatly enhance the offerings of popular music on the existing BBC radio stations.

But the new BBC channel was so fundamentally unsatisfactory that there was still a need for pirate radio. For world news and classical music, the BBC was the finest institution in the world. When it came to popular music, its leadership was fairly well clueless, and even had that not been the case, the crippling needletime agreement with the musicians union guaranteed that a BBC pop music station would be musically dysfunctional, forced to try to work around the very evident fact that fans wanted to hear the actual hit records, not "live" recreations thereof. In 1964, just after Radio Caroline appeared offshore and in direct response to that appearance, the BBC renegotiated the needletime contract, increasing its overall network needletime from twenty-eight hours to seventy-five hours per week. But that still represented only 20 percent of the then-weekly 375 hours on Radio 2, Radio 3, and Radio 4. Three years later, with the new fourth channel added, needletime hours were spread even thinner. The next needletime agreement, which came into place in the early 1970s, upped those weekly allotments only from seventy-five to eighty-two hours out of what was then a total of 530 weekly radio broadcasting hours on the BBC network. So at that time Radio 1 was broadcasting ninety-five hours per week, but it controlled only thirty-four hours of needletime, which is to say, less than five hours of recordings could be played in a thirteen- or fourteen-hour broadcasting day. The positive result was that Radio 1 could offer live performances from the golden age of the rock era. The negative result was that "live" performances were limited too, and thus the Radio 1 disc jockeys were obliged to fill out the remaining time with "recipes, competitions, phone calls and, so help us, talking parrots."

As Chapman points out, the rationale for the BBC's cultural high-mindedness had been turned on its head. Decades before, the operational idea was that the broadcasting of live performances of classical music, whether played by studio ensembles or on location from concert venues, had an authenticity that could not be matched by recordings. But that aesthetic did not transfer well to hit songs. Different principles obtained, whereby a most authentic rendition was preserved as a repeatable object performed in a particular way by a particular artist on a particular recording, rather than being rendered and continuously recreated in live performance. For example, instead of playing Jimi Hendrix's recording of "Purple Haze," Radio 1 might present a live rendition of "Purple Haze" performed in the studio by Bernard Herrmann and the Northern Dance Orchestra. (Under those circumstances, I'd prefer the talking parrot.) In an article on needletime published in *Melody Maker*, Robert Partridge reported that even into the 1970s, representatives of the recording and broadcasting industry in Britain were still living in the past, arguing over whether or not a record could be overexposed and whether or not the audience preferred a live cover version of a song or the original record itself.

**Radio Caroline continues.** So O'Rahilly kept going in the face of the Marine Offenses Bill. He was an Irish citizen, not a British national. Radio Caroline North could be supplied from Dundalk in the Irish Republic and Radio Caroline South from Ijmuiden in the Netherlands. His business office relocated from London to Amsterdam. Some staff members resigned in the face of potential fines and jail terms that could be incurred by British citizens for violating the Marine Offenses Bill, but many stayed, and as the years passed, only a few were ever penalized for their actions.

The defiant Radio Caroline had a long and erratic further history. The station broadcast into 1968, but then both of its ships were seized by a Dutch creditor. The *Caroline* was scrapped, but O'Rahilly eventually reacquired the *Mi Amigo* and resumed broadcasting late in 1972. The following year, 1973, brought full-blown assimilation. Authorized commercial radio came to the UK with the establishment of eight ILR (Independent Local Radio) stations, including an AM and FM music station, Capital Radio, for the London area. At this time Radio Caroline was operating off the Dutch coast, at times in collaboration with Radio Veronica, sharing ship facilities and transmitting facilities as circumstances demanded, in the face of a succession of equipment failures and damages incurred from storms.

In August 1974, just as a Dutch Marine Offenses Act was about to become law, the *Mi Amigo* pulled up anchor and relocated to the English coast, once again near Essex. O'Rahilly announced that the station's business office would now be situated in Spain, which was one of the few European countries not to have signed the Strasbourg Convention. (Spain ratified the treaty only much later, in 1988, in the process of bringing itself into line with the European Economic Community.) Supplies would ostensibly be tendered to the *Mi Amigo* from Bilbao. That proved to be a treacherous journey, and instead fishing vessels from Belgium and the Netherlands brought food, fuel, and water, while the deejays themselves sneaked back and forth into England via harbors in small towns or landings on beaches. Radio Caroline remained on the air throughout the mid- to late 1970s, with numerous interruptions as both the broadcasting equipment and the ship deteriorated. Finally, on March 20, 1980, the *Mi Amigo* sank.

In 1981 O'Rahilly purchased an Icelandic trawler, the *Ross Revenge*. A myriad of transnational legal struggles ensued, and only in August 1983 did Radio Caroline resume broadcasting, now as an AOR station ("album-oriented rock," or "adult-oriented rock"). The station and its audience were aging. At the same time, a consortium of British, Irish, and American businessmen put together a new offshore Top 50 station, eventually commencing broadcasting into England from the North Sea as Laser 558. Immediately popular, Laser 558 threatened to draw substantial audiences away from the licensed, commercial, land-based pop music stations of the ILR, as well as from Radio Caroline. One year later, the government stationed a surveillance ship in the vicinity, in an effort to photograph and then to identify ships delivering supplies to the pirate stations, so that these participants in the operation could be prosecuted for marine offenses. A few months later, Laser 558 ceased broadcasting, owing to electric failures on board and more importantly owing to debts owed creditors. Not coincidentally, the government withdrew its surveillance.

Radio Caroline continued on, and a renovated rival returned to the sea in 1987 as Laser Hot Hits. That year a Territorial Sea Act extended British waters from three to twelve miles, and both operations were obliged to relocate to comparatively rougher and more dangerous anchorages, further out into the North Sea. A hurricane of mid-October 1989 badly damaged the Laser ship. The staff carried out repairs, but bankruptcy ensued.

On Easter weekend, 1989, Radio Caroline broadcast a twenty-fifth anniversary show, counting down a "Top 1,001." During the late 1980s O'Rahilly's ship had also been hosting a second station, broadcasting into the Netherlands and Belgium, and on August 19, 1989, a Dutch ship came alongside. The Dutch crew forcibly boarded the *Ross Revenge* in international waters, cut down and hauled away its aerial array, and vandalized the broadcasting equipment, either by throwing it from the deck or by smashing fixed items with sledgehammers. Radio Caroline and its continental affiliate were off the air. Radio Caroline's engineers rebuilt with materials that either had been hidden away or were not fully damaged, and six weeks later it resumed broadcasting, but only temporarily, as two new factors came into play. Panama, it turned out, had cancelled the ship's registration in 1987, to comply with a new agreement not to register ships that broadcast without authorization from the high seas. As a stateless ship, the *Ross Revenge* lacked the legal standing that would allow its lawyers to pursue charges of assault against the Dutch boarders. Then, in 1990, the British Parliament strengthened the Marine Offenses Bill, passing a new broadcasting bill that included a clause allowing the Royal Navy and the Army to board offshore foreign radio ships in international waters, to make arrests, and to seize equipment. Suffering also from ongoing equipment and staffing problems, Radio Caroline went off the air in November 1990, with the new broadcasting bill scheduled to take effect on January 1, 1991.[29]

Thus ended unauthorized offshore broadcasting in northwestern Europe, without any tidy resolution to the push and pull between prohibition and assimilation. The enthusiastic pursuit of broadcasting from international waters took full advantage of a loophole in nationally controlled pop song distribution systems and unquestionably contributed to the dismantling of state radio monopolies and the legalization of commercial pop music stations. But even as offshore activities declined, because of both the enforcement of marine offenses laws and competition from licensed stations, small, localized, onshore, unauthorized radio broadcasting proliferated. This was in part a continuing manifestation of longstanding hobbyist activities on land, but it was also in part a reflection of a new escalation of commercial chaos on the airwaves. In the Netherlands, for example, there were estimated to be some six thousand pirate radio stations in the 1980s, many of them broadcasting music and talk shows in the Amsterdam area with advertising support. "Control and prosecution is a difficult and often hopeless undertaking."[30] Contemporaneously in the London area, a vogue for soul music in dance clubs brought forth an associated vogue for privately run, land-based pirate dance stations in greater metropolitan London, one of which, KISS-FM, actually managed to gain a commercial license, despite severe governmental opposition, when a new round of licensing opened up in 1990.[31] The ships had been quashed, but their disobedient activities carried on.

In 1978 a firm called Music Radio Productions introduced a board game, "The Pop Pirates." The rules of the game pretty well summarized the whole era. Players were to equip a ship for life at sea by purchasing transmitters, aerials, and anchors, and by hiring a captain, a crew, and a staff of disc jockeys. Chance cards governed equipment failures, the supply of provisions, storm damage, drifts into territorial waters, the size of audiences, the success or failure of marketing endeavors, and so forth. The ultimate goal was to sail the course and win a license to broadcast from land.[32]

**PART III**

# Recordings

# 6 · Illegal Copying of Phonograph Records

The mid- to late 1940s were a quiet time for the illicit distribution of songs. Once the song-sheet story died down in 1942, with legitimate song-lyric magazines having taken over the field, accounts of unauthorized activities were largely absent from the entertainment industry's trade papers and fan magazines, except for a handful of items that appeared in *Variety* and *Down Beat* during the latter half of the decade, detailing isolated instances of illegal activities in the phonograph-record industry. These instances marked the start of a multilayered situation that grew into a global phenomenon and global problem (either or both, depending on one's perspective) that continues into, and no doubt will continue beyond, the present day.

The remaining portion of this book traces that situation, the wholesale, disobedient (and sometimes criminal) distribution of recorded songs through a succession of formats—phonograph records, various sorts of audiotape, compact discs, and digital files. If life were neat and tidy, this would be a linear thread, leading from the 78 r.p.m. disk to the MP3 file, but as it turns out, this line of development is so hopelessly confused with occurrences of fan-based album bootlegging that the two threads cannot be untangled. In the late 1960s the term "bootlegging" came to be used in a specialized sense. Insofar as it applied to recordings, it denoted not only the distribution of existing songs without authorization, but also the unauthorized distribution of otherwise unavailable and often newly made renditions, taken, for example, from a taped concert or broadcast, or from copies of unreleased studio sessions. From this perspective, a survey of recorded songs, distribution, and disobedience involves a juxtaposition of media layered across content. The act of copying existing records, tapes, CDs, or digital files differs from the act of bootlegging newly released recordings in rock, folk, punk, and related genres.

Intermingled within these threads, but not always lining up into the same weave, is a larger theme, the push and pull between equivalency and transformational use. Unlike song sheets, unlike fake books, unlike pirate radio, unlike even the defensible aspects of music photocopying, a substantial portion of record piracy, in the broadest sense of that term, involves equivalency, the merely venal copying of someone else's song products. Time and again, examples of this practice lack any component of transformational use: a new musical convenience, a new musical portability, a way to personalize or customize songs and song products, the distribution of otherwise unavailable repertories, and so forth. Instead, it's just a way for nonowners to make a buck, manufacturing a cheap knock-off, and for consumers to save a buck, buying that cheap knock-off. Conceptually, the resulting contest between legitimate and illegitimate channels of production and acquisition calls to mind the safe company and the safecracker, or any other such situation involving a back and forth maneuvering between control and theft. One side comes up with a new lock, in an effort to fully control access to the goods. The other side figures out how to unlock it.

In these instances of unambiguous equivalency, song owners have not been confronted by characters in the manufacturing and distribution chain with whom the public might sympathize. Neither beloved educators nor clergy were pirating phonograph records. There have been no parallels to the modestly heroic offshore deejay, riding out a storm while short on food and water in order to deliver broadcasts to an eager listening public. So, song owners have had a free hand to stomp down on venal record piracy as hard as they can, shouting "bootleggers! crime! piracy!"; calling in the FBI and any other available governmental authorities; and pursuing fines and jail sentences.

In this portion of the fight, obsolescence is the only possible outcome. If unauthorized song products are merely copies, lacking any promise of a transformational quality or a transformational use, then assimilation cannot be an outcome. Why would any song owner assimilate a copy of its own song product? The illegal copying of records came to an end only when that format gave way to tapes and compact discs. The illegal copying of tapes came to an end only when that format gave way to compact discs. The illegal copying of compact discs is—at the time of writing—coming to an end only because this format is giving way to digital song files, at which point the game changes, from safes and safecrackers to a new era of transformational use. That story comes later.

Exceptionally, there was, for phonograph records, a minor episode of transformational use. In the early 1950s, Dante Bolletino (on his amusingly named Jolly Roger label) and a few other entrepreneurial bootleggers released historic recordings that legitimate major record companies had declined to put out, thus providing consumers with a desirable song repertory that was, at the time, otherwise unavailable. These reissues were only peripherally related to the large-scale piracy of current hit songs, but they deserve mention for heralding a later era of album bootlegging and the future possibility of a significant transformational usage for an unauthorized recorded song product. The predictable pattern kicked in: first prohibition, putting Bolletino and other small-time operators out of business, and then assimilation, as the major companies initiated their own historic reissue projects.

Otherwise, equivalency held forth, and protracted battles were the norm. The intended hammer was the Copyright Act. Legislators made a succession of efforts to shore up the act, because it afforded inadequate protection to recordings. Nearly all of these efforts failed. So the fighting often shifted into other arenas. Just as attorneys for song owners and the government rather quickly turned away from infringement in their battle against song sheets and instead took up charges of trade violations or conspiracy, and the introduction of new laws against the illicit practice, so now the owners of recorded songs took up these same paths, raising the legal stakes and expanding the territories for prosecution. In response, unauthorized distributors tested new loopholes in the system.

Concurrently, song owners took up a strategy parallel to the nationwide campaign conducted by Arthur Hoffman and the MPPA during the latter part of the battle over song sheets: they went after legitimate retailers who carried the illicit products. This strategy proved much more effective than attempts at the suppression of unauthorized manufacture and distribution, and for several years at least, phonograph-record piracy was tamped down. Then along came tapes, and the situation exploded again.

From the 1940s into the 1960s, the contest was pretty well confined to national boundaries. Therefore I focus on American copyright law and American record piracy during this period, while ignoring accounts of similar activities in, say, Formosa, the Philippines, Cuba, Italy, or Lebanon.[1] Later, for tapes, CDs, and song sharing, globalization adds layers of complexity that become crucial to the story.

In these later decades of globalization, the situation becomes hopelessly muddled. Piracy (in the sense of copying, an equivalency) and bootlegging (in the sense of new releases, a transformational use) come to be regarded as distinct activities in some contexts, while being conflated and treated as one and the same thing in other contexts. But for phonograph records, in roughly the first decade and a half of the wholesale unauthorized copying and distribution of recorded songs, the situation was as yet uncomplicated, in large part because the manufacturing process restricted opportunities for introducing unauthorized goods into the distribution chain.

**The manufacture of phonograph records.** For many years, there was scarcely any wholesale phonograph-record piracy going on, probably because the act of pressing a record was a highly specialized, fragile, and expensive process, and the vast majority of pressing plants were tightly controlled by authorized manufacturers. Although most music was recorded in professional studios, the act of "cutting" or "waxing" a record was something that could be done in a one-off manner, with transportable equipment taken to a remote location. But mass manufacture, leading to a finished product, was a complicated industrial process, requiring a professional pressing plant. To take up this process from the point just before production begins: during recording, the grooves holding a recorded performance have been cut into the soft surface of a disk—early on, the surface was wax, and hence the phrase "waxing a record," but during the period in question, lacquer was used rather than wax. Once that happens, the soft disk surface is electroplated. This is the master recording. (From the mid-1950s onward, master recordings were made on tape and then transferred to disk. But never mind that for the moment.) The grooved master disk provides the basis for a negative copy, a sturdy, ridged, electroplated version confusingly also known as the master. From this negative master comes a third item, a sturdy, grooved positive copy known as the mother or the matrix. The mother disk/matrix disk in turn serves as the mold for a fourth step, the production of an indeterminate number of metal ridged stampers, each of which can withstand the heat generated in the process of stamping out the final product. Roughly 1,000 to 1,500 copies are made from a stamper before it wears out and a new stamper is put into the production line.[2] Add to that multistage process the design, printing, and attachment of labels to the center of the disks, the making of sleeves for the disks, the design and printing of artwork for multidisk collections, and the precautions necessary to reduce scratching or breakage in the transportation of these objects, and it is easy to see that phonograph-record piracy was not suited to any sort of fly-by-night operation.

The move from lacquer 78 r.p.m. recordings to vinyl long-playing recordings in the 1950s did little to simplify the process of pressing records on any large scale, although one isolated report, from Cleveland in 1960 (noted below), suggests that it became possible to streamline phonograph-record production on a small scale. But, because large-scale distribution required professional manufacture, the path to illegal wholesale distribution invariably led directly through legitimate (or at least nominally legitimate) record-manufacturing plants. For those engaged in bootlegging—or, as some trade reporters put it, "lacquer-legging" and "disklegging"—the question was whether the manager of a legitimate plant could be persuaded to make illegal pressings.[3] What happened—and this is an absolutely crucial element that distinguishes the phonograph-record distribution chain from other song-distribution chains described previously—was that the recording industry came to rely upon manufacturers for maintaining security, for being one of the strong links in that chain, because copyright, as it then applied to phonograph records, was a weak link, indeed virtually impotent.

**Recordings and copyright.** Until 1972, the U.S. Copyright Act applied only to published music. In order to be protected, any given piece had to be published "in intelligible notation," as the Supreme Court defined it. That phrase denoted a musical notation that would be intelligible to human eyes—that is, written or printed—rather than a musical notation that would be intelligible to a machine that decoded the surface of a phonograph record, via the movement of a needle through the hills and valleys within the grooves, converting those grooves into intelligible sound. This in turn meant that, in the realm of popular songs, sheet music could be protected by copyright and recordings could not. Consequently, for instances of the wholesale unauthorized copying and distribution of recorded popular songs, the main provisions of the Copyright Act did not apply. Instead, the music industry and the government were obliged to work around these central provisions. Recordings were only protected in a secondary way, through a licensing provision.

Ironically, in light of many other stories here, the licensing provision of the Copyright Act of 1909 came about not to support a monopolistic consolidation of the music industry, as would so often be the case, but to prevent such a consolidation. While the Copyright Act was making its way through several revisions in Congress during that first decade of the twentieth century, the Aeolian Company, a manufacturer of piano rolls, tried to corner the market by coming to an agreement with approximately eighty music publishers to gain exclusive rights to the manufacture of piano rolls for each and every copyrighted piece in the publishers' catalogues. These perforated sheets, when inserted into a player-piano mechanism, allowed an instrument to make music without any human intervention beyond starting up the device. A performer played a "recording piano" whose mechanism made marks on a roll, after which an operator punched holes into the rolls wherever the marks appeared. Because the resulting object was, in effect, a recording, Aeolian was positioning itself to gain contractual control of all recordings, from a legal point of view.

To break the prospective monopoly, Congress added a licensing provision to the Copyright Act. Once the owners of a copyrighted piece of music knowingly allowed that piece to be recorded for commercial distribution—or "mechanically reproduced," as the concept was expressed in legal terms, to apply to both piano rolls and phonograph records—then anyone else could make a "similar use" of that copyrighted work, so long as the manufacturer paid the owner a royalty of two cents per copy. (The courts sometimes found themselves tied up in knots over the meaning of "similar use." This would become a factor later, in the fight against tape piracy; see chapter 7.)

**The pursuit of criminal infringement.** Because recordings were for so many decades one step removed from direct copyright protection, and because state and then federal legislation to close that loophole came to involve a myriad of complexities, efforts to pursue illegal copying through the provisions of the Copyright Act were even more convoluted for recordings than for printed music. There were several areas for concern.

First, the song owners often found themselves operating in the dark. Because of the weak link between copyright and recordings, record piracy was poorly defined in legal terms. The lack of full-blown trials for criminal infringement in the realm of disks meant that there were no opportunities for higher courts to review cases and to write opinions on decisions made in Federal District Court. More than two decades later, when incidents of tape piracy began to make their way through the courts, the law remained poorly defined. Commenting on that forthcoming era in "Tape Pirates: The New 'Buck'-aneer$," Steven L. Sparkman lays out a number of areas of ambiguity, and he relays a record executive's frustrated comment: "It's costing us thousands of dollars to protect what rights we have—and we don't know what they are."[4]

Second, there was a justifiable apprehension among the song owners that the courts might decide in favor of the bootleggers, again because of the weak link between copyright and recordings. What if a judge were to grant bootleggers ownership of their song products, rendering these products legal and thus putting an end to authorized monopolies? Occasionally this actually happened. As it turned out, those decisions were always reversed on appeal, favoring the song owners once again. But a fear of opening that door was enough to steer the industry away from this legal path, probably on many occasions.

Third, proving infringement was time consuming and expensive. There is, as noted earlier, a huge disjunction between, on the one hand, a commonsense notion of criminal copyright infringement, emerging from, say, reading in the newspaper that so-and-so was caught in possession of some tens of thousands of unauthorized copies of a pop song recording, and, on the other hand, the actuality of presenting elaborate testimony from witnesses and musical experts in Federal District Court, to make the requisite watertight connection between a printed, copyrighted song and its expression on a phonograph record. In any given situation, would prosecution be worth the cost?

This question led directly to a final concern, that when a case did go forward, the result might be disappointing to the song owners. Charges might be dropped owing to a lack of proper evidence documenting manufacture, distribution, or sales. Or a determination of guilt might be achieved, only to result in a mild slap on the hand and the resumption of unauthorized activities. Remember, however venal the activity of illegal copying might seem from the perspective of the legitimate recording industry, and however harshly the industry might characterize the infringing defendants in press releases, the participants in disk and tape piracy were no different from those involved in distributing song sheets and fake books. Generally, they made a rather mild impression on federal judges who were otherwise immersed, day-by-day, in truly despicable and often murderous crimes.

**Remedies other than criminal infringement.** To strengthen their hand, prosecutors normally ventured into other legal areas, just as in the era of song-sheet bootlegging, but taking in an even greater variety of options. If the Copyright Act failed to bring sufficient weight to bear against defendants accused of record piracy, then perhaps an intimidating result could be achieved through charges of unfair competition, misappropriation, conspiracy, mail fraud, wire fraud, grand theft, possession of forged instruments, interstate trafficking in counterfeiting, and dealing in stolen property rights. All of these paths would be taken up in the fight against the wholesale distribution of unauthorized disks, and the pursuit of tape piracy would add still further options, including RICO, the Racketeer Influenced and Corrupt Organizations statute.

**Industry agencies.** Overseeing these contests were two associations that should now be familiar from previous stories, the MPPA and the NMPA. Both represented publishers, who controlled copyright. Joining them were a number of other agencies. Prominent among these were the Harry Fox Agency (HFA), representing the record-licensing arm of the publishers, and three organizations representing record production: the Recording Industry Association of America (RIAA), the Association of Record Manufacturers and Distributors of America (cleverly sustaining the nautical, antipiracy theme with their acronym, ARMADA), and the National Association of Record Manufacturers (NARM).

In the first two decades following the passage of the Copyright Act, the MPPA and NMPA oversaw its licensing provisions. Then, in 1927, the NMPA founded the Harry Fox Agency to oversee the licensing of mechanical rights and the collection of royalties. Harry Fox had been based in Cleveland as vice president of his brother Sam's music-publishing company. He followed Sam to Manhattan and headed his new agency, HFA, while also serving as general manager of the MPPA, thereby tying together those two major organizations. Harry Fox died at the age of seventy in 1953, having returned to Cleveland during the course of a long illness. Consequently he was only involved in the first hints of strife over phonograph-record piracy. But his institutional legacy, HFA, took on a longstanding role in actions against phonograph-record piracy and its successors in other formats.[5]

From 1952 the newly formed RIAA joined HFA in early battles against record piracy. Later, in the era of CDs and song sharing, the RIAA would become by far the most important and most aggressive voice operating on behalf of the song owners and the recording industry. ARMADA and NARM came into the picture in the early 1960s, supporting HFA as well.[6]

**Record piracy begins.** A black market for hit records came to the notice of song owners in New York City early in 1946.[7] This is the earliest report that I found, and nothing much seems to have come of it. In 1947, Francis Craig's rendition of "Near You" became a hit record in the Nashville area, where it began to circulate on unauthorized pressings. The plant that was pressing Craig's disk could not handle the unexpected demand and consequently farmed out extra pressings to "regional wildcat factories." Capitalizing on Craig's hit, these factories skimmed off profits by making extra copies from the masters supplied to them. Then they sold the extra copies independently via "dark-alley avenues to retail counters and coin-machine use" (that is to say, both for private sales and for jukeboxes in public venues).[8]

The next year, 1948, brought a new episode of copying hit records "borrowed" from legitimate firms for unauthorized "nocturnal pressing." Record counterfeiters reportedly were "flooding Los Angeles with pressings of hijacked masters."[9]

**Early attempts at new legislation.** During the first decade and a half of phonograph-record piracy, even the largest runs of bootleg pressings were little more than a minor annoyance for the industry as a whole. A report of January 1947 estimated that the recording industry had sold 350 million disks in 1946.

Having recovered fully from its Depression-era slump, the postwar recording industry had reached a position at which it was probably the most profitable segment of the entertainment world, with income from sales of phonograph records thought to have surpassed the entire radio industry's income from sales of advertising time. Disk sales grew still further throughout the 1950s, and during the five-year stretch from 1954 to 1959, these sales increased by a factor of more than 100 percent.[10]

Consequently there was no great urgency for legislators to attempt legal remedies, shoring up protection against record piracy. In Los Angeles in 1948, during the alleged flood of counterfeit disks, a U.S. congressman introduced a bill making it unlawful to bootleg phonograph records, but that bill stalled. He reintroduced it in future years, but eventually the bill died. After all, relative to the whole, the "flood" was a mere trickle. From a legislative point of view, why bother?

When that path failed, representatives of the recording industry appealed to the FBI to help, but the FBI refused to intervene, its agents pointing out that the Copyright Act of 1909 provided no legal mechanism for prosecuting phonograph-record piracy. Instead they referred matters to the Internal Revenue Service and advised the manufacturers to pursue excise taxes on the record sales, "which bootleggers naturally do not pay."[11] This path was not worth the effort involved in securing documentation.

So the recording industry was obliged to avert its eyes from a first wave of pirated hit songs of the day. Instead, the earliest episodes of prosecution involved, ironically, a transformational usage rather than a mere equivalency, in the unauthorized reissue of historic out-of-print recordings.

**Unauthorized reissue projects.** In the early 1950s a few entrepreneurs recognized that there might be a decent market for unauthorized 78 r.p.m. reissues of out-of-print recordings by Jelly Roll Morton's Red Hot Peppers, Bix Beiderbecke, Billie Holiday, the big bands of Glenn Miller and Benny Goodman, and other artists standing at the intersection of jazz and popular music. Such reissues began to circulate in New York, Los Angeles, Cleveland, and other cities. Some were copied from vintage Victor pressings, and lawyers for the label's owner, RCA, sent threatening letters to the firms.[12] In Chicago, records on the bootleg Blue Ace and Hot Jazz Club of America labels made their way onto the radio, as reported under the headline "Disk Pirates Now Dare Service DJ's."[13] This action underscored the potential transformational use, providing both education and entertainment by taking this out-of-print, historic music and making it available to a broad audience via broadcasting.

Other reissues in this same vein originated from the catalogues of Columbia and Decca, and Columbia soon took similar action against Dante Bolletino, whose Jolly Roger label provided perhaps a bigger threat to the corporation by putting out Louis Armstrong's Hot Five and Hot Seven music not on 78 r.p.m. disks, but in the latest new format, on ten-inch LPs. The normal pattern occurred. Rather than taking over the market by putting out its own legitimate product, Columbia first collaborated with the Harry Fox Agency and Julian Abeles (lead counsel for both HFA and the MPPA) in suppressing the Jolly Roger label. They gained a victory in 1952, when New York Federal District Court Judge Edward A. Conger fined Bolletino $5,000 for copyright infringement.[14] That was sufficient to put the little Jolly Roger label out of business. Meanwhile, someone at Columbia had immediately recognized the value of Bolletino's idea, and assimilation kicked in while prohibition was only just getting underway. In the spring of 1951, Columbia rereleased Armstrong's historic recordings, now packaged as a four-LP set: *The Louis Armstrong Story*. Later repackaged on compact disc, this project remained viable for decades.[15]

**Unauthorized pop song pressings in the 1950s.** The unauthorized reissue projects dedicated to classic jazz and big bands involved comparatively small pressings, thousands of disks rather than hundreds of thousands of disks. At the same time, a more wholesale sort of pop song record bootlegging was going on in several major American cities. Without giving details of artists and titles, *The Billboard* reported in September 1951 that four plants in the New York metropolitan area were producing more than fifty thousand bootleg records per week under the direction of an unknown man who was utilizing four different aliases and at least as many different bank accounts, with counterfeit labels for these disks being printed in Philadelphia. "Several independent pressing plants are known" to have pressed pirated disks at times when legitimate business was slow."[16] In a similar vein, *Variety* reported early in 1952 that a strike at the Columbia Records pressing plant in Bridgeport, Connecticut, had somehow opened the door for illegal pressings of Johnny Ray's biggest hit record, pairing "The Little White Cloud That Cried" on one side with "Cry" on the other.[17]

Further into the decade, while covering additional incidents, a report in *Variety* pointed out that hit records were most susceptible to piracy because of the urgency entailed in efforts to capitalize on popularity. This was especially true when a hit song derived from a source other than the major corporations, such as Columbia, Victor, Decca, and Capitol. Smaller and so-called independent record companies were unlikely to have large manufacturing and distribution systems in place for those occasions when a record became a hit and the need arose for fast action in the area of pressing and delivery. In these situations, the back door to piracy was more likely to be wide open.[18]

The late 1950s brought details of a typical attempt at prosecution, with a seemingly substantial violation begetting a minor slap on the hand. In Chicago, George Hilger printed huge quantities of counterfeit record labels representing songs from more than a dozen legitimate firms. He then shipped these labels to Carl J. Burkhardt, whose Rite Record Company in Cincinnati offered a soup-to-nuts service in the production of disks. Burkhardt pressed either 12,500 or 125,000 records and delivered them back to Hilger. (Reports in *Variety* and *The Billboard* are not in agreement; evidently one paper dropped or added a zero.) Among these were copies of a dozen then-current Top 40 hits, including "La Dee Da," by Billy Ford and his Thunderbirds; "Bad Motorcycle," by the Storey Sisters; and the pairing of "I Am Lonely" and "Get a Job," by the Silhouettes.

Acting on information from the MPPA, Cincinnati police seized one thousand pirated records and five thousand labels at Burkhardt's company and the uncertain larger number of disks from Hilger's home (12,500 or 125,000). In Illinois, the state attorney's office arrested Hilger and Charles English, owner of a distributing company in Chicago. Reluctant to pursue civil or criminal infringement, the state instead charged Hilger with counterfeiting a trademark and English with possessing records bearing a counterfeited trademark. These were misdemeanors bearing maximum penalties of a $200 fine and one year's imprisonment.

The revelations that followed made for good newspaper copy, if nothing else. The two men's activities were connected through the same sales company. Also, English turned out to be Charles Eglise, allegedly a Mafia lieutenant and currently under investigation in a jukebox racketeering scandal that was making headline news in the *Chicago Tribune*.

But in the end, it was much ado about nothing. No action was taken against Burkhardt and his Rite Record Company. English/Eglise was released as well, while his company received a $100 fine. Hilger got a six-month suspended sentence and the maximum fine allowed, $200, but on the recommendation of the prosecuting attorney, that was reduced to $50.[19] Here, then, was yet another example of a penalty for piracy that might be regarded by the bootleggers as office overhead. In February 1959, the Senate Rackets Committee reviewed the case, expressing "wide-eyed wonderment" that Hilger could have gotten off "so lightly after conviction for so profitable an undertaking."[20]

From the late 1950s into the 1960s, Abeles and others complained to legislators that phonograph-record piracy was rampant. In 1959 *The Billboard* reported on the ongoing practice of independent pressing plants receiving orders for, say, fifty thousand copies of a record, and then continuing to press disks beyond that number, selling the additional copies through illicit channels. "One favorite practice which has been noted in the Manhattan area is for dealers to put the bootleg merchandise out on Saturday afternoon and evening 'when all the tourists are strolling around,' as one disk man put it."[21] Seemingly, in Times Square, the more things changed, the more they remained the same: bootleg song sheets in 1929, bootleg records in 1959, bootleg tapes in 1979, bootleg CDs in 1999.

In May 1960, a summary of the outcome of the Hilger and English case was attached to an account of a new, personalized approach to piracy: "meanwhile, from the Cleveland area, comes a new report this week, that a large truck is making the rounds there offering to 'press your favorite records from your favorite labels' on the spot. The truck reportedly carried the hottest new items and makes new cuttings of them to order."[22] Evidently the technology for copying records was becoming portable. I found no further information on this activity.

While most accounts suggested general failures to identify or to prosecute bootleggers, and lenient outcomes when prosecution went forward, occasionally the hammer dropped. Here the most notable outcome concerned a group of men whose activities were coordinated by Eugene Atwood (also known as Brad Adwood).

Atwood headed his own company in Hollywood, California. In June 1960, at the instigation of ARMADA, he and two men in charge of a New Jersey company, Bonus Platta-Pak, were accused of distributing counterfeit pressings of "Ding-a-Ling" and "Wild One," by Bobby Rydell, and "When You Wish upon a Star," by Dion and the Belmonts.[23] In October 1960, ARMADA then tipped off a Los Angeles County district attorney, who gathered together thirty-five detectives from the police department for a Sunday morning raid that yielded two hundred cubic feet of bootlegged records.[24]

Rather than pursing infringement, prosecutors filed felony charges of various sorts, raising the possibility of substantial fines and harsh sentences. In Hackensack in June 1961, Atwood and his Bonus Platta-Pak associates pleaded no contest during their trial, after a printer testified to receiving artwork for the counterfeit labels from William Thompson, one of the defendants in the California case. In December 1961, Atwood, Thompson, and another participant in the California arm of the operation were found guilty. Collectively Atwood received fines totaling $3,500, a one-year prison sentence, and five years' probation, variously for violation of the California trademark statute, conspiracy to sell records with counterfeit labels, selling counterfeit records, attempted grand theft, and conspiracy to commit grand theft and to cheat and to defraud. Three men faced lesser combinations of these charges, while Thompson was convicted of conspiracy to violate the business and professional code. They received fines ranging from $500 to $1,000, and sentences ranging from probation to one year's imprisonment.[25]

So this approach, pursuing every available avenue pertaining to theft, fraud, trade violations, and conspiracy, had the potential to threaten bootleggers in a way that infringement actions could not, at least in an era before the criminal infringement provisions of the Copyright Act were reinforced. Prosecutors and industry representatives hoped that the result would send an intimidating message to other bootleggers.

There were a number of other incidents of a similar nature during this same period. Two deserve brief notice for the manner in which press coverage suggested that record piracy might be linked to organized crime. In 1960, Vincent Graffeo, a seventeen-year-old "teen hoodlum," was shot to death allegedly to prevent him from testifying about a racketeering crime school that was operating in Brooklyn. Reportedly, some "graduates" of this school were receiving lessons in record manufacture and distribution.

That same year, at the Newark, New Jersey, airport, three men met a messenger from Utica, New York, who was delivering samples of pirated versions of LPs by Frank Sinatra and Johnny Mathis. Detectives trailed the men to Brooklyn, seized the sample disks, and arrested eight people, one of whom headed a Brooklyn firm that produced album covers and record labels. Additional arrests followed, including two brothers who ran the Peerless Album Company, which also produced album covers in Brooklyn; the owners of the Graphic Processing Corporation, which printed record labels and album covers in Manhattan; and an official of the pressing plant in Utica where thousands of copies of the Sinatra and Mathis albums were confiscated, thus foiling, before any disks were sold, what was said to be an operation financed by the Mafia.[26]

These allegations echo earlier claims from the era of song sheets, and they will continue into later eras. All I can say is that looking through numerous sources on organized crime, racketeering, and the Mafia, I failed to find any discussions of record piracy. Was it unrelated? Or was it perhaps, in the large context of organized crime, not important enough or not threatening enough to deserve mention? These are pure speculations.

**Further attempts at legislation.** In 1952 the newly formed RIAA persuaded New York State Senator John D. Bennett to introduce a bill that would shore up federal law by making the unauthorized distribution of phonograph records a criminal offense in this crucial state, central to the music industry. The bill passed both houses of the state legislature, but Governor Thomas E. Dewey then vetoed it, without explanation.[27] In the following year, an article in *The Billboard* attributed the governor's veto to Sidney Bobbe, a lawyer for an independent classical music label, Eterna Records. Bobbe reportedly persuaded Dewey to exercise his veto power because the bill would penalize "clients engaged in the business of re-recording obsolete classical musical records no longer available on the market in original form."[28] Here was a direct parallel to the situation of Dante Bolletino, but with support for unauthorized manufacture and distribution allegedly supplied from a high office of government, and no hint of impending prosecution. No one seems to have noticed the contradiction and its underlying aesthetic judgments, that it was all right to reissue out-of-print classical music, but it was not all right to reissue out-of-print jazz and popular music.

On the other side of that coin, a federal court judge in Chicago ruled in mid-1952 that a phonograph recording of a song constituted a publication of that song, and such a publication somehow transferred that recording into the public domain. I won't go into the complicated legal train of thought that led from recording to publication to the public domain. Suffice it to say that this decision would be overturned on appeal, but not before sending a message to record bootleggers that their activities were legal, at least temporarily.[29]

In the mid-1950s, a bill similar to Bennett's died on the desk of New York State Governor Averell Harriman, just after reports of the circulation of pirated copies of hit songs recorded by the McGuire Sisters and Sarah Vaughan.[30] Exceptionally, a state bill successfully passed in Illinois, making record piracy a criminal offense. Efforts continued in the early 1960s to introduce federal legislation in Washington and state legislation in New York to make commerce in record piracy a criminal offense subject to five or ten years in jail and a $10,000 fine. These bills came to naught.[31]

**Pursuing retailers.** Given the general lack of legislative support, the most effective strategy against phonograph-record piracy proved to be a two-fold approach: to continue attempts to identify and to prosecute unauthorized manufacture and distribution, but also to initiate attempts to identify and to prosecute legitimate retail outlets carrying bootleg products. The first major incident involved Glenn Miller, in a variant on the jazz reissue projects. Miller's Army Air Forces orchestra had made numerous broadcasts during World War II, both on the Armed Forces Network and on commercial networks. Miller died, evidently in an airplane crash—the plane was never found—while leading his group in Europe in 1944, and a decade later his estate took the lead in fighting against the appearance of bootlegged reissues of recordings made from those wartime broadcasts. The bootlegger, Joe Krug, was arrested, and song owners filed suit against both Sam Goody and Portem Distributors for violation of the Copyright Act. At that time, Sam Goody, as an individual and a corporation, was the largest retailer of phonograph records in New York.

Initially, everything went badly. In Federal District Court in Manhattan, Judge Irving R. Kaufman ruled that a phonograph record was not a copy of a musical composition within the meaning of the copyright law, and therefore it was not a violation of copyright law to sell an object that could not be defined as an infringing copy. This meant that so long as Krug paid the appropriate publishing firms the statutory royalty rate of two cents per recorded track, he (and any fellow bootleggers) effectively had carte blanche to manufacture and to distribute recordings. The question of Goody's culpability was rendered moot.

The U.S. Court of Appeals for the Second Circuit overturned Judge Kaufman's decision. Krug was put out of business. The judgment then went against Goody, and retailers were put on notice for the first time that they had an obligation to check that their store goods were legitimate. The Supreme Court declined to review the case.[32]

Following upon this success against Sam Goody, the RIAA, ARMADA, NARM, and music publishing organizations expanded their efforts at this end of the distribution chain, endeavoring to suppress the retail sale of unauthorized disks. In June 1960, bootleg disks were found in food and drugstore chains in New York and New Jersey, including A&P Supermarkets. Another such business, Alexander's, was selling illicit singles for forty-eight cents each and Connie Francis's LP *Italian Favorites* for $1.48; reportedly the firm shipped these back to the unidentified distributors upon being notified that they were dealing with bootleggers.[33] A few months later, two businesses in New York City ordered unauthorized copies of "Never on Sunday," "The Twist," "Cathy's Clown," and other hit songs from a pressing plant in New Jersey. The bootleggers then sold these 45 r.p.m. singles through chain stores such as F. W. Woolworth and Co. A raid by Bergen County, New Jersey, authorities yielded disks, stampers, masters, and business records.[34]

The most important of this group of cases got underway earlier. In 1958, the Rite Record Company of Cincinnati—the same plant that would be absolved of guilt in Hilger's case—manufactured disks for the Jalen Amusement Company, which held the concession for record sales in twenty-three H. L. Green chain stores throughout the United States. The Warner Bros. music publishing group sued Jalen and the H. L. Green stores for unlicensed disk manufacturing. This action expanded to involve, on one side, additional publishers, and on the other side, many prominent retailers, including the May Company, J. C. Penney, S. H. Kress, Mayfair Markets, Safeway Stores, and J. J. Newberry. The suit against Jalen and Green slowly made its way through the courts. In 1962, New York Federal District Court Judge Thomas F. Murphy ruled in favor of Warner Bros. In 1963 the Court of Appeals upheld Murphy's decision.[35]

In his brief on this case for that Court of Appeals, Judge Kaufman wrote about the lack of a mechanism for dealing with the piracy of hit songs via illegal pressings of phonograph records. Kaufman complained of "a legal problem vexing in its difficulty, a dearth of squarely applicable precedents, . . . and an almost complete absence of guidance from the Copyright Act."[36] It would be another decade until the Copyright Act was rewritten to take record bootlegging into account. But, in the interim, the pursuit of retailers had significantly discouraged the black market, at least temporarily. For a few years little was heard on record piracy until it returned in a new form, as tape piracy.

# 7 · *Illegal Copying of Tapes*

In December 1970 the FBI raided a warehouse in Manhattan and arrested Salvadore DeChristopher on charges of violating a federal statute outlawing interstate traffic in counterfeit labels. The FBI seized twenty thousand counterfeit records, one hundred thousand labels, fifteen thousand covers, and machinery used to shrink-wrap copies of the Beatles *Let It Be* album and Paul McCartney's self-titled album, *McCartney*.

A decade later, in mid-March 1980, members of the police department in Suffolk County, New York, conducted raids on two locations, one of which led to the seizure of "three automated record presses valued at $40,000 each, able to produce a total of 6,000 LPs during an eight-hour shift; thousands of lacquers and metal parts; a shrink tunnel for wrapping; tens of thousands of finished LPs, and hundreds of thousands of labels." Counterfeit and bootleg albums by McCartney and his group Wings, and by Led Zeppelin, were reportedly on the presses when the police arrived.[1]

So record piracy did not just go away. But the late 1960s brought two major developments. Tape piracy overwhelmingly overshadowed the unauthorized distribution of phonograph records from that point onward, and the new genre of album bootlegging emerged.

The present chapter traces the first of these developments, the history of tape piracy. In this era, which extended into the 1990s, accounts of the seizure of unauthorized tapes paint the picture of an epidemic of illicit musical manufacturing reminiscent of the earlier era of bootleg song sheets. By comparison with phonograph-record piracy, a set of five new elements came into play, layered on top of the existing factors:

Tape production was much simpler and cheaper than phonograph-record production. Consequently it was comparatively easy to set up a plant devoted to unauthorized manufacture, rather than being confined to working through the back door of legitimate manufacturing plants. This punched a huge hole in the recording industry's control of the distribution system. Illicit manufacture proliferated.

Tape packaging tended to be far less detailed than disk packaging. On the one hand, this made counterfeiting easier. On the other hand, legitimate product might not look much different from bootleg product. It could be difficult for authorities to distinguish the one from the other, and consequently, unauthorized distributors did not have difficulty slipping their goods into established systems. Illicit distribution proliferated.

A new transformational possibility emerged. Cartridge tapes and cassette tapes could be played in vehicles. This happened through legitimate channels. But the new market for these mobile formats was huge, and within months of the introduction of eight-track cartridge players into automobiles, unauthorized eight-track tapes were in circulation. Illicit sales proliferated.

Another new transformational possibility emerged, but through unauthorized channels. The songs on any given tape might correspond exactly to the contents of a record album, but they need not do so. Instead, a tape maker might compile or reorder recorded songs into any desired program that fell within the available duration, which could range anywhere from half an hour to several hours. Freed (albeit illegally) from licensing agreements and from obligations to any particular record label, pirate manufacturers could do something other than strict copying. Illicit new compilations appeared, as greatest hits, party tracks, and dance mixes.

Finally, the legal stakes escalated. The proliferation of tape piracy brought renewed efforts to offer protection to recordings through new state and federal copyright legislation and to increase maximum fines and jail terms substantially for those convicted of violations. From time to time during this period, tape bootleggers operated within gaps in coverage between state and federal laws, or old and new laws, and a few firms endeavored to legalize bootlegging through appeals to legal principles involving disclaimers and the concept of similar use. By 1978 the safe havens and loopholes had been closed via appeals to higher courts.

Presenting a history of these developments entails the use of a good deal of technical knowledge and industrial jargon that might seem, without explanation, impenetrable and perhaps off-putting to a general readership. By way of illustration, here are four selections from news reports of this era. I present them briefly, initially without any explanation, and then turn toward a lengthy explanation of their contents by offering a history of competing tape formats and a description of the recording and manufacturing process:

1. Modern Records was a legitimate label established in 1945 by the Bihari brothers in Los Angeles. It featured African American music in swing,

rhythm and blues, and other styles. In 1967, Modern began to fill custom orders for duplicating four-track and eight-track cartridge tapes, and in April 1968 the company introduced an equivalent service for cassette tapes: "'One master and 10 slaves will be used initially,' says Saul Bihari."[2]

2. In 1973, a raid headed by the FBI and the Los Angeles city attorney's office on Superior Audio Distributors yielded "ten Arvin recording slave units, one T11 tape recording master, nine T11 recording tape loaders, seven Trayco high speed winders, three Audiotek high speed winders, and three ElectroSound splicers."[3]

3. In 1981, a jury in Fort Lauderdale found the owners of Gale Distributing, Inc., guilty of engaging in unfair competition with RCA, CBS, and four other major recording conglomerates. From 1974 to 1975 "[Marvin] Nestel and [Jeanette] Schultz had purchased 'pancakes' of pre-recorded tapes from various pirate manufacturers, wound them into eight-track cartridges and distributed the finished product throughout the country."[4]

4. By the 1980s, seizures had become so widespread that the RIAA had taken to issuing annual statistical reports. Here is their list for the period extending from April 1982 through March 1983.[5]

72,334 bootleg records and cassettes
17,786 counterfeit cassettes
3,816 counterfeit 8-track tapes
18,738 pirated 8-track tapes
3,993 pirated cassettes
900 pirated disks
9,950 master tapes
1,100 pirated LP jackets
110 counterfeit and bootleg stampers
11,300 labels
200 pancakes
3,200 bootleg insert cards
30,645 LP jackets
200 pieces of manufacturing equipment, including:
    12 duplicators
    16 slaves
    15 shrink-wrap machines

In considering these accounts, I resisted great temptation to call this chapter "Masters, Slaves, and Pancakes," or perhaps "Loaders, Winders, and Jackets," knowing that either title would be colorful, but perversely misleading and uninformative. Obviously some technological and terminological explanations are in order, to make sense of this industrial jargon in advance of laying out the highlights in the battle against tape piracy.

In writing about phonograph-record piracy, I briefly explained the process of pressing a phonograph record, but I presumed that everyone would know what a phonograph record is. Even though this once ubiquitous format has virtually disappeared from home use, replaced by compact discs in the 1990s and then by MP3 files in the new century, the technology has survived and remained visible, because at the same time that home use declined, the turntable achieved a second life of its own as a musical instrument within hip-hop culture. The image of a dance party featuring a deejay "scratching" LPs on two adjacent turntables remains a powerful icon at the time of writing, and indeed from 2008 into 2009 Southwest Airlines invested heavily in a television commercial in which a dancer, desperate to impress a woman, overbalances his backflip and wipes out the two turntables, sending them crashing to the floor. With this sort of continuing visibility, I think there is no need to offer answers here to the questions, What is a turntable? What is a phonograph record?

But tape recording is a different matter. Many aspects of this medium are arcane, and even those aspects that were once familiar to a general audience are now fading from view. All of this deserves explanation.

The essence of the recording process works this way: sound waves from the performer(s) vibrate a diaphragm in a microphone, which converts those vibrations into electrical signals; the recorder's "head" converts the electrical signals into magnetic patterns and then imprints those patterns onto (initially) a spooled magnetized wire and (in later years) a spooled magnetized tape, either of which—wire or tape—runs past the head at a (hopefully) steady speed. For playback, reverse the process, but insert an amplifier: as the wire or tape runs past the recorder's head, the head reads the magnetized patterns and converts these patterns back into an electronic signal; then, just as for turntables and radios, an amplifier increases the power of that signal and sends it to a speaker; the speaker converts the signal from an electronic impulse into a vibration of the speaker cone. That vibration produces sound waves.

The successive formats for this process were wire recording, reel-to-reel tape recording, cartridge tape recording, and cassette tape recording. Certainly wire recorders are now every bit as obscure as bootleg song sheets. Although reel-to-reel recording was never big in home usage, it was the state-of-the-art format for studio recording throughout much of the latter half of the twentieth century, and it figured prominently in the early years of industrial computing.

So I presume that most readers will at least have a general image of the mechanics of reel-to-reel tapes. Cartridge tapes were, at one time, hugely popular, but now have gone the way of song sheets and wire recordings. For this reason, and because of the jargon involved in their manufacture, and also because I have somehow managed to experience a lifetime of music without ever once having played a cartridge tape, I presume that a detailed explanation is in order, particularly given their prominence in the realm of tape piracy. Finally, there are cassette tapes. In 1987, 58 percent of recorded music sales in the United States were for cassettes—more than 400 million units.[6] Two decades later, these too have virtually disappeared, becoming antiquarian and archival items. Consequently, in tracing the history of tape piracy, I have also included an account of the development of cassettes.

One last general comment: through the eras of tape recording, as competing formats and new uses emerged, there was a continuous give and take among the considerations of cost, convenience, and quality. The thicker the tape, the sturdier it would be. But the thicker the tape, the less the overall footage that could be wound onto a reel, and the shorter the overall duration of the recorded music. The wider the tape for any one track of music, and the faster that track ran past a tape head, the more information that could be read at any given instant, and the higher the quality of the resulting sound. But the wider the track, the fewer the number of tracks that could be laid across a piece of tape, and the faster the speed, the quicker the tape ran out and (again) the shorter the overall duration of the recorded music.

Unlike phonograph records, magnetic tape carried a hissing sound that resided in the background on high quality systems, but came into the foreground in cheap systems. This too was a component of wide and fast: the more musical information streaming past the head at any given moment, the greater the ratio between music and hiss, and the less noticeable the hiss.

The thicker and wider the tape, and the faster it ran, the better it sounded and the less it hissed, but the more it cost to produce and purchase, and the faster it ran out. Competing formats and uses yielded compromises and defined tolerances. If a tape were made thinner, it might be cheaper, more tape could be wound onto a reel, and longer programs could be recorded. But thin tape was much more likely to break, and that was a nuisance.

The conventional speeds were halved from 30 inches per second downward: 30 and 15 i.p.s. for studio work, 7.5 and 3.75 i.p.s. for home use, and 1.875 i.p.s., originally intended for speech only, not music, but later incorporated into cartridge designs for pop song usage. If cheap, narrow, and slow were combined—if the magnetized surface of a cheap, slow-running tape were subdivided into multiple tracks—then a single tape could hold several hours of music. At what points and in what situations would consumers find this option tolerable? The answers varied.

Here are a few possibilities, among very many. A professional stereophonic studio master recording from around the year 1960 would have been made on a wide tape, spooled onto a ten-inch reel and holding approximately an hour of music when running at 15 inches per second. The format was generous enough to allow a thin blank area in the middle of the tape, which discouraged the magnetized patterns from bleeding over from one channel to the other, to insure the highest possible fidelity and stereo separation. A high quality home tape from that same era would be half as wide, spooled onto a seven-inch reel, but again holding approximately an hour of music, because it would run half as fast, at 7.5 inches per second. If a home user instead purchased extra-thin tape and halved the speed again, four hours of music could be crammed onto a single reel, with some loss of high fidelity. And so on, and so on. The following survey of formats—wire, reel, cartridge, cassette—illustrates various approaches to these types of choices.

**Wire recording.** Because wire recording never caught on, I am content to use the normal term, tape recording, for the entire era. But in the earliest manifestation of this process, it would be most accurate to use the term "magnetic recording," a process that dated back to 1894, well before the invention of magnetic tape. That year the Danish telephone technician Valdemar Poulsen came to understand the principles for a form of recording that utilized magnetized steel wire. In 1898 Poulsen received a patent for the "telegraphone." In 1900 Poulsen presented a prototype at the Paris Exhibition, where he made what is now the oldest surviving magnetic recording, preserving the voice of the Emperor Franz Joseph. No form of amplification was available and thus, as with a telephone, the listener held a receiver against his or her ear to hear the recording. The device would not begin to be usefully applied to music for another quarter-century.

In the mid-1920s, the invention of electronic amplification, powered by vacuum tubes, opened up the possibility for functional magnetic recorders, and researchers at the U.S. Naval Research Laboratory patented an improved method for magnetization that yielded a durable magnetic imprint and a reduction in background noise. Kurt Stille and Ludwig Blattner made magnetic recorders utilizing solid steel tape in Europe in the 1920s, as did Semi J. Begun for the company C. Lorenz AG in Berlin in 1935. In the United States, Bell

Laboratories and the Brush Development Company devised techniques for magnetic recordings, respectively, in 1937 and 1938, and both Brush and the Webster-Chicago Corporation worked throughout the war years on military applications of magnetic wire recorders. But the main developments came from Germany.[7]

The fear of new technology was a recurring motif in the history of the music industry. In October 1944, *Variety* ran an anticipatory report about a wire recorder produced by the Armour Foundation. This machine was scheduled to become available to civilians after the end of World War II, at a cost of $35. It would be able to record—and even worse, the author feared, to rerecord an estimated one hundred thousand times—nearly seven hours of music on a spooled wire two miles long. The prediction in 1944 was that the wire-recording device threatened to deliver a "knock-out blow to recording companies and record sales."[8]

This proved not to be the case. As noted previously, phonograph records had become probably the most lucrative objects in the entertainment industry. "It'll be some time yet before sound on tape, wire, or other methods puts a halter on" record sales.[9] The 1950s brought Top 40 radio, a medium devoted to promoting the sale of hit songs. As the decade ended, retail sales for disks were estimated at $484 million. The feared knockout blow had not been delivered by wire recording.[10]

## INDUSTRY STATISTICS

For decades the recording industry has maintained their practice of giving out annual sales figures on the unrealistic assumption that retailers would receive list prices for every sale. So the actual gross income received by record stores for the year 1959 was probably something substantially less than the estimated $484 million. But here and in the chapters that follow, I have accepted the industry's annual figures, because I believe that, for the purposes of this book, the actual numbers do not matter much. Rather, what matters are proportional relationships from year to year and from era to era, the rises and falls in sales; the relationship of these rises and falls to technological developments in the industry, to musical trends, and to larger developments in the American and global economies; and the complex claims of causality that linked sales figures to piracy, especially when times were tough.

If a knockout blow were to be delivered, it would never have come from wire recording. The medium was too fragile. In my capacity as an archivist at the Pennsylvania State University, I had an opportunity to observe the conversion from wire spool to compact disc of a recording of an anti-Truman speech given by the labor leader George McCulloch in 1948. What a nightmare, even for the technician in the Fred Waring Archives, who previously had had the experience of converting some three hundred of Waring's musical wire recordings into digital form. The wire is as thin as thread. If it comes off the spool, it nonetheless retains the impulse to spool and becomes hopelessly tangled, a kitten's delight. Rewinding is difficult, because the wire may get caught within the top or bottom edge of the spool, and it may break in the attempt to pull it out. Our technician's method of splicing is to tie a square knot in the wire, although that of course poses potential obstacles to a smooth respooling. His aim is to get the best possible transfer to digital form on the first try, because there may not be a manageable second opportunity.

Having seen something like this, I find the thought laughable that wire recording technology would ever have caught on for widespread home use, and that it would in some way threaten the recording industry. But its potential did pose a genuine transformational threat, from a generic standpoint. If a more viable medium were invented, would record producers and radio broadcasters have to yield some of their monopoly on the dissemination of songs? What if individuals were to choose to create their own programs, from records and broadcasts?

The year 1951 brought another harbinger of things to come with the introduction of the Minifon P55, a portable wire recorder powered by three batteries, each of a different voltage and with a different but brief life span. That aspect was a nuisance. The Minifon P55 measured 7 × 4 × 1.6 inches. So its portability was nothing like that of modern portable musical devices, but it was smaller than any number of modern-day laptop computers. The Minifon P55 utilized a hair-thin wire that was half as thick as the already threadlike wire made for standard machines, and if the batteries were working properly, it ran at 11.8 inches per second, rather than the speed of 24 i.p.s. that had become standard for wire recorders. Notwithstanding the increased opportunities for tangling the wire, the slow speed and thin wire yielded the possibility for capturing long-running programs on a single spool. The authors of the "Vintage Audio History" website explain that during a brief period of the heightening Cold War, the Minifon P55 was the ultimate spy machine. It even came with an optional spy device, a microphone that looked like a wristwatch.[11] The Minifon P55 was functional, it was lighter and smaller than conventional units, and it could be disconnected from the electric grid. Here was a harbinger of the future. Could a machine like that be plugged into a car battery and operated on the road? Could someone sneak one into a concert?

**Reel-to-reel tape recording.** The work toward mechanisms for using tape, rather than wire, got underway in Germany in 1928, when Fritz Pfleumer received a patent for affixing magnetic powder to a paper strip or a film strip. In 1935, the German company Allgemeine Elektrizitatsgesellschaft (AEG) began to manufacture a Magnetophon tape recorder. Proceeding from Pfleumer's idea, a German firm, BASF, and a Japanese firm, TDK, demonstrated paper and plastic tape coated with magnetic oxides. In 1936 both companies began to produce small quantities of these products. That year BASF recorded Sir Thomas Beecham and the London Philharmonic while the orchestra was on tour in Germany, and then broadcast the event in Germany, not live, but recorded on tape.

Proceeding from this work, the American 3M (Minnesota Mining and Manufacturing) Company began in 1944 to work on a commercially viable method for affixing magnetic iron oxide dust (i.e., rust) to a reel of plastic or paper tape. In September of that same year, 1944, perhaps coincidentally only a month before *Variety* issued its fearful notice on wire recorders, American servicemen found a prize at Radio Luxembourg. The Germans had occupied the station, disrupting its commercial broadcasts of pop music to northwestern Europe. In fleeing the Allies, the Germans left behind an advanced version of the AEG Magnetophon. This tape recorder served as a model for engineers at the Ampex Corporation, who in 1947 made the first high quality magnetic tape recorder for use in American recording studios. The Brush and Magnecord companies were also selling rival machines by 1947, and in that same year the 3M product, magnetic tape, became commercially available.[12]

As with earlier developments in records, radio, and wire recording, the major manufacturers of phonograph records resisted the introduction of magnetic tape, for fear that it would supplant the phonograph record. Consequently smaller labels were the first to take up the new format in the recording studio. Gradually through the early to mid-1950s tape recording became the medium of choice for all professional recording studios, and by decade's end, both inexpensive and high-end home machines were on the market. In 1962, when multitrack studio taping was becoming standard practice in the industry, an instructional piece appeared under the title "Radio Taping, Illegal but Fun." Its author, A. L. Seligson, was writing for individuals getting into the field of monophonic (one-track) and stereophonic (two-track) home taping. While focusing almost entirely on techniques for making high quality tape recordings of FM radio broadcasts, Seligson cautioned his readers that the music industry "has for some time apparently settled into a live-and-let-live attitude" with regard to the question of personal taping from radio, provided that this activity did not lead to commercial distribution. "Don't plan to go into the recording business with your FM tapings, and don't charge your friends admission to come and hear them."[13]

Reel-to-reel tapes never caught on for widespread personal usage. Although their operation demanded nothing near the fussiness of wire recording, open-reel recorders required a degree of skill and fussiness that many people found off-putting, probably, above all, owing to the invariable nuisance of properly threading the tape through the machine's tape rollers and tape head and then onto the empty take-up reel. Also, it was not uncommon for the brakes on the reels to malfunction during fast-forwarding or rewinding, with the result that tapes would break, requiring an awkward process of splicing; even worse, under the force of sudden braking, tapes could become mangled while being drawn violently into the center of the reel. For all its problems of scratches and breakage, a phonograph record was still much easier to deal with than a reel-to-reel tape. What was needed, for tapes, was a closed-reel system that consumers could just "plug and play," to use the anachronistic term.

Portable reel-to-reel recorders followed studio and home machines onto the market. Necessarily they only held small reels—usually of a three-inch diameter—and consequently the running time for any one tape was rather limited, particularly if the operator wanted to maintain some decent level of musical fidelity by running the machine at 3.75 i.p.s. Portable open-reel re-corders used standard batteries rather than the eccentric three-pack of dif-ferent batteries that the Minifon wire recorder required, and they produced what was, for many listeners, an acceptable sound. So a certain amount of practicality was developing, and the path to sneaking a recorder into a con-cert was opening up. But I found no evidence whatsoever that this possibility had manifested itself in the wholesale unauthorized distribution of reel-to-reel concert performances of popular songs. That new mode of distribution was yet to come, from 1969 onward, with cassette tape recorders carried into rock concerts. And on the other main front of mobility, there was still no way in the world that anyone could safely thread tape though a portable open-reel recorder with one hand while holding a car's steering wheel with the other. That would require a closed system: a cartridge or cassette. Reel-to-reel tapes represented a crucial and long-lasting stage in the development of professional recording, but in leading areas of tape piracy, including album bootlegging, song products for automobiles, and unauthorized anthologies, reel-to-reel tapes had no significance.

**Cartridge tapes.** On the path toward a viable, self-operating, "plug and play" cartridge system, RCA in 1958 introduced a closed system reel-to-reel design known as the RCA Victor tape cartridge or the magazine loading cartridge. The device ran at 3.75 inches per second with the tape divided into four tracks, yielding thirty minutes of stereophonic sound or an hour of monophonic sound in each direction. An auto-reverse mechanism eliminated the need to flip over the tape and rethread it. But this proprietary system never caught on. The tapes operated exclusively on RCA playback machines. For tapes of less than the best fidelity, they were expensive, ranging from $4.95 to $8.95 per album. Repertory was extremely limited. Owing to difficulties in production, the project encountered delays, with only sixteen RCA albums available in this format more than a year later, in mid-1959. Eventually only a very small portion of the RCA catalogue ever became available on its proprietary cartridge tapes. Competing manufacturers held back their participation, and the machine never caught on.[14]

The successful design for tape cartridges was developed for use in radio stations. In Toledo, Ohio, in 1952, Bernard Cousino designed an endless-loop tape cartridge. Anchored by a freewheeling hub in the center, the tension-driven tape came off the upper portion of the hub, ran continuously through an opening alongside one edge of the cartridge case, and then rewound back onto the lower portion of the hub. Cousino coated the plastic, nonmagnetized side of the tape with graphite, to lessen the friction as any one loop of tape coming off of the inside of the spool tape ran past the loop of tape spooling immediately around it. Cousino used two methods to delineate starts and stops: he integrated subaudible cueing tones into the recorded programs, and he spliced aluminum foil into the magnetized plastic tape at desired spots.[15]

In 1954, George Eash, who had shared space in Cousino's electronics shop, revised Cousino's design. He received a patent for his revisions in January 1957 and then began to market his device as the Fidelipac, which also came to be known as the NAB cartridge (for National Association of Broadcasters) or, more simply, as a "cart." Vern Nolte of the Automatic Tape Company has also received credit as a pioneer in this invention.

Eash's Fidelipac utilized quarter-inch-wide audio recording tape, which was then standard in reel-to-reel home recording. The cart ran at 7.5 i.p.s., also the standard for home musical use. But the Fidelipac had a specialized twist: half of the width of the tape held the recorded program, whether an advertisement, a station-identification jingle, or any other sort of brief "spot," while the other half held cues, electronic signals that allowed the cart to operate automatically, as, for example, to skip past blank areas of tape, or to rewind to the beginning of a jingle after it is played, or to start up another cart or some other type of equipment in the studio. Once stereo became standard (not long thereafter), the Fidelipac gained another degree of specialization, carrying three tracks rather than two: left channel, right channel, and cues.

Apart from the convenience of easy filing and retrieval that carts offered for radio presenters, their cueing feature also allowed a single individual to host a radio show simply by pushing a button to integrate ads and jingles into the show, where otherwise at least two people would be required: a deejay at the microphone and an engineer cueing up the sound. With carts at hand, one person could do both jobs. Give the news or weather or a station ID, hit the button cueing in an ad on a cart, and as that ad is ending, start spinning the turntable and cue in the next record. Then repeat that same process, again and again, with variations. It was a highly useful device. As equipment for radio stations, the cart remained viable into the twenty-first century.[16]

In 1962, Earl "Madman" Muntz invented the Stereo-Pak four-track cartridge system, aimed at consumers rather than professional broadcasters. Each cartridge held two distinct stereo programs, with the tape head moving up and down to align itself with the different paired tracks. The tape speed was 3.75. So, a lowered fidelity of sound was offset by a reduction in production costs and accordingly a lower retail price, for two full programs of music could be preserved on each tape. The rubs, here, were several: fast-forwarding threatened to damage the tape; rewinding was impossible, owing to the one-way-only design of Muntz's tape loop; and a listener had to throw a switch manually to get from one pair of stereo tracks to the other.

Even though some of the essential elements of a reasonably carefree "plug and play" device were still missing, Muntz's system had considerable attraction. Manufacturing both players and tapes, he began to license albums from major record companies and to duplicate these albums onto his four-track cartridges. He pioneered the introduction of tape players into automobiles, marketing the tapes as CARtridges and reaching an agreement with the Ford Motor Company that for a brief period led to his dominance of this field. But the four-track system soon lost the battle of formats to an eight-track design. In 1970 Muntz ceased the manufacture of four-track cartridges.[17]

The breakthrough to vast commercial sales came from the inventor of the Lear Jet, William P. Lear, Sr., reportedly after having taken a ride with Muntz in an automobile outfitted with a four-track cartridge player. Bill Lear, as he was known, formed a consortium whose members included his own Lear Jet Corporation; the 3M company, which supplied the tape; the Motorola corporation, which manufactured the players; RCA Victor, which supplied the recordings; and, once again, Ford.[18] Proceeding from previous designs, Lear minimized consumer intervention and maximized playing time. The player operated through the radio system in Ford automobiles, and when a cartridge was inserted into that player, the connection switched automatically from radio to tape. Lear squeezed eight tracks into the width of a quarter-inch tape, where previously four, and earlier two, had been. So the quality of sound was reduced still further. But what did that matter, if you were roaring down the road at seventy miles per hour, or stuck in city traffic, idling alongside trucks, with the sounds of refuse pickup, taxi horns, and the occasional siren added into the mix? Irwin J. Tarr, manager of merchandising and planning for RCA Victor, explained that "with only 400 feet of tape, listeners will be able to hear as much music as is now being carried on one or two long-playing records."[19]

Lear eliminated the need for Muntz's manual switching system, instead inventing a complex geared system that moved the tape head up and down. This system adopted Cousino's method of using splices of conductive foil to signal the automated internal movement from the end of one of the machine's four stereo programs to the beginning of the next program. To underscore the attractiveness of this feature, the possibility of endless playing with neither hand obliged to leave the steering wheel, the "8" in the Stereo 8 logo was turned on its side, appearing as the symbol for infinity. Alternatively, a button situated beneath the radio's tuning dial allowed listeners to switch, as desired, to any one of the cartridge's four stereo programs.

There were disadvantages. Cartridge players might "eat" a tape, causing it to jam or break. The vibration of an automobile in motion might affect the quality of the playback, perhaps knocking the tape head out of alignment with the narrow tracks running past it, so that the "ghost" of one program spilled into the sound of another. The dirt and extreme temperatures involved in the routine operation and storage of a vehicle might cause cartridge tapes to deteriorate, particularly with a foil splice separating from the plastic after its glue hardened into uselessness. But the tapes were cheap. Just buy another one.

Here was a reasonably successful "plug-and-play" system. A *New York Times* article of April 1966 showed, in one photograph, a little girl selecting a cartridge from a jumble piled on the passenger seat, and in the adjacent photo, the little girl sliding that eight-track tape into the player, which then would start automatically, sounding through speakers mounted in the car doors. This was, as reporter Jan Syrjala put it, literally "child's play."[20]

As car radios had previously done, cartridge players transformed the automobile industry. Upon introducing its 1966 models in September 1965, Ford began to offer an optional stereo tape system, while RCA made available fifty prerecorded cartridges. The system cost an addition $245, and more than 20 percent of those purchasing Lincoln and Thunderbird models took the plunge. In 1966 the Chrysler Corporation introduced a cheaper car-tape system through its accessories dealership, Mo-Par. The Mo-Par "hang-on" device could easily be attached to (and presumably just as easily stolen from) the dashboard of any Chrysler model. In September 1966 General Motors followed Ford by introducing tape units into its 1967 Buick, Chevrolet, Oldsmobile, and Pontiac models. The only holdout within General Motors was the luxury division, Cadillac, which offered only an AM-FM stereo radio until April 1968, when buyers were offered the alternative of ordering, as a dealer-installed accessory, an eight-track stereo tape deck built by Delco. Other manufacturers joined in, with Norelco, for example, offering its miniaturized Car-Mount model, which was mounted beneath the dashboard like Mo-Par's machine for Chrysler, but which offered recording capabilities via a plug-in microphone and a recording button, so that, for example, a businessman on the road could dictate reports. The Car-Mount player was fully detachable, thus doubling as a handheld portable recorder.[21]

Picking up on this frenzy of activity, *Billboard* magazine introduced a weekly feature page entitled "Tape CARtridge" (initially capitalized thus, as Muntz had promoted the word). As the mobile hardware grew in popularity, catalogues of prerecorded eight-track tapes grew accordingly, with cartridge versions of LPs coming to be released not long after the release of those same LPs. With RCA having sold about five hundred thousand tape cartridges drawn from a catalogue of two hundred albums during the months leading up to mid-January 1966, the London, Mercury, Capitol, Decca, and Columbia labels followed suit, releasing albums from their catalogues on cartridge tape.[22]

In 1970, Audio Magnetics, a manufacturer of cassette, cartridge, and reel-to-reel tape, introduced a line of thirty-six-minute and seventy-two-minute blank tape cartridges. "'We feel there will be a great response for blank 8-track cartridges to complement the pre-recorded music market,' said Ray Allen, sales vice president."[23] That did not happen, but the format flourished throughout the late 1960s and early to mid-1970s, and in a reversal of the usual process, from home to car, eight-track cartridge players began to gain a modest popularity for home usage. Gradually the format was supplanted by the tape cassette, but not until 1982 did the cartridge lose its commercial viability for general sales.[24]

**Cassette tapes.** In 1963, slotted in between the introduction of Muntz's four-track cartridge and Lear's eight-track cartridge, the European record producer Philips introduced a miniaturized, closed, reel-to-reel system, the audiocassette. Mass production of blank, recordable tapes began in Hanover, Germany, in 1964, and prerecorded cassettes made their debut late in 1965. Parallel developments occurred in the United States through Mercury, which Philips had acquired earlier in the decade. The new format entered the American market with the Carry-Corder, a small unit that both recorded and played cassettes, and with the mass production of blank tapes priced at $2.65 each. At the very same time that manufacturers of eight-track cartridges were entering into agreements with the leading auto makers, audiocassettes presented cartridges with a new competitor. A Philips cassette player for automobiles became available in the summer of 1966 at a price of $150 (less than the Ford-Lear cartridge package, and comparable to the Chysler–Mo-Par dashboard undermount). In September 1966, Mercury released forty-nine albums in cassette format, at $4.95 per album.[25]

Like nineteenth-century phonographs, the Carry-Corder was designed for taking and playing dictation, not recording and playing music, and despite the then ongoing mania for stereophonic sound, it was a monophonic device. For music, the Carry-Corder and many similar early cassette machines produced a low-fidelity sound with a substantial hiss overlaid across the content. The tape was 0.15 inches wide—only slightly more than half the size of home-use quarter-inch reel-to-reel tape. It moved at the slowest typical home-use speed, 1.875 inches per second. And when utilized for music within these parameters, it held the magnetized signals for two pairs of stereo tracks, one program running in each direction, with an unrecorded guard band physically separating each track. Such specifications for a tiny, slow-running width of tape would have been considered disastrously unpromising for musical use in conventional open-reel machines. But these specifications remained in place for cassettes, and engineers, working around the obstacles they had been given, transformed the Carry-Corder and its cousins into a vast array of useful musical machines.

Unlike the phonograph, audiocassette players were meant from the start to be portable, and this too was a disadvantage for musical use early on, because a small machine meant a very small speaker, and in the 1960s, most small speakers were of poor quality, producing a tinny sound. Here three paths to improvement emerged: the late 1960s and early 1970s brought substantial improvements in speaker quality, large and small; the separation of the playing component from the amplifier and the speaker yielded a player that could be plugged into decent-quality automobile systems and a "cassette deck" that could be plugged into high-fidelity home systems; and on still another path, speakers could be eliminated altogether in favor of headsets.

As with the eight-track cartridge, these developments moved from portable use to home use, rather than the normal other way around, but they continued further, to studio use, as makers of audiocassette machines achieved professional standards of high fidelity sound. A succession of noise-reduction systems under the Dolby brand greatly reduced cassette tape hissing, with only minimal distortion of the musical timbre, in the introduction of a slight heaviness at the lower end of the frequency spectrum; most listeners never noticed it. Experiments with magnetized materials led to the introduction of improved tapes capable of holding a higher quality of sound on their miniaturized width. Wollensak, the camera division of the 3M Corporation, developed a transport system that would run the tape reels smoothly at a reliable speed. An auto-reverse system was introduced, so that cassettes, like cartridges, could, if desired, play endlessly, without a need to move hands from the steering wheel.

As with cartridges, some aspects of the cassette format remained flimsy, no matter the improvements. Most commonly, a machine "ate" the tape, mangling it. But also like cartridges, cassettes were cheap. Just throw away the ruined tape and buy another one.[26]

It took quite a while for cassettes to overtake cartridges in the automotive world. In October 1971, when the American branch of the Japanese electronics firm Toshiba announced a new line of cartridge players, the weekly report in *Billboard* was still called "Tape Cartridge," not "Tape," and Toshiba was "convinced the bulk of the new business will be in 8-track."[27] But in audiophile and studio circles, cassette decks were in rapid ascendance, and in the realm of personalized listening, the cassette brought a transformational change every bit as important as the introduction of tape systems into cars. Just as speaker design improved by leaps and bounds, so the trebly earphone plug of the transistor-radio era gave way to high-fidelity miniaturized stereophonic headsets during the 1970s. These headsets were incorporated into an iconic, portable, pocketable cassette player, scarcely larger than the cassette itself: the Sony Walkman, introduced in 1979. With the success of the Sony Walkman, cassettes in the early 1980s not only captured the entire market for tapes, driving cartridge manufacturers out of business, but also rivaled and for a period of time outsold LPs.

**Tape manufacture: Cases, pancakes, hubs, speed winders, loaders, masters, and slaves.** Manufacturing tapes was far simpler and less expensive than pressing phonograph records. The process was more or less the same for reel-to-reel tape as for cartridges and cassettes (the objects of tape piracy), but of course with the reel-to-reel tape being spooled onto open plastic or metal reels rather than being loaded into closed cases.

First, acquire the cases. Some firms molded their own, but most purchased cases in bulk from nonmusical firms, that is, companies dedicated to plastics manufacturing. In the same way that the Xerox Corporation had scarcely any reason to concern itself with music photocopying, many tape-case manufacturers had no incentive to cooperate with song owners, especially if that cooperation might lead to reduced sales. At one point Julian Abeles and his law partner John Clark complained on behalf of the recording industry that they were getting little support from this front end of the distribution chain, and *Billboard* ran an editorial against manufacturers and distributors selling cases to pirates.[28]

With cases at hand, acquire a "pancake" (an industrial-sized spool) or a "hub" of blank tape. With a "speed winder" and a "loader," offload an appropriate length of tape from the pancake or hub into individual cases. Make a "master" version of a tape. (Many firms copied LPs onto tape to create their own masters.) Put one case into each "slave" (a high speed tape duplicator), and then connect any number of slaves to a tape player holding the master. Copy the master. Because of the capability of slaves to record at high speeds rather than at normal playback speeds, a whole album might be copied in, say, five minutes. With numerous slaves operating simultaneously, many copies could be made in a short period of time.[29]

Finally, print a normally minimal amount of artwork and information on an adhesive label. Affix the label to the case. Shrink-wrap it.

Some firms were engaged in this entire process. Others set up shop for a portion of the process. For example, a large-scale bootlegging firm might offer pancakes and hubs of prerecorded tape, selling these to smaller operations and thus allowing those smaller operations to function with cases, pancakes, winders, and loaders, without also having to invest in duplicating equipment. A report on a 1973 price list from Superior Audio Distributors of Eagle Rock, California, shows how that ambitious company tried to fill all available whole-sale and retail needs. At the time that Superior was raided and shut down, it was offering blank eight-track tapes at twenty-five cents each; individual prerecorded tapes from a selection of 750 albums at $2.25 each, with bulk purchases of five hundred or more copies reducing the cost to $1.75 per album; 3,600-foot-long tape hubs holding multiple copies of prerecorded albums at $6 per hub, with a minimum order of ten hubs required; speed winders at $120 each; and eight-track loaders for prerecorded tape, at $1,295 each.[30]

**Tape piracy begins.** The process was far simpler and much cheaper than record pressing. Evidently the attraction for bootleggers was overwhelming. Stereo 8 cartridges only first reached the market in the fall of 1965. Already in June 1966 Columbia Records was filing suit against Cartridge City, Ltd., and Cinematic, Ltd., of Nassau County, New York, for the unauthorized distribution of Columbia albums on bootleg cartridges.[31]

A report from 1971 indicates how much these activities mushroomed. A raid by U.S. marshals on the National Manufacturing Company in Phoenix yielded 150,000 tape cartridges, seventeen winding machines, duplicating equipment, and machines for labeling and wrapping tapes. The company was operating a 17,200-square-foot facility. "The highly organized plant had special areas for office work, maintenance, testing, quality control, labeling, shipping, and receiving—and even a kitchen and lounge area." Its employees operated on continuous shifts, around the clock.[32]

And some participants were quite brazen in advertising their goods, perhaps even foolishly so. In 1970, Al Berman, general manager of HFA, complained that a catalogue of 320 unauthorized albums in Stereo 8 was circulating nationally among wholesalers and retailers, including music by Creedence Clearwater Revival and Bob Dylan's album *New Morning*, the latter at that moment being available via authorized channels only on a Columbia LP; the illicit distribution of *New Morning* in cartridge form had gotten underway even before Columbia had released a legitimate Stereo 8 version of the album. Around the time that the bootleggers put out a Christmas supplement to their catalogue, U.S. District Court Judge Ben Krentzman issued an injunction in Federal District Court in Tampa against those accused of selling the cartridges in Florida for about $3 each, roughly 60 percent of the going price for authorized prerecorded tapes.[33]

As tape piracy proliferated, a number of individual actions and class-action suits followed along lines established in the battles against phonograph-record piracy of the late 1950s and early 1960s: massed groupings of publishers filed complaints against massed groupings of cartridge and cassette manufacturers and distributors, or against massed groupings of retail outlets handling unauthorized tapes. During the late 1960s, Berman developed a new strategy in collaboration with Abeles and Clark. Rather than naming specific songs infringed upon in any one given action, they sought the statutory licensing fee—which was then still two cents per track, as it had been for sixty years—plus triple that amount in damages for all recordings discovered to have been made without permission. Via this use of open-ended, generic complaints, the act of unlicensed manufacturing could lead to substantial fines.[34]

Defendants in one of those mass actions attempted to disconnect recordings from copyright law. In Los Angeles in 1968, thirteen publishers filed suit against an array of companies, including Muntz Mobile Stereo Pak, Superba Tapes Co., the U-Tape-A-Tape company, and others. The owners of Superba Tapes admitted in Superior Court that their firm sold recordings by the Tijuana Brass, the Sandpipers, the We Five, and other groups without authorization from the song owners. But they then contended that because recordings were not protected by the Copyright Act, they had a right to copy the material. In his essay on tape piracy, Sparkman discusses the complicated and at that point largely unanswered line of questioning raised by this line of argument: if a recording could only be licensed, not copyrighted, and if the dissemination of that recording constituted publication of the performance on that recording, did that throw the recording into the public domain? An affirmative answer would be a bootlegger's delight, allowing anything to be copied. Superior Court Judge Robert Thompson thought otherwise and issued a temporary injunction against the defendants, who agreed to pay royalties owed and to discontinue their infringing actions.[35]

As in the previous era of phonograph-record piracy, authorities also turned to legal formulations other than copyright in their attempts to suppress unauthorized tapes. For example, in 1968, fifteen publishers charged two businesses in the Los Angeles metropolitan area with tape piracy. The battle against Phoenix Tapes and Hollywood Music Programmers went all the way to the U.S. Supreme Court, which ultimately upheld the decision of a California District Court of Appeals, that the act of copying recordings from the Capitol label without permission constituted unfair competition. Manufacturers and distributors should not be allowed to "wait for a recording to be produced and then duplicate it and sell it at maximum profit and with minimum effort and expense."[36]

**A transformational use: Illicit compilations.** A key development, insofar as tape piracy might offer a truly positive (if unquestionably illegitimate) contribution to American culture, was the creation of party tracks, dance mixes, platter packs, or whatever this type of product might be called: an unauthorized anthology of hit singles of the day, cutting across industry-defined boundaries in ways that legitimate manufacturers would not condone or approve until many years later, when that sort of compilation began to be promoted in authorized forms in supermarkets and chain stores and on late-night television. In the late 1960s and the 1970s, these unauthorized compilation recordings were attacked by representatives of the song owners as being nothing but a rip-off, a way to offer the most profitable songs at bargain-basement prices without even paying licensing fees, let alone production and development costs. But of course it was much more than that. Unauthorized compilations wrested programming control away from the recording industry and into the hands of distributors who might have some very nice ideas about putting songs together in an attractive sequence. Unauthorized compilations allowed people to listen to hit songs without having to wade through all the other stuff that they did not really want to hear. Here, three decades early, was one of the fundamental principles underlying song sharing.

For example, in Federal District Court for the Southern District of New York in May 1970, seventeen publishers filed suit against Eastern Tapes, Cartridge Counter, Inc., and six individuals, accusing them of holding clandestine meetings with customers, making undocumented cash sales, using false names, and placing orders through a telephone answering service. Here was a typical clandestine bootleg operation, no different for tapes than for song sheets or fake books, or, for that matter, horse racing. What was interesting was the song product. Eastern Tapes and Cartridge Counter were manufacturing and distributing a series entitled "Super Sounds," eight-track tape compilations of unauthorized copies of twenty current hit songs. Venal or not, this was a wholesale commercial realization of the transformational possibilities of tape recording.[37]

**Home taping.** The recording industry was not just concerned over wholesale illicit activities. Corporations and agencies in the United States and Europe were worried about individual uses of tape recording, namely, the possibility that home taping would detract from sales of prerecorded tapes. In a preemptive anticipation of losses, the industry proposed the establishment of levies on sales of blank tapes and tape recorders. For the first time, the grand contest over songs, distribution, and disobedience began to take on a major global component, with Europe rather than the United States leading the way in this instance.

The RIAA, the British Phonographic Industry (BPI), the International Federation of the Phonographic Industry (IFPI), and other such organizations prompted governments to introduce legislation for tape levies, the proceeds to be distributed according to various formulas. Variants of this legislation passed in France, Germany, the Netherlands, Portugal, and Spain, but proposals failed in the United States, Canada, the United Kingdom, and the rest of Europe, for several reasons: because of the lack of reliable documentation of the extent of piracy (more on that in a later chapter); because of questionable plans for distributing proceeds not only to performing rights organizations, but also directly to recording corporations; and because of the complete impossibility of distinguishing in advance whether an individual would be purchasing tapes and equipment for legitimate or illegitimate home use.[38]

With the blanket tape licensing scheme failing in most countries, these organizations turned from legislation to public relations and put together a morality campaign against the practice of individuals making their own tapes, most aggressively in the United Kingdom, where the BPI introduced a now-infamous slogan, "home taping is killing music." This effort also was ineffective. Taping for personal use did indeed have its nasty side, in, for example, the practice of buying an LP, taking it home, taping it, and then returning the LP the next day, arguing that it was defective or using some other excuse. Taping for personal use might stretch the intended relationship between public and private spheres, in, for example, the practice of borrowing an LP from a library and taping a copy before returning it. Taping broadcasts was a gray area, depending upon usage and ill defined by the law. But there were entirely legitimate uses as well. An individual might buy an LP and tape it to create a usage copy, the LP remaining as a preservation copy and being subjected to less wear. A record collector might tape a long out-of-print disk obtained from a friend.[39]

From this line of thought came a link back to bootlegging. Even though the industry made strong efforts to discourage the practice, it was also perfectly fine, in addition to making usage copies and collectors' copies, for individuals to make their own party tapes (or any other desired anthology) for personal use, whether for edification, education, or just pure enjoyment. But at this point, bootleggers and the real world intervened. Why would anyone bother to take the time to make a compilation of dance tracks, if a desirable prere-corded bootleg tape compilation were already available? Most people had bet-ter things to do with their time, and never mind the law.

**The revision of copyright law.** With tape piracy blossoming from 1966 onward, and with the as-yet-unrevised Copyright Act of 1909 remaining rather feeble in the face of wholesale infringement via recordings, the state legis-latures of New York and California introduced new criminal laws that took effect, respectively, in September 1967 and 1968, making it a misdemeanor to "knowingly transfer or cause to be transferred any sounds recorded on a phonograph record, disc, wire, tape, film, or other article on which sounds are recorded, with intent to sell, or cause to be used for profit through public per-formance, such article on which sounds are so transferred without the consent of the owner."[40]

In the New York Supreme Court, prosecutors achieved the first convictions under the new state laws against disk pirating in 1968 when Santos and Irma Maldonado, operators of the Orchard Music Shop in Manhattan, were found guilty of selling counterfeit and pirated records, "chiefly in a Latin groove."[41]

The new California law laid untested until 1971, when Donald and Ruth Koven, and Ruth's son Donald Goldstein, pleaded "no contest" to charges in-volving tape piracy. Judge Erich Auerbach gave them probation, suspended sentences, and fines ranging from $125 to $625. Auerbach noted that these were light penalties, because the law was new, but he warned future offenders to expect more severe sentencing.

The next case suggested otherwise, reinforcing the fears of song owners that the new law might lack bite. Jack Byram, a salesman for Capitol Records, was found to have been operating his own business on the side, selling unauthor-ized eight-track tapes of albums by the Carpenters, Carole King, the Rolling Stones, and James Taylor. Byram received three years' probation and a $350 fine.[42] In Georgia, which then had no such law, authorities complained in 1973 that "roadside tape salesmen [could] be found on almost any Sunday drives."[43] Gradually between 1971 and 1978, forty-nine states—all but Vermont—passed laws against record piracy. Writing for the *New York Times* in that last year, 1978, Edwin McDowell reported that among roughly one hundred prosecu-tions in the Los Angeles area, where record and video piracy was then thought to be centered, less than one-third had resulted in convictions.[44]

Steps were finally taken at the federal level as well. In 1971, a year in which six states had joined New York and California in enacting laws against record and tape piracy, Senator John L. McClellan, chairman of the Subcommittee on

Patents, Trademarks, and Copyrights, introduced a bill designed to respond to the proliferation of eight-track tape bootlegging. Congress passed McClellan's bill in early October 1971, and with President Richard Nixon's signature, it became the Sound Recording Amendment, extending copyright protection to new recordings, providing for substantial fines and the confiscation of equipment used for record piracy, and making violators subject to misdemeanor charges. This bill took effect on February 15, 1972. Crucially, a song no longer had to be "published" in order to be protected by copyright. Now a song need only be "fixed," as, for example, on a disk or on a tape, in order to be protected, at least for new recordings. The Sound Recording Amendment remained valid through 1974, after which its provisions were incorporated into a general overhaul that resulted in the new Copyright Act of 1976. The amendment eventually covered recordings made prior to February 15, 1972.

Legislators were also persuaded that the consequences of wholesale record piracy were dire. Criminal copyright infringement could now be a felony, rather than a misdemeanor, and the financial stakes were raised. In March 1975 the Justice Department closed the gap between old and new recordings. The illicit distribution of a recording made prior to February 15, 1972, was now subject to a $1,000 fine and one year's imprisonment, while unauthorized distribution of a recording made from that time onward was subject to a $50,000 fine and a maximum of two years in jail. When a further revision to the Copyright Act went into effect on January 1, 1978, the first offense for criminal copyright infringement became subject to a fine of up to $25,000 and one year's imprisonment, regardless of the date of the authorized recording.[45]

**Closing the legal gaps.** There were potential gaps in and among the state and federal copyright laws. These involved disclaimers, applications of the definition of "similar use," and distinctions in coverage between old and new recordings. Over the course of the 1970s, bootleggers tested these gaps, and judicial authorities closed them.

Some bootleggers took up the use of a disclaimer in their tape packaging. Evidently aware of the details of judicial decisions outside of the sphere of music, they experimented with the idea that if they distanced themselves from the song owners, they could distance themselves from prosecution. The first such cases took place in Illinois in 1970 in actions filed separately by Capitol Records and CBS against Gary Spies, the owner of Tape-A-Tape. Spies took care to claim that he was not counterfeiting. He was not passing off someone else's product as his own. Rather, he was following the law (well, at least some portion of the law), "which requires those who make and sell copies to take precautions to identify their products as their own." Accordingly, Spies attached the following disclaimer to all of his tapes: "No relationship of any kind exists between Tape-A-Tape and the original recording company, nor between this recording and the original recording artist. This tape is not produced under a license of any kind from the original recording company nor the recording artist(s) and neither the original recording company nor artist(s) receives a fee or royalty of any kind from Tape-A-Tape. Permission to produce this tape has not been sought nor obtained from any party whatsoever."

The court disposed of Spies's argument. "His bold admission of what he is doing no more insulates him from the plaintiff's action here than does the proclamation by a thief that he has committed a theft vitiate his criminal act." Three years later, Federal Court Judge Edwin A. Robson fined Spies $176,592 for unpaid royalties and damages based on the number of copies duplicated, which authorities were able to document, somewhat exceptionally within the context of the normally shadowy world of bootleg bookkeeping.[46]

As noted earlier, the licensing provision of the Copyright Act of 1909 allowed that once a recording had been made, anyone else could make a "similar use" of that copyrighted work, so long as the owner was paid a royalty of two cents per copy. In California in 1970, the Tape Industries Association of America, an organization of unauthorized manufacturers, advocated the usage of "disclaimer" labels that was currently getting Spies into trouble in Illinois. Prior to the arrest of the Kovens and their son in Los Angeles, the association attempted to void the new California state copyright law protecting recordings, on the grounds that the "similar use" provision of the federal Copyright Act "precludes California and all other states from proscribing the mere duplication of unpatented and uncopyrighted material." A specially appointed three-judge panel rejected their argument. The law was "a tolerable and permissible state regulation directed against theft and appropriation of a saleable product," and it did not impinge upon federal copyright legislation. The U.S. Supreme Court eventually upheld this decision.[47]

But then, in New Jersey in 1973, bootleggers gained a victory along these lines when Judge Irwin L. Kimmelman ruled, in reference to pre–February 15, 1972, recordings, that "in the absence of patent protection or copyright protection, exact copies or duplicates may be made by anyone."[48] Over the course of the next year and a half, this ruling provided a temporary safe haven for bootlegging all but the newest recordings, until Judge Joseph F. Weis, Jr., of the Third Circuit Court of Appeals in Philadelphia ruled that bootleggers did not qualify to be protected under the concept of "similar use." "Duplicators or pirates," wrote Weis, "do not 'use' the composer's work in a 'similar' fashion—indeed, they do not utilize the composer's work at all. It is a recording which is used . . . the statute only authorizes the use of the copyrighted work, that is, the written score." Weis explained that a "similar use" would entail the creation of new arrangements of songs and the securing of musicians to record those songs.[49] A related case in 1974 concerned a repeat offender, Albert Cecchi, the owner of Melody Records in Fairfield, New Jersey, and A&G Packaging, in Newark. Cecchi, who also operated under Jewish pseudonyms as Al Cohen or Morris Siegel, was denied the right to utilize the compulsory licensing provision of the Copyright Act as a safe haven. The act of his paying royalties for mechanical reproduction, said the court, did not legitimize his unauthorized copying and distribution of songs.[50]

Judge Kimmelman's ruling had pointed to a gap in legal coverage between existing recordings and new recordings, as of mid-February 1972. Even before that date, the recording industry and the government began to work on closing this gap. In November 1971, Atlantic Records, A&M, Warner Bros., and Columbia Records filed suit against fifty-two record and tape outlets and eighty individuals and corporations to establish that the provisions of the California state penal code still held and there would be no lapse in protection in the three months before the McClellan bill was to go into effect.[51]

Where appropriate, authorities were prepared to divide their seizures between the appropriate agencies, so that illicit copies of new recordings were governed by federal law and illicit copies of earlier recordings by state law. For example, in January 1973, the FBI, Los Angeles police, and members of the Los Angeles city attorney's office made a joint raid on Superior Audio Distributors in Eagle Rock, California. They confiscated more than seventy-five thousand eight-track tapes. Aware of the provisions of the Sound Recordings Amendment, the FBI seized only those albums dating from February 15, 1972, or later, in preparation for a grand jury indictment against Superior Audio. This constituted the majority of the tapes seized, including copies of Carly Simon's *No Secrets*, which at that particular moment was number 1 on the *Billboard* "Top LPs & Tapes" chart; Stevie Wonder's *Talking Book* (number 4 on that album chart); Diana Ross's *Lady Sings the Blues* (number 14); Helen Reddy's *I Am Woman* (number 19); Bette Midler's *The Divine Miss M* (number 27); and the O'Jays' *Back Stabbers* (number 81). At the same time, Los Angeles police took away the unauthorized copies of albums recorded prior to February 15, 1972, aiming to employ the antipiracy provisions of the California state penal code. Among the items falling into this category were copies of the Rolling Stones'

*Hot Rocks* and Al Green's *Let's Stay Together*, both still hanging onto the album charts with steady sales a year after their release, respectively, at number 116 and number 136.

Superior Audio also advertised a number of Latin albums, including *Mario Lanza's Greatest Hits*. These tapes carried an address in Plaza Blanca, New Mexico. As John Sippel, the *Billboard* reporter, pointed out in his detailed coverage of the raid, there is no such city.[52]

Finally, one audacious bootlegger, Richard Taxe, attempted to make his way around the new laws by claiming that his song products were altered from the original recordings, and therefore could be copyrighted on their own. Perhaps foolishly, Taxe used the recording industry's preferred press outlets to market his new corporation, Sound Alike Music, gaining announcements in *Variety* in June 1973 and *Billboard* in January 1974. Sound Alike Music, he explained, would copy existing albums, add instrumentation, and then apply for copyright for the resulting "original" recorded musical arrangements. His factory in west Los Angeles, *Billboard* reported, had six large injection molding machines for manufacturing cartridge cases and thirty duplication machines with audio sidewinders, capable of producing thirty thousand prerecorded tapes daily. In a puzzling bit of promotional logic, Taxe stated that his tapes, which would sell for $2.49 each, would take a segment of the marketplace away from tape pirates, as if his practice were otherwise.

It turned out that Taxe had been under investigation for more than a year. In August 1973, an FBI agent purchased eight tapes on Taxe's Sound 8 label, and these proved to be duplications of Warner Bros. and Atlantic records. Early in 1974, just as he was gaining his notice in *Billboard* as an ostensibly legitimate operation, an FBI raid on four locations for manufacturing and warehousing yielded about eighty-five thousand illicit prerecorded tapes and documentation of about 150,000 tapes already shipped to stores in numerous states between April 1973 and January 1974. The FBI then instructed law-enforcement agencies to confiscate these shipments, which included copies of albums by Black Sabbath, Deep Purple, Alice Cooper, Seals and Crofts, and Led Zeppelin. "Sound Alike" turned out to be "sounds the same."

In Los Angeles Federal District Court, Judge Irving Hill found Taxe and his associates guilty of conspiracy to violate the Sound Recordings Amendment, a misdemeanor; violation of the Sound Recordings Amendment, a misdemeanor; and mail fraud, a felony. Taxe received four years in prison and a fine of $26,000 plus court costs. His brother Ron Taxe and two other men received sentences ranging from six months to a year in prison, and fines ranging from $2,000 to $4,000.[53]

**Tape piracy continues.** With nearly universal state laws and the new federal Copyright Act in place, with the disclaimer and "similar use" loopholes closed, and with the gap between coverage of old and new recordings eliminated, the late 1970s and early 1980s brought forth harsh decisions in a final well-publicized round of fighting against tape and record bootleggers. Three cases deserve mention: that of David Heilman, for the magnitude of the fine imposed; "Operation Turntable," for the severity of the prison sentences; and "Operation Modsound," for bringing a counterfeit product into a major retail record chain, Sam Goody (once again).

In 1972 nine publishers initiated a class action suit against David Heilman, who eventually copied and distributed more than one thousand recordings in diverse genres, including rock music, "oldies," country music, and hit songs of the big-band era. Many of these he packaged into unauthorized anthologies. Among the cassettes, eight-track tapes, and LPs that he created from hit songs were a six-album set of Beatles tunes and a sixteen-track anthology combining songs by the Beatles, the Rolling Stones, and Bob Dylan. Heilman advertised these compilations in men's magazines.

In 1974, in keeping with what was coalescing as a standard interpretation of the law, the Wisconsin Supreme Court held that Heilman's actions were a form of unfair competition and misappropriation, and it issued an injunction against his activities. Subsequently he was held in contempt of court for shifting part of his business to Illinois in an attempt to evade the injunction, and for violating a similar injunction in California. This resulted in a $136,000 judgment against him in 1975, but Heilman continued to sell tapes as late as 1977, utilizing pseudonyms, receiving funds through post-office boxes, and depositing his funds into out-of-state bank accounts to disguise his operations. In February 1979 Heilman was convicted of copyright infringement in Federal District Court in Chicago and fined $9,000; this was, in the context, a minor blow. But the following month, the civil case of 1972 finally came to an end in Milwaukee County Circuit Court. The nine plaintiffs were awarded a judgment of $6,740,728 against Heilman and his corporation.[54]

In April 1979, "Operation Turntable" got underway. A jointly funded team obtained warrants to search four businesses belonging to a ring manufacturing and selling unauthorized cartridge and cassette tapes in Florida, as well as related private residences in Florida, South Carolina, and Maine. The FBI, a Florida-based U.S. district attorney, and the Duvall County Sheriff's Department collaborated on documenting charges of copyright infringement, conspiracy to violate the Copyright Act, the interstate transportation of stolen property, dealing in stolen property rights ("under Florida's larceny statute, 'property' is defined as anything of value, both tangible and intangible," reported *Variety*), wire fraud, conspiracy to violate the Racketeer Influenced and Corrupt Organizations (RICO) statute, and substantive violation of RICO. While some of the seventy-four defendants got off with suspended or brief sentences and probation, others went to prison for periods ranging from one to eight years. *Variety* announced a portion of these outcomes under the headline, "Stiffest Sentence Ever for Recorded Piracy Meted Out."[55]

The most high-profile case was Operation Mod Sound, initiated against a bootlegging distributor, but expanding to include the Sam Goody corporation. The investigation began, according to testimony from FBI agent Robert B. Levey, with the establishment of a bogus retail outlet, Modular Sounds, in Westbury, on Long Island, New York, in 1978. In the course of purchasing pirated goods from more than fifty individuals, Levey became involved with George Tucker, the head of Super Dupers Co. of Hasbrouch Heights, New Jersey. After gathering as much information as possible, three hundred federal agents conducted a simultaneous raid in December 1978 on nineteen sites in New York, New Jersey, Connecticut, North Carolina, and Georgia, seizing copies of albums by Elvis Presley, the Bee Gees, Linda Ronstadt, Donna Summer, Chicago, Kiss, Fleetwood Mac, and others.

Details of Tucker's involvement came out later through the testimony of a Canadian man, Norton Verner, who had been mistakenly granted immunity of the basis of false testimony from Tucker and with the intent of Verner becoming a government witness in a forthcoming trial against Sam Goody, Inc. Verner testified that he had met Tucker at least ten times in the course of arranging to purchase approximately sixty thousand pirated eight-track cartridges for something in the range of $80,000 to $100,000 (accounts differ on the exact figures), including copies of the soundtracks to *Saturday Night Fever* and *Grease*. Verner knew that the copies were illegal.

Charged with numerous counts of wire fraud and copyright infringement, Tucker pleaded guilty to one count each in August 1979. His sentencing was postponed when he offered to cooperate with the government's investigation into Sam Goody, Inc. As the year turned, Tucker got into an ugly fix when in an appearance before a grand jury, he denied working with Verner, only to recant his testimony before another grand jury, the next month. A trial followed, at which Verner testified that Tucker had warned off the company manufacturing the illicit tapes in advance of the FBI raid, and consequently that segment of the raid had produced no results. In September 1980, Tucker received five years' imprisonment and a $25,000 fine, variously for wire fraud, copyright infringement, making false statements to a grand jury, and obstructing a government investigation.

Meanwhile, the investigation of Sam Goody, Inc., was underway. In 1979 Arnold Rich, corporate counsel for the American division of the European recording conglomerate PolyGram, reported that the company had received a large shipment of returns of counterfeit cassettes and eight-track tapes from Sam Goody. This was, reported *Billboard* in February 1980, "the first known instance of such massive alleged bogus goods being found in normal industry pipelines." The reporter explained that it could be difficult to distinguish legitimate products from fraudulent ones, and dealers should watch out for inauthentic numbers printed on labels supplied from manufacturing plants, off-color covers, or other aspects of shoddy packaging. As the investigation expanded, complaints came from Columbia for albums by Billy Joel, James Taylor, and Paul Simon; from the RSO label, for Eric Clapton and Andy Gibb; from Arista Records, for Barry Manilow; and so forth.

In February 1980, the Justice Department's Organized Crime Strike Force brought indictments against Sam Goody, Inc., the corporation's president, George Levy, and its vice president in charge of procurement, Samuel Stolon, on charges of racketeering, interstate transportation of stolen property, and the unauthorized distribution of copyrighted sound recordings. Four other individuals, including Verner, allegedly acted as middlemen, buying counterfeit recordings from illicit manufacturers and then reselling the recordings to retailers, including Goody, but they were not charged.

The same day that Tucker was sentenced, the Goody corporation and its two executives entered "not guilty" pleas to felony charges. At a well-publicized trial in Brooklyn, Judge Thomas C. Platt dismissed charges against Levy, for lack of evidence, while the jury found the company and Stolon guilty of some of the charges. But that summer Judge Platt accused the prosecution of covering up false statements made by an FBI agent, and Platt ordered a retrial. In November 1982, following an extended period of outraged posturing and accusations emanating from all sides, the parties reached a bargain. Most of the remaining charges were dropped, and the Goody record chain and Stolon pleaded "no contest" to the charge of shipping twenty-three thousand counterfeit copies of the *Grease* soundtrack from New York to a company facility in

Minneapolis. Judge Platt fined the company $10,000 and sentenced Stolon to one year in prison. Four months later, another judge suspended Stolon's sentence, ordering him instead to spend three years on probation and to perform two hundred hours of community service.[56]

This was the last widely publicized individual case in the battle against tape piracy. It was by no means the last case. LP piracy continued on a seemingly intermittent basis, while tape piracy continued on a widespread and continuous basis. But trade papers and newspapers offered only a few further reports on individual cases. None of these added to the story insofar as revealing new methods of unauthorized distribution, or new approaches to prosecution.[57] Instead, the early 1980s witnessed a transition in the coverage of pop song piracy, from reports on individual, localized events, to statistical reports and unspecified, generalized assertions concerning activities taking place on a national or global basis. Had the practice of "scare journalism," publicizing specific stories of severe fines and lengthy prison sentences in an attempt to intimidate tape and record pirates, been effective in tamping down activities? Or had pop song piracy become so commonplace, despite the prohibition efforts, that it no longer made for interesting news? Probably it was a bit of both. Certainly the door was not closed. These practices continued, with phonograph record and tape piracy leading straight on and uninterruptedly into compact-disc piracy. And in crucial ways, the door opened further, becoming a global concern rather than a national or American and European concern. Before getting on to this next era, compact-disc piracy, I must rewind the tape, as it were, and tell the story a second time from the late 1960s onward, with album bootlegging rather than tape piracy as the focus.

# 8 • *Bootleg Albums as Unauthorized New Releases*

Layered across a transition in press coverage of tape and LP piracy, from specific accounts to generalized overviews, was the incorporation into news reports, both specific and general, of unauthorized new releases of previously unavailable recordings, beginning in 1969 with a Bob Dylan double LP, *The Great White Wonder*. This was the first bootleg album, in the new sense of that term. It took its name from the packaging: a cardboard record jacket with nothing but *G. W. W.* stamped on it, and blank white labels on the disks. *The Great White Wonder* presented a pastiche of music illicitly obtained by its compilers, Dub and Ken. Sides one and three held appallingly low-fidelity recordings that Dylan had made in Minneapolis in 1961. A portion of side two presented rejected takes from a few of Dylan's studio sessions for Columbia. None of this was terribly important. But the remainder of side two and all of side four held seven songs of tremendous musical and historical interest, and rightfully these caused a sensation. Here were half of the fourteen unreleased demo tracks that Dylan had made in Woodstock, New York, in 1967 with the band later to be known as "The Band" (with Robbie Robertson on guitar). The group would soon achieve great fame, first accompanying Dylan and then touring and recording on its own.

*The Great White Wonder* was not only the first bootleg album, but, for its content, one of the most desirable bootleg albums ever. It sold for decades, in significantly greater numbers than the typical bootleg album, and with the added irony of bootleggers bootlegging the bootleggers in repackaging this music in new formats for successive generations of Dylan fans.[1]

*The Great White Wonder* showed the way for a host of new unauthorized recorded song products that have offered something other than mere equivalency. Yes, these products have involved unauthorized copying, but they bring into play a constellation of transformational qualities as well.

Album bootlegging offers a fairly harmless way for fans of popular music to collect souvenirs. Sneak a tape recorder into a concert. Trade the tape with friends. Become an entrepreneur and turn that tape into a homemade release, putting out a few hundred copies or at most a few thousand.

Album bootlegging appeals to collectors. Once the practice of sneaking recorders into concerts and taping radio broadcasts becomes commonplace, and once bootleggers gain paths into obtaining unreleased studio recordings, then a fan devoted to a band can try to gather everything that the band ever recorded. Of course that is an impossible goal, but the fun is in the gathering.

Album bootlegging can provide an opportunity for an aspiring musician to promote songs at a point early in his or her career. A musician or a band might encourage the practice, tacitly or even explicitly. (Those who subsequently manage to achieve fame and fortune may then change their tune, clamping down on bootleg products; more on that later.)

Album bootlegging offers a path into enhanced enjoyment and appreciation. An illicit concert recording might substantiate the buzz on the street, that this band was best heard "live," or perhaps that this other band was best before it lost some member who never made it into the studio. A set of tapes obtained under the counter from an engineer at a major studio might illuminate the interpersonal dynamics of a band and the making of a famous song, through the experience of hearing rejected takes and conversations taped in the course of music making. More generally, motivations for creating, distributing, or obtaining bootleg albums might entail striving after any imaginable sort of social, cultural, sociological, historical, linguistic, or musicological interpretation for which the largest possible sample of available recordings can enrich the possibilities for understanding music and meaning.

On the most abstract and threatening level, album bootlegging challenges the notion that popular artists and recording companies should have monopolistic control of their cultural product. It threatens to wrest away that control, allowing music fans to second-guess artistic and financial decisions as to what performances should be recorded and what recordings should be released.

Here are a couple of examples, written from personal experience in much later years. In 2003, I had the privilege of recording the poet Amiri Baraka in concert at Penn State, under a contractual agreement with the group's manager that they would have control over the ultimate fate of the recording. Everything came together. The sound was terrific. The balance was perfect. I didn't mess anything up, except for not knowing that tenor saxophonist and pianist Archie Shepp was also going to sing briefly. (That one minute in two hours of music was off mic.) The performance was magical. The crowd was out of its mind with joy. Baraka's rendition of "I Am the Blues" is by far the best recording he ever made. Okay, maybe that's not saying much, because he rarely recorded, and when he did, it was in some poor circumstances. But even if Baraka had recorded frequently and well, this track would be a contender for honors. As for Shepp, he has indeed recorded frequently and done very well, and yet I would be so brash as to claim that this is also one of the best recordings he ever made.

This recording still sits on my shelf, unissued, and heard only by my friends and the friends of the two professors who organized the concert. Baraka is unapproachable. His manager is unapproachable. The band's manager is unapproachable. Phone calls and e-mails go unanswered. I am not the sort of entrepreneur interested in creating my own bootleg issues, and even if I were, I would never consider it in the face of that signed agreement. Maybe my children's children can post the whole thing on the Internet when the involved parties are all dead and gone. Then their generation can lament: what a tragedy that our generation never got to hear this.

A second story. In the winter of 2004–5, I served as the consultant for a jazz auction. Among the treasures that came into the auction were a number of reel-to-reel tapes from John Coltrane's family. Four of these reels held the entire studio session for the renowned album of pop songs *John Coltrane and Johnny Hartman* on a high-quality stereophonic reel-to-reel tape that had evidently been dubbed directly from the master tape, presumably so that Coltrane could take it home and listen after making the recording in March 1963. The tape included numerous alternative takes that up until that moment were believed to be permanently lost. On another reel was the lost master tape of the sextet version of a portion of "A Love Supreme" that Coltrane recorded the following year. In addition to capturing extraordinary music, these tapes provide rich insights into the music-making process, with conversation among the musicians and recording engineer Rudy Van Gelder, and moments of rehearsal.

Just before the sale, lawyers for the Verve Music Group, owners of the Impulse! label for which these recordings were originally made, came into the auction house and obliged the Coltrane tapes to be withdrawn from the event. Years have passed. Hopefully, someone will eventually see their way to releasing the music, on Impulse! or otherwise.[2]

These are, I think, fine examples of experiences that motivate the disobedient distribution of bootleg albums. It isn't just about making a buck. What is a person to do, when the musicians are intransigent and for unknown reasons act against what might actually be in their own best interests? Or when a record company is intransigent and acts against what might actually be in its own best interests?

Similar lines of thought have motivated decades of bootlegging Dylan, Led Zeppelin, the Rolling Stones, and so forth. As one practitioner, known as the Byrdman, put it in commenting on the act of producing concert releases, in response to the charge that album bootleggers were engaging in the presumptuous usurpation of artistic rights: "They performed it in front of an audience, people heard it . . . it's not an invasion of privacy."[3] Certainly I would agree, from my own experiences, that musicians and recording companies can demonstrate poor judgment in deciding what to release and what to withhold. This transformational quality of the practice of album bootlegging, enabling such decisions to be overturned, is perhaps that activity's greatest strength, and it clearly separates this disobedient practice from unambiguously criminal practices in the realm of record and tape piracy.

**Distinguishing bootlegging from piracy.** Until the advent of *The Great White Wonder,* the terms "bootlegging," "piracy," and "counterfeiting," had been used interchangeably, except when a clear distinction might be made between, on the one hand, "counterfeiting," whereby an unauthorized copy is specifically intended to be pawned off as if it were the real thing, and on the other hand, "bootlegging" and "piracy," whereby the item in question may not be pawned off as the real thing. A bootlegged or pirated object might hold the words to or the sound of an authorized cultural product, but it might be packaged in such a way that it would never be mistaken for that authorized product.

Once *The Great White Wonder* came on the scene, and similar projects followed, some people involved in the world of popular-music recordings, both in the news business and in legal circles, tried to maintain a consistent terminological usage. Counterfeiting would keep its meaning: to pawn off an illegal copy as if it were the real thing. Pirating would involve an illegal copy packaged in such a way as not to be confused with the authorized object. But bootlegging would denote a new, unauthorized release, not the copying of an existing recording.

This approach became particularly true for news coverage of unauthorized releases in the *New York Times*, which has always provided a model for editorial precision and consistency in any area. *New York Times* reporters were clearly striving to maintain the distinction, once it emerged, but it proved difficult.[4] And not even in legal circles were these distinctions maintained with consistency.[5]

Clinton Heylin's book *Bootleg: The Secret History of the Other Recording Industry* is the definitive study of unauthorized album releases. Heylin scrupulously maintains a consistent approach to terminology, and, when appropriate, he calls attention to instances in which one concept might run into another. Thus, for example, Heylin explains that Dante Bolletino's releases of Louis Armstrong's music on the Jolly Roger label represent piracy, the illegal copying of an existing legal product, because Columbia Records owned the sessions that Bolletino copied. These same releases foreshadow bootlegging, because at that time Columbia had shown no interest in reissuing these long out-of-print tracks, and therefore Bolletino was supplying recordings that were otherwise unavailable.

Having noted this semantic distinction, I admit to purposefully ignoring it in many portions of this book. In the big picture, a survey of the wholesale disobedient distribution of songs over the course of some eight decades (and still growing), the terms appear casually and carelessly mixed together. I think that it would be absurd to try to impose some sort of linguistic discipline on that reality, particularly given the extent to which people involved in these contests have conflated the two practices, bootlegging and piracy, whenever it suits their purposes.

**Album bootlegging blossoms.** On the heels of the resounding success of the Bob Dylan double LP, Dub bought high quality portable recording equipment, anodized the microphone black so that it could not be easily seen, and pointed it at the public address systems in concert venues for shows that the Rolling Stones performed in Los Angeles, Oakland, San Diego, and Phoenix. The second show in Oakland proved to be the best of the lot, and Dub released it as *LiveR Than You'll Ever Be*. Rock critic Griel Marcus hailed it in *Rolling Stone* magazine as the best album the Rolling Stones had ever made, and musically it upheld the group's reputation as "the greatest rock-and-roll band in the world." Here was an ideal manifestation of the possibilities of album bootlegging, in which the talented bootlegger produces a new song product that is not just enjoyable, but also serves as a crucial historical artifact, capturing the Rolling Stones at one of their peaks. In fact, Dub did such an accomplished job of making this recording that rumors subsequently circulated to the effect that it was actually an unauthorized release of a legitimate production.[6]

Following upon this release came a bootleg album that was truly professionally made. *The Royal Albert Hall Concert 1966* captured Bob Dylan actually in concert at the Free Trade Hall in Manchester, England (mislabeled as the Royal Albert Hall in London), via tapes obtained through the back door and then transferred to LP. Here was a realization of another path: legitimate recordings, withheld from the public for who-knows-what artistic or financial reasons, and then made available via illicit distribution.[7]

The pseudonymous Rubber Dubber was another musically and technologically talented bootlegger who took things even one step further than Dub in the effort to capture bands "live" and at their best. ("Dub," by the way, is recording jargon for making a copy of an existing recording; it's a clever moniker for an album bootlegger.) Rather than sneaking a tape recorder into concerts, Rubber Dubber brought a truck carrying professional recording equipment into the parking lot and attended concerts while carrying only two microphones. These microphones operated via built-in FM transmitters, thus allowing Rubber Dubber to broadcast directly from the concert to the equipment in his truck. He then offered a series of state-of-the-art bootleg albums. Lawsuits and the passage of the Sound Recordings Amendment put him out of business in 1972.[8]

As the story of the Coltrane tapes illustrates, high-quality copies of master recordings may exist in various forms, perhaps taken home by a musician for personal review, or perhaps warehoused in such a way that the inventory is not tightly controlled. Around the same time that Rubber Dubber was broadcasting to himself from rock concerts, Dub and Ken duped a record-industry employee into coming over to their house with a bundle of unreleased studio recordings by the Rolling Stones, the Who, Led Zeppelin, Dylan, and others, ostensibly for a private listening session. Dub and Ken hid microphones in the living room, drilled holes in their floor, ran wires into the basement, and turned on their tape recorder, ultimately releasing the whole lot. Here, in more wholesale fashion, was another example of album bootleggers wresting artistic control from songwriters, performers, and record companies, and instead putting out everything they could get their hands on.[9]

As album bootlegging spread, in its own modest way by comparison with large-scale record piracy, globalization became a factor, with the European marketplace eventually matching the American one in importance. The stylistic breadth of album bootlegging also expanded, moving retrospectively back into rock and roll, and forward into British punk.

**Europe enters the scene.** Years earlier, in 1961, the Rome Convention had provided an international agreement "for the protection of performers, manufacturers of records, and broadcasting organizations." This agreement extended some legal protection from songwriters to performers, manufacturers, and distributors, requiring remuneration, based on national law, for recordings disseminated to the general public. But only fifteen countries signed it, including the United Kingdom and Germany. The United States, France, and the Netherlands were among those who abstained.[10]

Dub, clever as always, became aware of the implications of this lack of participation. He began to stamp "made in Holland" onto his bootlegging label, TMQ (Trademark of Quality). He chose the Netherlands because that nation was a nonsignatory of the Rome Convention, while also having come to be known for taking a very open stance to unauthorized song distribution (witness, for example, the success of Dutch offshore pirate radio, described earlier). More generally, the Dutch were sympathetic to many aspects of "counterculture." So a fake "made in Holland" statement might not ruffle many feathers in the Netherlands, and it might clear a path for Dub exporting his song products to Europe.

Thus TMQ disks ostensibly "made in Holland" (actually, California) stood in the bins of a newly rising and legitimate London-based distributor, Virgin Records, until March 1973, when authorities raided the Virgin store on Oxford Street. Ultimately the corporate head, Richard Branson, had to pay a fine of £1,045 for carrying these products.

Concurrently, bootleg albums truly made in Holland circulated with little opposition. The most important of these included a release of a Jimi Hendrix session, as *Sky High*; the first bootleg album of the Velvet Underground; and, from an earlier era, rejected takes somehow obtained from Sun Records, featuring Elvis Presley and Jerry Lee Lewis.[11]

Another geographical variant on motivations for album bootlegging was the practice of making available in one country or continent some selection of recordings that previously were only available in another country or continent. A bootlegger named Richard led the way in issuing high-fidelity copies of rock songs that had been issued in Europe but never released in the United States. The most important of these were a Beatles album, *Not for Sale*, and a Pink Floyd album, *The Dark Side of the Moo* (punning on Pink Floyd's *The Dark Side of the Moon*, and with a cow pictured on the cover).[12]

**The genre expands.** In 1977, album bootlegging achieved a symbolic status as a genre in its own right with the publication of a two-hundred-page discography, *Hot Wacks*. This volume listed bootleg album titles and track titles, identified sources insofar as that was possible, rated the albums, and in some instances offered commentary on them.[13]

At around the same time, album bootlegging moved more expansively into rock and roll. One major stimulus was the cleaning out of a warehouse holding high-fidelity RCA tapes from Presley's movies. Learning of the imminent disposal of these tapes, album bootleggers somehow procured the tapes and released everything. Presley's death in 1977 led to an absolute frenzy of increased activity in this area, including even a parody by Richard (the same man who brought European tracks into the United States without authorization). He created "the very best of the very worst" Elvis recordings, on the "RCA Victim" label. Here was a bootleg album by a participant in the genre who had the humor to poke fun at his colleagues' worst practices, when their products did not rise above venal copying. The tongue-in-cheek album notes announce "50,000,000 fans can't be wrong," "a new rip-off repackaging job," and so forth.[14]

In England, the practice of bootlegging came to be essential to the documentation and understanding of numerous short-lived punk bands. For some of these groups, a bootleg release might present the only record, both literally and figuratively, of their best work, or of any of their work, period. Examples include *No Fun*, capturing the Sex Pistols at a performance in June 1976 in Manchester, and *Spunk*, a compilation of their first studio demo recordings. Heylin notes that the Sex Pistols' legitimate recordings were perhaps never as good as these bootlegs.[15]

**Album bootlegging as self-promotion, or not.** Another transformational justification for bootlegging is that it might offer an alternative or an additional way for a musician or a band to distribute songs. This could be the case for anyone who did not have a contract with a major label, or perhaps had only recently secured such an affiliation. In circumstances like these, bootlegging might actually help to boost a career.

Bruce Springsteen reportedly encouraged bootlegging during his rise to fame, on the belief that the circulation of bootleg albums would help to promote his music. Heylin speculates that Springsteen and his management facilitated this practice by allowing numerous FM broadcasts of his early concerts. These broadcasts could then be taped privately and bootlegged.

But then, having gained the fame he desired, Springsteen reversed his position in the late 1970s and began to crack down on bootleggers. The most important of these was the pseudonymous Vicky Vinyl (Andrea Waters), who had turned a September 1978 Springsteen broadcast from Passaic, New Jersey, into an acclaimed three-LP boxed set, *Pièce de Résistance*. Springsteen and his label, Columbia, sued Waters in June 1979, eventually winning a more than $2 million civil judgment for damages. This put her out of business. She had no resources at all, let alone $2 million.[16]

Not long thereafter, in 1982, President Reagan signed a new law for sound recordings, raising the maximum criminal infringement penalties to five years imprisonment and a $250,000 fine, and making the first offense a felony rather than a misdemeanor. As far as the law was concerned, transformational uses were irrelevant. Album bootlegging and record piracy were one and the same thing.[17]

Early on, album bootlegging was predominantly an LP culture, rather than a tape culture, in that the LP jacket design was often an important part of the artifact, except, for example, in the case of fans trading homemade Grateful Dead tapes. (This group encouraged bootlegging.) Then, as CDs began to take hold in the general marketplace, album bootlegging followed suit. Since the late 1980s the bootleg album has mainly been a song product on digital media, whether CDs or beyond. For example, a succession of high quality CD releases of Led Zeppelin concerts got underway in 1988, beginning with *Live in Zurich*. Over the course of the next three years, more than one hundred Led Zeppelin bootleg albums came out. The band had steadfastly declined to issue representative live performances, and so bootleggers filled that artistic void. There were also significant new releases of sessions by the Who, captured in rehearsal in Leeds, England, and by Lou Reed, from a radio broadcast taped in 1972.[18]

Meanwhile there were crucial developments concerning globalization, not only in opening new doors for record piracy, but also in opening new doors for album bootlegging. These developments involved discrepancies in relationships between the legal coverage of studio recordings and the legal coverage of "live" recordings, and discrepancies in the duration of copyright from one country to the next. Consequently, important new developments in album bootlegging—including concert recordings that fell into the public domain, a series of so-called protection gap albums, and the oxymoronic achievement of the first "legal bootleg" record label—came into being as subcategories of various transnational aspects of the distribution of songs on compact disc. So before delving into that latter portion of the album bootlegging story, I need to return to the thread of changing formats into which that bootlegging story is woven, and present the new central object, the compact disc.

# 9 • *Illegal Copying of Compact Discs*

In 2002, following straight along the lines of reports on song-sheet peddling in Times Square in 1930 and 1939, the *New York Times* offered a report on sidewalk sales in lower Manhattan. By way of illustration, the paper showed a folding table heavily laden with illicit compact discs.[1] Here was a metaphor for the extent to which patterns in the unauthorized distribution of songs might remain intact as the decades pass. A number of typical expressions of monopoly and disobedience reengaged, transferring to the new musical medium. Meanwhile, older media receded into obsolescence, and existing contests over their unauthorized manufacture and distribution faded away.

Some aspects of characteristic distribution chains carried over from the earlier formats. On the one hand, the manufacture of prerecorded CDs was even more specialized than the process of pressing phonograph records, and in the first decade in which CDs were popular, there was no feasible alternative for that authorized process. The result was a situation similar to that prevailing in the era of phonograph-record piracy. Entrance to unauthorized copying could only be gained through the back door of legitimate factories. On the other hand, CD burners and blank discs eventually came onto the market. Their use proliferated and became progressively less expensive through the course of the 1990s, and this altered the situation somewhat, opening up possibilities that had flourished in the era of illicit tapes. In addition to operating through the back doors into legitimate companies, unauthorized manufacturers could set up their own production sites, although the vast preponderance of manufacturing remained in the hands of the authorized factories.

In either case—persuading a plant operator to manufacture illicit CDs, or setting up a do-it-yourself operation—possibilities for transformational use, rather than mere equivalency, also carried over directly from tapes to CDs in the realm of unauthorized compilations. In addition to continuing the practice of album bootlegging, unauthorized song producers created new anthologies of existing recordings, variously as greatest hits, dance mixes, and party tracks. In 1996, for example, the RIAA sued ASR Recording Services in Canoga Park, California, for "unauthorized top-hit compilation albums" of songs by such artists as the Beatles, Boyz II Men, Mariah Carey, Michael and Janet Jackson, Elton John, Madonna, the Pet Shop Boys, Queen, U2, and Vanessa Williams.[2]

Joining these compilations was a closely related new entity, the "DJ mix." As live musical performance became increasingly sidelined by recorded music, the sphere for disc jockeys expanded from radio into nightclubs, weddings, bar mitzvahs, and so forth. It was cheaper than getting a band, it was simpler than getting a band, and from the point of view of both personalities and sound, it was generally speaking less hassle and more reliable than getting a band. In releasing piracy statistics for the year 1995, the RIAA bemoaned: "while traditional cassette piracy continues to decline and has reached a five-year low, the seizure of counterfeit and bootleg CDs has almost doubled, reflecting the increasing popularity of that format, especially for illicit DJ mixes."[3]

A different line of continuation, involving transnational conflicts, carried forth from offshore pirate radio into the era of compact discs. In a previous era, pirate stations had broadcast pop songs onto northwestern Europe shores with, for example, a Panamanian ship registration, ownership in Liechtenstein, and the financial backing of an American Top 40 entrepreneur. For these governments and businesses, the lure of income might outweigh the niceties of supporting a nation that was receiving unauthorized broadcasts. Now, in the same way, a Taiwanese compact-disc manufacturer might accept illicit orders, with a busy production line and the resulting financial gain outweighing transpacific niceties. Insofar as many CD manufacturing plants were located outside of the centers of the recording industry, the United States and western Europe, the monopolists found themselves in a situation that they could not fully control.

While these various aspects of monopoly and disobedience continued, or reengaged, other aspects of songs, distribution, and disobedience in the CD era were new. The most important new factors involved globalization, and the transnational relationship of copyright to recordings. When the manufacture of sound recordings became an international endeavor, with most plants initially based outside of western industrial countries, and when a multitude of nations disagreed in diverse ways in their conceptions of copyright protection, then legal and legislative loopholes opened unauthorized back doors to song distribution much wider than ever before. For example, some nations might afford legal protection to their own musicians and music, but not to foreign performers or foreign works. Or some nations might afford "live" recordings a different level of protection from that offered to studio recordings. Or some nations might classify recordings—whether "live" or made in the studio—as having fallen into the public domain, even while these same tracks remain protected in other nations.

Once the production of songs became an international endeavor, these factors weighed in heavily on the functionality of the distribution chain. At the extreme, what was piracy for one nation might be redefined as legitimate business for another. A consequence of these transnational loopholes was that the physical location of contests over songs, distribution, and disobedience shifted considerably away from factories and distributors to customs stations, in efforts to halt the importation of unauthorized discs.

**Digital copying and digital copyright.** The advent of compact discs also brought a transformational musical factor into play. The fact that a digital file could be copied without any noticeable degradation in sound quality led to a transformation of the ways in which song owners lobbied for copyright protection.

For phonograph records, each generation of copying resulted in a loss of audio fidelity. When legitimate plants were doing illicit manufacturing through the back door, this was not necessarily a factor. An unauthorized disk might be pressed from exactly the same run as a legitimate disk, and the resulting sound quality might be identical. But for someone like Dante Bolletino, the act of creating a new master from an existing 78 r.p.m. Louis Armstrong record meant that Bolletino was starting the pressing process five steps removed from the original (master/negative master/mother/stamper/record). Necessarily, the final song product could not sound as good as a disc pressed from the original 78 r.p.m. Columbia master. Bootleg projects such as these were typically distinguished not only by their low-end packaging, but also by their characteristically inferior sound quality.

For tapes it was usually much worse. Unauthorized master tapes were normally made from existing records. Like Bolletino's product, this removed the fake "master" five steps from the original master. For tapes, each additional stage of duplication then not only degraded the sound further, but also introduced a higher level of tape hiss, layered across the music. Furthermore, the vast majority of bootleg tapes were carelessly made. Their sound quality was notoriously mediocre.

Unlike records, unlike tapes, compact discs could be copied over and over without any significant degradation in sound quality, so long as care was taken in transferring the digital code from one object to the next. In this new duplication process, there would no longer be any meaningful distinction between "masters" and "slaves."

Manufacturers were deeply concerned over the possibilities that this raised. Insofar as the metaphor of the safe maker and the safecracker applies, it was as if safe manufacturers would be publishing all of the combinations to all of their locks, and yet still trying to protect the contents. After that, song sharing was just around the corner. Recognizing the prospect for losing control of song products, the recording industry joined other facets of the software and entertainment industries in supporting the Digital Millennium Copyright Act (DMCA), which became law in October 1998, coincidentally just as Shawn Fanning was beginning to test Napster on a localized college network.

The DMCA aimed to prevent individuals from overriding technical measures that would protect a digital file from being copied, to prevent individuals from circulating methods for breaking such protection, to require manufacturers to use the technology provided under DMCA licensing, and most ominously, to automatically define as criminals those manufacturers who did not participate in DMCA licensing. Two months later, in December 1998, the RIAA introduced the Secure Digital Music Initiative, an ultimately failed effort to create software code that would protect copyrighted music in all digital formats and for all digital players and recorders. Other proposed initiatives of the ensuing decade were oriented toward digital television broadcasting and digital film, but these too introduced efforts to prevent the illegal copying of songs. Surveying the whole, Tarleton Gillespie offers this warning in his book *Wired Shut: Copyright and the Shape of Digital Culture:* "At the core of these changes is a fundamental shift in strategy, from regulating the use of technology through law to regulating the design of the technology so as to constrain use." He argues that this goal—not to restrain those who make illegal copies, but to prevent the possibility of making illegal copies—cannot be achieved.[4]

**The invention and introduction of compact discs.** The compact disc was about a decade in the making, and nearly another decade in catching on. Antonio Rubbiani first demonstrated a form of video disk technology in Italy in 1969. The next year, the Philips Corporation began to work on ALP (audio long play), a format that was conceived as a future rival to the LP. This new format would use laser beams rather than needles to record and to read musical information stored on a disk. Later in the decade, Philips proceeded from technological developments created for the laserdisc, a format for film storage that never caught on widely. Philips began to adapt this technology to an audio format, and its staff coined the name for the product: a "compact disc."

In 1979 Philips entered into an agreement with Sony for the purpose of establishing international manufacturing standards; this was, coincidentally, just as the Japanese electronics manufacturer was releasing the Walkman (and a decade before it got into the artistic end of the record business, purchasing Columbia Records). The standards agreed upon by Philips and Sony defined, among many other things, the rate at which continuous sound would be "sampled" into microscopically brief moments and converted into digital files representative of those countless moments; a standard size, twelve centimeters in diameter (about five inches); and a standard duration, approximately seventy-four minutes in length (some CDs held as much as eighty minutes of music).

In the first half of the 1980s, the market for prerecorded cartridge tapes faded away in favor of prerecorded audiocassettes. Philips and Sony introduced compact discs to the general public in 1983, but CDs caught on only gradually in the United States, and even more slowly in Europe. For several years, the LP remained overwhelmingly dominant as the preferred medium for prerecorded music, and only in 1988 did CD sales surpass LP sales in the United States.

In the area of home recording, CDs burners were not yet on the horizon. So cassettes headed that market, with blank tapes surpassing LPs during the 1980s in terms of the annual volume of units sold. Then, in 1990 Philips and Sony introduced the recordable compact disc. In 1992, for the first time, compact discs led cassettes in both value and units shipped.

By the end of the 1990s, cassettes and LPs were disappearing from the American market. CDs accounted for 87 percent of the volume of units sold in the United States in the year 2000, and 91 percent in 2001. Europe followed suit. Consumers embraced home, automobile, and personal CDs players (notably, a new Sony Walkman, for compact discs rather than cassettes). Consumers not only purchased new releases on CD, but also discarded first their LPs and later their tapes, replacing shelves and stacks of these now antiquated media with shelves and stacks of reissues of songs on compact disc. The potential for sales was immense. Recording companies could release not only new songs, but all the old ones, again, in the new format. Industry growth soared. And naturally the landscape of illicit releases followed suit, shifting from LPs and tapes to compact disc.[5]

**The manufacture of compact discs.** In the era of phonograph records, the complexity of the manufacturing process made this a particularly strong link in the distribution chain, insofar as the recording industry was able to maintain its supervision of this process. Yes, some stuff leaked out the back door, but the situation was manageable. For CDs, Philips and Sony developed a highly complicated manufacturing process based in part upon "class 100 clean rooms," robots, vacuum chambers, galvanization, polycarbonate injection, and so forth. So, in principle, if things were the same, this situation should have provided an even stronger link, insofar as control of the distribution chain was concerned. But things were not the same. Globalization entered the picture, and prospects for supervision were removed a country if not a continent away. Moreover, in the early years of CDs, the factories suited to such production were situated almost exclusively in Asia. Thus the recording industry, centered in America and Europe, was obliged to depend upon manufacture in countries that routinely failed to share Western conceptions of copyright and ownership.

The digital portion of the recording process begins with a sound file. In the twenty-first century, multitrack studio tape recording has given way to multitrack computerized recording, with the musicians' microphones and amplifiers feeding directly into software programs that capture sound in a digital form. Either way—whether via analogue recording converted into a digital file, or via direct digital recording—the result is an unimaginably long string of zeros and ones, as computer programs pass representations of sound through several stages of conversion.

With that sound file in hand, the manufacturing process begins. A compact disc preserves the numbers as patterns of smoothness and indentations— "lands" and "pits"—reflected past a laser beam. A movement from pit to pit or from land to land signifies a zero; a movement from pit to land, or vice versa, signifies a one. Encoding the microscopic pits onto a smooth disc, and then taking that disc through stages of mass manufacture, is a wickedly intricate process that requires an obsessively smooth glass disc created in a sterile room, because any stray particles might cause the laser to misread the lands and pits.

Portions of the manufacturing process recall aspects of record pressing. The pits reside in a layer coated onto the blank glass disc. Hardened by baking, this disc generates a metallic negative copy, smoothness and bumps rather than smoothness and pits. A positive master copy is "grown" around the negative copy; this is the "mother." A negative image is "grown" from the mother; this is the "stamper."

With the stamper in place, a polycarbonate molder produces roughly five hundred to one thousand discs in an hour. To produce the quantities that came out of major factories, approximately 10 million units per year, a factory would need to have at least two and possibly three such production lines operating all day, every day. (And to keep a factory of that capacity busy, illicit orders might fit the bill.)

Robotic arms shepherd the mass-produced discs through a cooling process. Then a reflective metallic layer coats the lands and pits, so that a laser beam can "read" them. Two more layers complete the process. A layer of lacquer prevents deterioration of the reflective aluminum alloy, and a layer of artwork provides a "label." This is not really a label in the traditional sense of a piece of paper affixed to a phonograph record or tape, but rather it results from the processes of screen-printing or off-printing directly onto the disc.[6]

**Globalization.** Having already gained the upper hand in the manufacture of electronic and computer hardware, Japanese, Korean, Taiwanese, and other Asian companies were initially in the best position to supply advanced robotic technology and the requisite sterile environments to realize this specialized manufacturing process on a massive, continuous basis. So East Asia dominated the early years of compact-disc manufacturing. Much of this production went to North America and western Europe. For example, by 1990 Taiwan had eight CD factories with an annual capacity of 80 million disks, but domestic sales in Taiwan at the end of 1992 accounted for only 10 million disks: "the remaining seven eighths of capacity can only be taken up by exporting," notes Heylin.[7] For the first time, the majority of recorded song products came into the West from abroad, through customs.

Unauthorized practices followed suit. Heylin notes that album bootlegging shifted from LPs to CDs in the late 1980s, via manufacture in East Asia. This immediately elicited a severe crackdown headed by the RIAA and the FBI and directed at U.S. Customs sites on the West Coast. In turn, a consequence of this crackdown was a shift in the balance of album bootlegging activities from America to Europe.[8]

When plants opened up on other continents, the disjunction between recording centers and manufacturing centers did not improve. Rather, the situation was exacerbated further with the fall of the Iron Curtain and a subsequent manufacturing free-for-all in central and eastern Europe, where attitudes toward copyright protection tended to be as casual as in a number of Asian nations. In March 1997, for example, a Dutch customs official put a halt to an attempt to import one hundred thousand pirated Bulgarian CDs that had made their way from Sofia, to Belgrade in Serbia, to Kiev in the Ukraine, to Amsterdam's Schiphol Airport.[9]

**Protection-gap CDs and other global disagreements.** To make matters worse for the song owners, a contested song product might not be illegal in its country of origin. For example, in Japan, which was growing into the world's second largest market for sound recordings (after the United States), the copying and distribution of American and European phonograph records and cassette tapes was an entirely legal activity until 1978. At that point new legislation began to offer some protections for foreign sound recordings, but only in 1992 were foreign works and recordings retrospectively brought into line with international norms and the protection afforded Japanese musicians. Similarly, the laws and treaties of other Asian countries such as Korea and Taiwan had no provisions at all for protecting foreign recordings until well into the 1990s, and piracy and bootlegging were unregulated in the first years of post–Soviet era markets in such countries as the Czech Republic, Bulgaria, and Romania. How were allegations of piracy during this era to be disentangled from these irreconcilable national approaches to copyright?[10]

Globalization compromised the control of distribution chains in ways other than the physical disjunction of separating song owners in one country or continent from song-product manufacturers in another. Disparate approaches to copyright protection also threw spanners into the works. Unquestionably the most distinctive song product to come out of a transnational legislative jumble was a quasi-legitimate, quasi-illegitimate form of album bootlegging that came to be known as the protection-gap CD.

The circumstances peculiar to this product coincided with the ascendance of the compact disc as the dominant medium for packaging bootleg albums. Hence the "protection-gap CD" rather than the "protection-gap LP," insofar as album bootlegging was concerned. In the broader picture of the unauthorized wholesale distribution of sound recordings, this product was already in place during the LP era, but for reissue projects rather than for album bootlegging. Activities had already gotten underway in the 1970s in Sweden, which then offered no protection for sound recordings. The leading figures were Carl Hällstrom and Jonas Bernholm, who focused on unauthorized reissues mainly in African American genres.[11] (Bernholm subsequently heaped coals on the heads of the authorized American record companies by paying royalties to minority artists who had in many cases never received royalties from the purported owners.)

As this situation developed further in Scandinavia, Austria, Germany, and Italy—and then, in some respects, throughout Europe—free trade rules of the European Economic Community (the forerunner of the European Community, which formed only later, in 1993) came into conflict with exclusive rights vested in recordings. The licensing fee due to a songwriter for the recording of that song is a nonexclusive right. Once a song is recorded, anyone else may record that same song, so long as the manufacturer pays the appropriate rights agency some pennies per track for each copy manufactured. By contrast, manufacture is an exclusive right. Once a record company enters into a contractual agreement with a performer, then only that manufacturer—say, EMI and its American affiliate, Capitol—may legally produce and sell the resulting song product—say, Beatles albums. The manufacture and distribution of this song product by some other entity constitutes a violation of that exclusive right.

In the 1980s, Denmark and Austria afforded only twenty-five years of protection for sound recordings, rather than the European norm of fifty years. Hence the term "protection-gap." When that twenty-five-year span expired for Elvis Presley, Fats Domino, Nat King Cole, and others, and when soon thereafter, the more widespread fifty-year span of European copyright protection of sound recordings expired for the early recordings of Louis Armstrong, Fats Waller, and Duke Ellington, European companies lost their exclusive rights to historic and lucrative material. These and countless other historic popular recordings fell into the public domain, so long as licensing fees continued to be paid to the song owners as required (if, say, the recording of "Love Me Tender" came into the public domain in Denmark, but the song itself remained under copyright.) "Protection-gap" reissue labels proliferated. The Englishman Keith Smith, for example, ran his ironically named Official Records out of Copenhagen, taking advantage of the foreshortened path to the Danish public domain to reissue unauthorized but legal albums of jazz, blues, rhythm and blues, rock and roll, country and western, and pop, while the Austrian entrepreneur Johnny Parth took a similar path with his cross-label, chronological editions of blues, New Orleans jazz, and gospel music on his pointedly named Document Records, based in Vienna. Parth, to take things a step further, advertised UK distribution from Hotshot Records in Leeds, England, and U.S. distribution from Arhoolie Records in El Cerrito, California.[12]

In 1988, British courts decided in favor of the recording industry, ruling that Cliff Richards's early 1960s recordings for EMI were protected by the laws of the United Kingdom and could not be distributed on a Danish label independent of EMI. But the ruling did not apply to bootleg releases of live recordings. This resulted in the widespread dissemination in Europe of protection-gap CDs, which came into being and quickly proliferated just as American authorities were cracking down on album bootlegging in LP format in the United States. (In addition to safes and safecrackers, Hydra provides another useful metaphor in the bootlegging and piracy story. Cut off one head and several more appear.)

Numerous factors exacerbated the situation from the point of view of the song owners. Generally speaking, a record company would not own a contracted group's live performances, unless this option were specified in the contract. On a more quirky level, Italian copyright law protected studio recordings for fifty years, but live recordings for only twenty years. Similarly, German copyright law only protected German nationals in this arena; recordings by non-Germans were fair game.

These circumstances gave album bootleggers the authority to manufacture and distribute historic live rock albums in Italy, and classic rock studio albums and contemporary live recordings in Germany. Many took this liberty one step further, paying the requisite licensing fees to the appropriate Italian or German recording rights agency and then distributing bootleg albums throughout the continent. An Italian firm established an oxymoronic entity, the first "legal bootleg" label, Bulldog Records, which got underway with a CD reissue of Bob Dylan's concert at the Manchester Free Trade Hall in 1966.

Practical considerations encouraged the exploitation of these loopholes in European copyright legislation. Heylin noted that, at the time, Italy hosted about half a dozen compact-disc processing plants, and these were underutilized by the recording industry. "Italian protection-gap labels were helping to keep Italian jobs in CD production—and the large multinationals were not." Layered on top of all this, competing illicit manufacturers situated in East Asia and elsewhere in Europe were bootlegging the bootleggers, imitating their approach, claiming that licensing fees had been paid in Germany (even if not), and claiming Germany as the country of origin for their song products (even if not). As Heylin explained, it became extremely difficult for authorities to determine which albums were legal and which were not. "If a Korean plant was making two Dylan bootleg CDs, one called *Friend to the Martyr*, the other *Going to Arlington,* [authorities] would have no idea which was the collection of studio outtakes from 1983 (the former) and which a legitimate German import of a live show from 1992 (the latter)."[13]

**Globalization and press coverage.** The globalization of the recording distribution chain led to both quantitative and qualitative changes in the press coverage of pop song piracy. Published accounts of phonograph record and tape piracy were abundant in the 1970s and 1980s by comparison with the coverage of song-sheet bootlegging in the 1930s and 1940s, which was substantial in those earlier decades, but limited mainly to *Variety,* the *New York*

*Times,* and a few other sources. Coverage of CD piracy reached an even greater level of intensity in the 1990s and into the new century, such that thousands of articles on the subject appeared yearly, variously in general newspapers and magazines, in entertainment periodicals, and in Internet sources. A substantial percentage of this coverage represented the easy flow of information in our modern society, in that the same story or the same subject would be recycled over and over again in different publications, on paper and in "virtual" form. But even accounting for such repetition, the coverage was intense.

And yet, most of this coverage lacked specificity, failing to convey a sense of what actually happened. What sorts of quantities of unauthorized CDs were in circulation, and who were the distributors and manufacturers? What percentage of CD exporting was legal, and what percentage illegal? How much damage were the illicit objects doing to legally distributed goods?

In earlier episodes of songs, distribution, and disobedience, there was no lack of hyperbole in the press coverage of events, but there was also a very substantial underpinning of concrete stories and useable statistical data that might be extracted from particular reports. In the earliest era, these accounts conveyed the sense that bootleg song sheets circulated in at least hundreds of thousands and probably millions of copies annually. Stories identified hundreds of the participants and the nature of their involvement, and court records fleshed out some of these stories. A sense of the whole emerged—or at least so I argued in an earlier chapter—of a failing relationship between sheet music and the then-new media of recordings, radio, and film. Whatever one's position on the ethics or legality of the situation, there could be little doubt that the bootleg song sheets were challenging and disrupting the normal practices of the music publishing industry.

Similar statements might be made for pirate radio, or record and tape piracy, or album bootlegging. Specific stories abound. It is possible to gain meaningful notions of the trauma that particular pirate stations caused the BBC, and why; or meaningful notions of the names of songs and types of song genres illicitly copied onto phonograph disks and tapes; or meaningful notions of the particular song products copied or compiled by unauthorized tape manufacturers.

That sort of press coverage began to fade away in the late years of record and tape piracy, and it more or less disappeared from the coverage of unauthorized CDs. Amid an onslaught of generalized hand-wringing over the illegal copying of compact discs, only a few articles provided any details. For a rare example, in 2002, following an investigation that had gotten underway in

1999, Ralph J. Marino, his wife Carol, their son Vincente, and their daughter Carol were accused of manufacturing ten thousand compact discs per week at their home in West Islip, New York. Entering with a search warrant, authorities found "1,500 pirated recordings, 36 CD burners, and three high-speed cassette duplicators."[14] I found scarcely any other such stories, and consequently very few trails that might be pursued, by name. It was as if a veil had been cast over everything. There was reportedly a huge amount of illicit activity going on, but no one seemed to be able to say much of substance about it. Individual participants had more or less disappeared. CD piracy was the work of vague groups of Taiwanese, Koreans, Bulgarians, Russians, whatever.

Press reports also offered an indiscriminate confusion of marketplaces. Which song products had an impact on the recording industry in the United States and western Europe, and which did not? For example, in the early 1980s the LP virtually disappeared from India, with a sole survivor from the previous era, the Gramophone Company, then competing against two hundred cassette-tape companies. A decade later, in 1991, as the first world was discarding LPs and tapes in favor of CDs, India had become the second largest producer of blank cassette tapes. Could a relationship be presumed between Indian cassettes and CD sales in the West? Did the mass production of cassette tapes in India significantly diminish those Western CD sales? Conversely, would pricey Western CDs have been purchased in India if cheap tapes were unavailable? (I think not, to all these questions.)

Several years later, in Tunisia and numerous other third-world countries, the "piracy share" of music sales was purported to exceed 90 percent.[15] The national recording economies of India, Tunisia, and these other nations constituted only a tiny percentage of the world market. What did it matter how their recordings were being made and sold, if this market had no significant effect on sales in the West? And yet a hefty portion of press coverage was given over to complaints concerning these peripheral markets, in sympathy with the song owners.

It is not an easy matter to explain this transition from specificity to vagueness. Perhaps there was a feeling that specific accounts no longer attracted a readership. Perhaps reporters felt overwhelmed by the extent of activities in bootlegging and piracy. Perhaps reports of album bootlegging were routinely conflated with reports of record counterfeiting and piracy in purposely careless ways, to generate inflated statistics on the level of unauthorized activity. Perhaps the consequences of globalization, including the shift in focus from factories to importation, made it difficult for governmental authorities, representatives of song owners, and the press to gather details in the same ways that they had in previous eras. Perhaps there was a purposeful confusion of marketplaces, as accounts of unauthorized recordings in economically peripheral nations intermingled with accounts of unauthorized recordings in the centers of record consumption.

To finish off this story of illegal copying that stretches from records to tapes to CDs, with album bootlegging laid across that thread, and before moving on to the utter transformation of the industry wrought by song sharing, I offer some thoughts on piracy statistics and industry growth, in an attempt to provide some sense of the extent of illicit activity and its value in relation to the whole.

In a very substantial sense, these questions concerning an absence of specificity and the possibly spurious nature of some complaints do not matter. The recording industry was conducting a public relations campaign to create a global notion of rampant piracy. That campaign unquestionably succeeded. Generalized claims concerning the vast extent and damaging value of pop song piracy came to be widely accepted, even when divorced from documentation. Whether that campaign was actually effective in suppressing piracy is a different sort of question, and probably impossible to answer.

## PIRACY STATISTICS AND INDUSTRY GROWTH

Back in the early 1970s, when album bootlegging took hold, authorities often found it convenient to ignore semantic distinctions between bootlegging and piracy. The same degree of offended tone, ominous significance, hysteria, outrage, and so forth might be meted out to the seizure of seventy-five thousand pirated tapes from Superior Audio Distributors in the Los Angeles area in 1972 as to the seizure of 109 bootleg tapes from the Feelin' Ceilin' head shop in Miami that same year.[16]

Two decades later, song owners were watching monopolies slip away owing to global situations that were out of their control. It was becoming increasingly difficult to send in the FBI or a parallel European authority to try to limit the damage. All that was left to do was to shout "piracy! piracy! piracy!" louder than ever before.

Typically, reporters seem to have accepted the shouts without questioning the recording industry's practice of arriving at estimated losses by conflating piracy and bootlegging, even when particular journalistic accounts carefully maintained the distinction between the two activities. Heylin meticulously traced this distinction throughout his history of bootleg records, and he argued convincingly that for the sake of what is now called "putting a spin on the numbers," an incorrect inference was purposefully being made in connecting the number of contested objects in circulation to the estimated numbers of copies of those objects. It seems that the majority of arrests and the majority of contested objects for record and tape piracy actually involved the unauthorized production and distribution of very small runs of bootleg albums and tapes—hundreds of copies, or at the very most a few thousand—rather than huge runs of mass-produced pirated and counterfeited copies of hit albums. As Heylin put it, describing the marketplace for album bootlegging: "Bootlegs represent no threat to the music industry. Only the most dedicated of fans is going to appreciate the 'point' of having all twenty-seven takes of *Can't Help Falling in Love*."[17] But the practice of album bootlegging proved to be extremely convenient in providing fodder for publicity releases from the music industry, whose estimates of alleged losses were inferred from the notion that each contested object had been copied in huge quantities, whether bootlegged or pirated, and each imagined illicit object might be assigned its full retail value.

In an unusually balanced instance of contemporary press coverage, Patricia Hollie in 1980 confirmed that there was a quantitative difference between bootlegging activities and counterfeiting activities, even if exact quantities were unknown. "Bootleggers have not really presented any competition to the major record producers. But counterfeiters, whose products look and sound like the legitimate recordings, are another matter."[18] Nonetheless, a string of estimated industry losses published in the *New York Times* accepted unquestioningly the conflation of figures, and Hollie herself carried this into her article. In 1971 the RIAA estimated that record companies were losing $100 million per year to tape bootleggers.[19] Two Brooklyn bootleggers arrested the following year were alleged to belong to a nationwide network doing $200 million worth of business annually in bootleg tapes.[20] In 1978 Stanley M. Gortikov, then president of the RIAA, admitted that "we have no accurate figures of the extent of piracy in America"; he said that "the figure we generally use is an annual street value of $200 million," which would have been roughly 10 percent of the figure for legitimate annual sales, then standing at roughly $2 billion.[21] Two years later the estimate had doubled and then tripled, with the ironic note that this figure was claimed to be conservative: "Conservative estimates now put the piracy rate at one in 10 for records and perhaps one in five for tapes. We estimate that unauthorized duplication cost the industry $400 million last year," reported Hollie in February 1980.[22] "Counterfeit recordings rob the industry of $400 million to $600 million a year," said Joseph Treaster one month later.[23]

So many questions emerge. What was the volume of the industry's legitimate output? What was its value? How many objects were being pirated and bootlegged? What was their value? Over the years and decades, were there patterns of growth and recession for legitimate output and value? Over the years and decades, were there patterns of growth and recession for illegitimate output and value? How did legitimate and illegitimate activities relate proportionally, the one to the other? What other musical or extra-musical circumstances might have affected volume and value?

Trying to get a handle on what was actually going on is very difficult. The information given out was incomplete and in some respects contradictory. That makes it difficult to separate spin from reality. I have tried to speculate on these questions in the pages that follow, but I would first acknowledge as clearly as possible that these speculations are constructed on quicksand.

While putting out what were probably wildly inflated estimates of the total value of unauthorized recordings, the RIAA began in the 1980s to give out detailed statistical summaries of seizures. In these reports the organization attempted to distinguish among the disputed activities of counterfeiting, piracy, and bootlegging. In the previous chapter, as a means of introducing the tape technology involving masters, slaves, and pancakes, I presented one of these lists, for the period April 1982 through March 1983. Here is that same list once again, offered for consideration now from the perspective of its implications for the total volume of output in the realm of counterfeiting, piracy, and bootlegging during that year:[24]

72,334 bootleg records and cassettes
17,786 counterfeit cassettes

3,816 counterfeit eight-track tapes

18,738 pirated eight-track tapes

3,993 pirated cassettes

900 pirated disks

9,950 master tapes

1,100 pirated LP jackets

110 counterfeit and bootleg stampers

11,300 labels

200 pancakes

3,200 bootleg insert cards

30,645 LP jackets

200 pieces of manufacturing equipment, including:

    12 duplicators

    16 slaves

    15 shrink-wrap machines

Altogether, authorities seized about 120,000 recordings. Perhaps the 72,334 items were pirated rather than "bootleg," and the compiler of the list used the wrong term; otherwise, the proportions seem wildly out of the normal, by comparison with all anecdotal accounts of album bootlegging. But never mind that. Let's just accept the total. What does this figure—120,000 illicit recorded objects—represent in relation to the whole?

In the early 1980s, the annual output of the music industry was somewhere in the neighborhood of 600 million units. So piracy, counterfeiting, and bootlegging in the course of that year represented .02 percent of the whole, approximately one illegal object for every five thousand legal objects. This is a far cry from the press releases given out at various times by the RIAA and spokesmen for the Harry Fox Agency, who claimed that piracy represented one in ten albums, one in five albums, a third of all albums, and in the most exaggerated moment, a half of all albums. Small wonder that years back, when Abeles was lobbying for a revision of the Copyright Act in the mid-1960s, a U.S. Senator took him to task for giving out exaggerated and unsubstantiated numbers. Abeles replied, and rightly so, that it was difficult to track numbers in any realm of bootlegging, but that fact does not explain the shameless exaggerations.

Of course, Abeles and his colleagues knew full well what they were doing, and why. If record and tape piracy were really such small change, why would the industry have put so much money and effort into fighting it? The reasons seem clear: to keep a lid on the practice, to intimidate, to send a message that dire penalties for disobedience were possible (even if not the norm), to attempt a monopoly, and to strive for complete control of the distribution of their product, which is something that the record industry fairly well maintained, for quite a while, at least in the main markets of the United States and Europe.

An RIAA report from the mid-1980s offers an opportunity to speculate on an additional set of questions. What if the statistics on seized objects were completely unrepresentative of the whole? What if the industry and legal authorities were doing a really incompetent job of suppressing unauthorized recordings, and the total amount of activity was far more than the total number of objects seized? This was possible. There is, I think, no way of knowing. I have my personal opinion, that the industry was crying wolf constantly, for the reasons given immediately above, when in fact there were only a few isolated wolves and most of the sheep were fine, thank you. But perhaps I am wrong.

In the mid-1980s the RIAA added a new category to its annual report, listing the number of labels seized. This statistic by implication gave a larger volume to piracy actions, indicating in effect how many objects the pirates and bootleggers might have created if they hadn't been stopped before the labels were affixed to recorded objects. The period April 1984 to March 1985 was a quiet year for confiscation: roughly sixty thousand objects and 550,000 labels. The next twelve-month period was an active one: about 550,000 objects seized, together with 4 million labels.[25]

Let's combine these figures, recordings seized and labels seized, to identify the implied extent of intended piracy and bootlegging during these two year-long periods. The first period, from April 1984 to March 1985, witnessed an illegitimacy level of about .1 percent of the whole, or roughly one potential illegal object for every one thousand legal objects. The second year, from April 1985 to March 1986, reached about .75 percent of the whole, or one potential illegal object for every 133 legal objects. So even during the latter period, which was from this perspective evidently a lousy year for the song owners, the relationship of piracy to legitimacy fell far short of the proportions claimed by those song owners.

This raises another set of questions. Were the owners grossly exaggerating? Or was piracy and bootlegging running rampant, scarcely checked by the efforts of law enforcement? My guess is the former, but again, I cannot know. My impression, from extensive reading in the area, is that these lines have been sharply drawn for many decades, and people tend to have their minds set on the situation, one way or the other, regardless of reasoned argument.

One question that can be answered with a reasonable sense of certainty is the following: how was the recording industry doing during this era, regardless of record and tape counterfeiting, bootlegging, and piracy? Generally, very well, with far more expansion than stagnation. Between 1964 and 1969, from the advent of cartridge and cassette tapes through their installation into automobiles and the explosion of pirate operations, legitimate sales of recordings doubled, growing at a rate of about 20 percent per year. Annually from 1970 to 1976, growth continued steadily at a slower but still vigorous rate, exceeding 10 percent.

In 1977 and 1978 sales soared, growing at a rate of 25 percent per year.[26] No doubt there was some substantial amount of piracy going on. This is documented. No doubt the vigorous campaign against piracy was necessary, to make people aware of it and to keep it manageable in relation to the big picture. But on the whole, the industry was doing very well, piracy or not.

Then came a period of decline. Sales fell off about 12 percent in 1979 and then more or less sat at a flat annual rate until 1984, when growth resumed. Was piracy the cause, despite all of the efforts at suppression, and despite all of the new state and federal antipiracy laws than came into play in the course of the flush decade immediately preceding? Perhaps. In her 1980 article on piracy, Hollie explained that during what was then a period of recession not only in the industry, but generally in the American economy, many production plants were accepting income from unauthorized sources and manufacturing illegal recordings in order to seize opportunities to continue running. But Tschmuck argued that the problem during this period was neither a general economic slowdown nor an upsurge in piracy. Instead, he attributed the decline in sales to a lack of technological and artistic innovation in the recording industry.[27] To what extent was the vehement public relations campaign against piracy an effort to deflect attention from other systemic concerns?

The advent of the compact disc revitalized the recording industry. As legitimate business flourished, so too did piracy flourish, in its lesser proportionate way. For the first half of 1988, the RIAA reported seizures of just over three hundred thousand unauthorized recordings and 4 million labels, in the context of a legitimate volume of about 380 million units for that half year. This boils down to an intended piracy rate of about 1.1 percent (one piratical object or label seized for every ninety-five legitimate objects sold). A year later, for the six-month period extending from January to June 1989, the numbers were 360,000 discs and tapes confiscated, 4.6 million labels confiscated, and 400 million legitimate units. This boils down to a rate of 1.15 percent (one piratical object or label for every eighty-seven legitimate objects). In 1990 the rate was higher still, as the RIAA reported unprecedented numbers of items seized. These proportions—the implied statistical relationship of disc and tape piracy to authorized issues—remain much smaller than the proportions claimed in press releases given out by the RIAA and its associates, but the proportions are considerably higher than those derived from statistics at mid-decade. Unauthorized copying was on the rise, if indeed there is any sort of meaningful relationship between quantities confiscated and overall piratical activity.[28]

Beginning in 2000, the quantities of CDs sold declined. In 2002 the IFPI asserted that 40 million pirate recordings had been seized at the European Union's external borders during the previous years, and the organization claimed that levels of record piracy were in excess of 50 percent in Bolivia, Brazil, Bulgaria, China, Ecuador, Estonia, Greece, Indonesia, Kenya, Latvia, Lithuania, Malaysia, Mexico, Nigeria, Pakistan, Paraguay, Peru, the Philippines, Romania, Russia, the Ukraine, and the former Yugoslavia. This report appeared in various sources under headlines such as the following: "CD Burning the Chief Cause of a $3.3 Billion Downturn in World Record Sales Last Year."[29] Clearly many reporters accepted the direct link, connecting the dots from piracy to declining sales, and accepting the notion that each album bootlegged in, say, Nigeria, signified an $18 loss in the West. Some people were raising the same questions that Tschmuck had brought up regarding record and tape sales. Were declining profits due to unauthorized copying, or to artistic stagnation and a saturation of the market for CDs?

So it was all a murky situation, muddied by the necessarily incomplete documentation of fly-by-night operations, muddied by the tactical politics of authorities attempting to control developments, muddied by a possible waxing and waning of interests in new musical formats and devices, muddied by the immeasurable factor of changing musical tastes, muddied by the measurable but causally uncertain relationship between the musical economy and the national economy, and muddied by the complexities of globalization and incompatible national legislation.

# 10 • *Song Sharing*

With song sharing, the history of songs, distribution, and disobedience arrives at unresolved current events and (at least to date) the most radically transformational instance of an unauthorized song product: MP3 files circulating via computer networks. In this setting, the globalization of unauthorized song distribution takes on an entirely new meaning, freed from orders placed through manufacturers in countries that do not fully participate in international copyright agreements, freed from orders placed through the back doors of manufacturers in countries that do participate, and freed from the oversight of customs officials. There is nothing tangible to import. The song product is no longer an object in a physical package. Instead, a "virtual" and virtually instantaneous distribution chain has come into being. Select any existing recording, copy it in digital form, and post it on the Internet.

This latest contested era of the unauthorized distribution of songs got underway in 1987 from without, through unforeseen musical consequences of research into video soundtracks. It blossomed with the introduction of Napster in 1998, and it has continued into the second decade of the twenty-first century in an at-times brutally punitive contest between song owners and individual listeners. Initially, Napster and its successors operated independently of and in a wholly different manner from the authorized distribution of recordings on compact disc. The resulting threat to the control and profitability of song distribution threw the music industry into a panic as never before.[1]

After several years, the expected pattern began to kick in, with some aspects of prohibition giving way to assimilation, as the song owners began to recognize the viability and inevitability of the new song product, which came into being in 2003 in an authorized form, as iTunes. But at the time of writing, full assimilation seems doubtful, and opposing positions appear to be irreconcilable, with no prospect for resolution. One outcome seems likely, if the prevailing habits of young people are a meaningful indicator: albums on compact disc will probably follow phonograph records and tapes into obsolescence, giving way to current youthful preferences for collecting individual songs stored on various types of digital media. Another major outcome remains up in the air.

Song files are circulating in obedient and disobedient forms—for a fee, and for free. Can they coexist without severe conflict? Will one or the other prevail?

Song sharing offers a diverse set of transformational qualities that contribute to and complement that largest transformation, a rethinking of the global distribution of recordings. One such quality has its origins in the compact disc, when songs began to be captured and expressed digitally through strings of zeros and ones. But the full implications of that transformation only came into being with the circulation of MP3 files. A recording has always been in some sense an unfathomable, miniaturized, virtually invisible physical object, whether tiny hills and valleys engraved as record grooves, or patterns of magnetized dust on a tape, or alternations of microscopic smoothness and pits on the surface of a compact disc. But MP3 files take this abstractness one step further. Only the invisible part remains, the electronic representation of a string of numbers. Popular songs have been removed from their containers and packaging.

The storage of recorded songs still depends upon objects, even if, say, the storage medium is now a computer hard drive or a handheld device's flash drive, rather than a compact disc. But recorded songs may now be "shared" around the world at the click of a button, as digital files, to any place that has telephonic or broadband or wireless connections. And individualized players may be miniaturized to a greater degree than ever before, because now these players only need to hold some sort of digital storage that can be made to be much smaller than a tape or disc; alternatively, the player itself may be effectively a new form of radio, a receptor for song files stored elsewhere and delivered over a shared network. The player is still a physical object, but the recording is not.

In the process of removing containers and packaging from songs, the concept of an album has been dismantled. Song files circulate as individual entities. Each user is free to create his or her own compilations. Do-it-yourself approaches that had operated in somewhat peripheral markets, as platter packs, party tapes, DJ mixes, and so forth, are now the prevalent mode, available to anyone who participates in song sharing. Tied into this possibility, and complicating it substantially in the realm of the morality of unauthorized downloading, is a widespread feeling that compact discs have been underachieving in their musical offerings and, correspondingly, greatly overpriced. In a survey of the song-sharing scene in 2002, Edna Gundersen passed along a typical comment, that many CDs had only one or two strong songs and lots of mediocre padding. As Fred Goodman put it most bluntly, writing for *Rolling Stone* in 2000: "Why pay eighteen dollars for a CD that has three good songs on it when you can get those songs for free through file swapping?"[2]

In turn, this logistical transformation, from albums to single song tracks, has wrested a crucial aspect of the artistic control of song distribution away from musicians, song owners, and record corporations. Many popular songs continue to be released within a conceptual framework defined by an album, but once a given song has been appropriated into a song-sharing network, the connection between that song and that album is severed.

In the chapter "Listening in Cyberspace" in his book *Recorded Sound,* Mark Katz calls this aspect of customization "singles listening." (In the context of portable playback devices utilizing headphones, the term "singles listening" has taken on a perhaps unintended second meaning: listening in isolation from others.) With singles listening, in the sense intended by Katz, programming shifts entirely into the hands of the individual, as it had done for some people in the era of tape recording, but now with a far greater potential for ease, convenience, and flexibility.[3]

Speaking of these possibilities in relation to Napster—though his comment applies to any MP3 usage—Griffin Mead Woodworth writes: "By allowing music to be removed from industrially determined contexts such as albums, radio playlists, concert performances, and even copyrighted catalogues, Napster has empowered the end-user—rather than the author or copyright holder—to determine the particular context (physical and otherwise) in which a piece of music sounds and, therefore, the associative meaning ascribed to said piece of music."[4]

Most crucially, with the advent of song sharing, the world of music has pretty well lost the shackles of ownership, which is a terrible thing for the song owners, but a wonderful thing for listeners. Song sharing offers unprecedented opportunities for exploring and sharing musical styles. Decades ago, people could go to a record store and ask to hear a song before buying it. Now, with song sharing, any recorded music may be available for browsing, whether for learning or enjoyment or some combination of the two.

Song sharing also offers an unprecedented combination of speed, ease, breadth, and economy: search for an artist, group, title, label, style, theme, instrument, lyric, or some other attribute of a song; identify a potentially appropriate song; and download that song, authorized or not. Katz describes the delightful results of making up musical genres and then conducting song-sharing searches on three imagined terms. "Swedish funk" led him to the song "Freaky Funksters" by the Electric Boys, a quartet from Stockholm. "Vietnamese hardcore rap" yielded "Around the Town" by "a California Vietnamese group inexplicably known as Thai." "Jewish gospel" brought forth no results. (Are there no songs associated with Jews for Jesus?)[5]

More seriously, Katz conceptualizes these possibilities as manifestations of transformational possibilities residing within the historical development of recorded music. All of these developments emerged in previous eras and from legitimate spheres. One line of development reaches back to the first home usage of the phonograph. Katz calls it "repeatability," the idea that the same performance may be played over and over again. This path takes on an additional dimension in the age of digital recording, in the manner in which digital sound files can be copied without a loss of fidelity. Another line of development concerns opportunities for moveable playback equipment. Katz calls this "portability," and I discussed it in detail earlier, in recounting the convenience of song sheets and fake books, and the development of cartridges and cassettes for vehicular use. A third line of development concerns individualized relationships to listening, the removal of sound from public performances. Katz considers this line to be a subcategory of portability, and he calls it "solitary listening"; I would be inclined to call this feature personalization, the opportunity for individuals to design their own listening experiences as they see fit. Either way, the point is that song sharing has carried the integration and flexibility of these various lines of development to its current apotheosis.[6]

**The invention and early distribution of MP3 files.** Song sharing was enabled by an invention that originated outside of music, in an effort to come up with a method for reducing the size of digital soundtracks designed for video games and for educational programs that would be played on television sets. The aim was to make these audio files small without severely handicapping the quality of the resulting sound. More broadly, this effort resided within the domain of motion-picture research.

In 1987, at the behest of the Italian researcher Leonardo Chiariglione of the Motion Picture Experts Group (MPEG), a team of German researchers at the Institute for Integrated Circuits of the Fraunhofer Gesellschaft came up with a solution to the problem. The German team created an algorithm for compressing the size of digital sound files by a factor of approximately eleven to one, mainly by eliminating those portions of the digital code corresponding to elements of recorded sound that the human ear would not have heard anyway. Recording equipment can capture sound at a rate much faster than the human ear can distinguish and in frequency ranges beyond the capacity of the human ear. So they carved those bits away.

Chiariglione's Motion Picture group incorporated the German algorithm for compressing sound files into a five-part, three-layered MPEG proposal for the standardization of digital audio and video files, with applications intended for film, television, and personal computers. The third of this five-part standard pertained to audio compression and the third of the three layers pertained to uses on personal computers. From this came the now well-known file name MP3, which itself is a compressed acronym for "data standards for the *M*otion *P*ictures Experts Group, part *3*, layer *3*." The staff had no idea or intention that their software would become the new standard format for pop-music song sharing.

In 1992, for the purpose of providing an industrial tutorial on MPEG standards, the consortium released a free software demo that converted music into low fidelity MP3 files. A Dutch hacker using the *Star Wars*–inspired name of SoloH copied the source code for the demo file from a computer server at the University of Erlangen, made his way into the computer server that Chiariglione was using, copied the MP3 code, revised that code so that it would convert high fidelity compact-disc audio files into reasonably high fidelity compressed MP3 files, and distributed the revised code on the Internet, where it was improved further by other hackers.

As noted above, being dependent on the compression of CD audio digital files to enable manageable file sizes, MP3 files had a somewhat lower "high fidelity" than their digital predecessors, CD audio files, but for most listeners the differences were slight, unimportant, and perhaps merely theoretical. Once created, an MP3 file could then be literally copied any number of times without further degradation of the original sound, so long as the user maintained the same type of MP3 file.[7]

Through the mid-1990s, MP3 usage proliferated, sometimes in legitimate ways, with aspiring bands distributing their own songs in the hopes of getting gigs or gaining the attention of the recording industry, but far more often in unauthorized ways, with people converting their CD audio tracks into MP3 format and then "sharing" their music over the Internet. As with song sheets and fake books, there was no consideration, on behalf of the music industry, that this new song distribution system might offer transformational possibilities. Instead, the usual process got underway. The song owners claimed a direct equivalency, constructed from the perspective of copyright rather than from the perspective of usage, whereby a recorded song on a CD was identical to that same recording shared over the Internet, regardless of all of the associated transformational qualities. From this perspective they pursued the usual immediate and longstanding response: an attempt at suppression. Fearful, and probably rightly so, that here was a new format for song distribution that they could not control, record corporations sought to outlaw its use.

Owing to early attempts by the RIAA to halt the circulation of MP3 files through threatening press releases and targeted personal letters, a good deal of the proliferation of unauthorized MP3 copies of copyrighted CD tracks was done in purposefully chaotic ways, to discourage prosecution. But the mid-1990s distribution of songs over the Internet in MP3 format was also unintentionally chaotic, because there was not yet a sensible system for storing, identifying, and exchanging song files. That would be Napster.

**Napster and its successors.** As a freshman at Northwestern University in the fall of 1998, Shawn Fanning noted that his dormitory roommate was skipping classes to concentrate on the then-laborious task of locating and downloading digital copies of obscure hip-hop recordings. Believing that he could streamline the process, Fanning created a computer interface that brought the MP3 format together with existing software for centralized peer-to-peer networking, with his website functioning as a hub for the examination, cataloguing, and exchange of digital song files stored on any participant's personal computer. Fanning gave the program his own childhood nickname, Napster.

Initially Fanning tested Napster on a campus computer network that could serve one hundred people. The reception was overwhelming. In less than a year, the trial group of one hundred grew into a user group of millions of people. In the course of that year, Fanning dropped out of Northwestern, worked on Napster at an office in Massachusetts, and then relocated to San Mateo, California (south of San Francisco, just above "Silicon Valley"). There he founded Napster, Inc., in partnership with Sean Parker.[8]

The structure of Napster depended upon a centralized computer server that provided a "search engine" enabling any participating individual to organize songs by title and artist and to identify the location of an MP3 song file on any other participating individual's personal computer. Because Fanning and Parker operated that central server, they were identifiable middlemen in the unauthorized distribution of songs. An avenue for prosecution had opened.

In December 1999 the RIAA filed suit against Napster for copyright infringement. In April 2000 the rock group Metallica did the same. To satisfy these complaints, Fanning and Parker would be obliged to attempt to exercise control over the content that passed through the Napster server. In a response to Metallica's complaint, Napster closed 313,377 accounts in May 2000.

The consequences of these actions are still unfolding, a decade later. There were three stages of response: a short-term backfire; a fleeting moment of victory for the RIAA and associated song owners; and a longstanding situation in which everything has been thrown into continuing chaos.

The short-term backfire was that the actions by the RIAA and Metallica initially served mainly to draw attention to Napster, which then gained in popularity. By one account, Napster had 58 million registered users and more than 450 million songs available for downloading in the summer of 2000. By another calculation, there were 4.9 million unique Napster registrants in July 2000. Presumably this disparity resulted from the common practice of users entering the site under a variety of pseudonyms, to discourage identification. By either calculation, Napster was growing.

The fleeting moment of victory for the song owners was the demise of Napster one year later, on July 1, 2001. The corporation was never fully shut down by a legal ruling, but it was effectively forced into bankruptcy through a complex court ruling that obliged Fanning and Parker's staff to block access to hundreds of thousands of song titles complied into a list by the RIAA in conjunction with its associated recording corporations. Policing this list was an impossibly expensive and time-consuming task. So Fanning and Parker figuratively and literally pulled the plug.[9]

The result was not what the RIAA hoped for. It was already too late. Broadband connections to the Internet were increasingly replacing dial-up connections, and the capacity of personal computer hard drives was growing by a factor of hundreds, with the result that downloading became faster, storage became easier, and the sharing of larger files—not just songs, but movies as well—became feasible. Digital song sharing was already abundant. Users had blocks of MP3 files on their own computers, and even if sharing had been somehow halted, the existing files remained. Furthermore, participation in digital song sharing was already an international phenomenon. Even if the RIAA had fully succeeded in suppressing files in America, non-American users would not be subject to such suits, unless the analogous institutions in their own countries joined the fight. Not everyone was sympathetic to the song owners.

Worse still for the record companies, no sooner did Napster cease operations than a half dozen or so rival networks strove to take its place, each one of which was more elusive than Napster had ever been. With the demise of Napster, digital song sharing became decentralized, in two ways. A single popular host for song sharing was replaced by a choice of new hosts, and—far more importantly—the new hosts used software programs that did away with the concept of a hub and instead spread MP3 files throughout the world in purposefully tangled ways. The most prominent unauthorized successors to Napster lacked central servers and thus eliminated identifiable distributors, at least for their musical components. The RIAA would have to seek other paths for prosecution of unauthorized song sharing.

The rival song-sharing sites included, among others, MusicCity's Morpheus, Audiogalaxy, KaZaA, BearShare, and LimeWire. Most of these had little traffic or did not even exist in February 2001, when Napster was flourishing. But when Napster died that July, the rivals leapt to prominence.

KaZaA and Morpheus both utilized Fast Track, a software program created by the Dutch programmer Niklas Zennstrom. His design shifted the distribution of MP3 files from centralized company computers to decentralized personal computers. KaZaA, which became probably the most widely used of these new services, made itself into an even more elusive target than other song-sharing hosts by disguising its ownership through a complex arrangement. Run by Nikki Henning, the corporation operated under the name of Sharman Networks from a business address located on the island of Vanuatu in the South Pacific.

KaZaA introduced a nasty twist into the song-sharing story. It offered two programs, KaZaA and KaZaa "lite." The fully functional KaZaA program was linked to spyware, invasive software that took over portions of the processing power of the personal computers onto which it was loaded. Presumably this was KaZaA's way of making money, by selling personal computer processing power to unidentified others. While countless individuals were downloading songs without authorization, those same individuals were unwittingly inviting a nonmusical and potentially highly invasive type of distributed computing to utilize the capacity of their computers, effectively turning the tables. So people who liked KaZaA's vast music selections faced a choice between putting up with the spyware or using the "lite" version, which offered a limited functionality.

LimeWire and BearShare utilized the Gnutella network, which had been developed by a subsidiary of the then-dominant e-mail corporation, America Online (AOL). Ironically, AOL at that point was in the process of acquiring Time Warner, the owners of Warner Music. Here was another example, not at all unusual in the music business, of goods produced by one subsidiary threatening to undermine goods produced by another. Gnutella did away with centralized company computers altogether, instead connecting personal computers directly from one to the next.[10]

Even if MP3 files were scattered through the electronic ether, each of these sites still functioned in some sense as a conceptual hub, and the recording industry attempted to suppress them by pursuing an argument similar to that applied to Napster: such sites should be responsible for policing the content of their digital traffic. But this path to prosecution hit a temporary roadblock in April 2003 when Federal District Court Judge Stephen Wilson ruled in Los Angeles that StreamCast Networks (which had created the Morpheus program) and the file-sharing company Grokster were not obliged to monitor their users. StreamCast and Grokster could not be held legally responsible if individuals used their products to infringe on copyright.[11]

In the course of upholding this decision in the Court of Appeals, Judge Sidney R. Thomas supplied an unusual judicial acknowledgment of the role that new products play in challenging copyright owners: "The introduction of new technology is always disruptive to old markets, and particularly to those copyright owners whose works are sold through well-established distribution mechanisms. Yet, history has shown that time and market forces often provide equilibrium in balancing interests, whether the new technology be a player piano, a copier, a tape recorder, a video recorder, a personal computer, a karaoke machine, or an MP3 player. Thus, it is prudent for courts to exercise caution before restructuring liability theories for the purpose of addressing specific market abuses, despite their apparent present magnitude."[12] Ultimately, however, Thomas's comment would be ignored, and the Grokster decision was overturned (see below).

Concurrently, in another behavioral parallel to earlier stories of songs, distribution, and disobedience, the recording industry, while working hard at prohibition, was making only halfhearted efforts to assimilate song sharing into a legitimate business model. There were just too many internal conflicts to overcome. As the century turned, the then-five major record corporations were Universal Music Group, Warner Music Group, EMI, Sony, and BMG. (They would become four in 2004, when Sony and BMG merged.) That year, 2000, while the fight against Napster was going on, the five corporations tried to get together to create a subscription service or several subscription services that would work as authorized alternatives to Napster.

These efforts became mired in complications. One was the control of files. Could songs be restrictively encoded, so that a song could not immediately be freely "shared" once it was downloaded by the subscriber? This proved to be an impossible goal and effectively a hacker's delight, as opposing parties enjoyed the challenge of breaking down encrypted barriers to access.

Another complication was the relationship between physical retail outlets and "virtual" Internet outlets. How could subscriptions to songs be priced without threatening price structures at record stores that were, at that time, the retail backbone of the industry? This too proved to be an impossible goal. As it turned out, record stores were dying, giving way to the acquisition of songs over the Internet in either format, CD or MP3, legitimate or not. By mid-decade most record stores would go out of business, with CD sales transferring to Internet-based corporations such as CD-Now, Amazon, and Half.com. Only a handful of nationwide physical retailers survived, with such chains as Wal-mart and Best Buy continuing to carry bins of compact discs.

Another complication was the difficulty of getting corporate rivals to cooperate in sharing repertory. Could five rival corporations pool their songs to create a subscription service whose offerings matched the expansiveness of Napster and its successors? As it turns out, that has yet to happen. Unrestricted, disobedient networks holding unauthorized sound files continue to be unrivaled in the breadth of the musical repertory that they offer.

The biggest complication was the cost. Under what circumstances would people pay for songs if they could get songs for free, and get away with getting songs for free? As the story of musical photocopying in the Catholic Archdiocese of Chicago perhaps shows best, song owners may make protestations of criminality and immorality as much as they wish, but even those dedicated to maintaining the highest standards of general behavior might not obey. If people were going to pay to download songs, it would have to be because the not-for-free product was attractive in design, convenient to use, more reliable than unauthorized products, and offering a broad catalog of widely desired titles. This would be iTunes.

**iTunes.** In the period between mid-2001, when Napster reached its greatest notoriety and largest audience, and mid-2003, when iTunes made its debut, Steve Jobs, the head of Apple Computer, tried time and again to win recording industry executives over to his conception of an authorized song-sharing service. In an interview for *Rolling Stone* magazine, Jobs painted a picture of the situation. "At first they kicked us out." Corporate executives were fighting to suppress unauthorized song sharing, unwilling to sell downloads outright from their own catalogues, and failing in a series of halfhearted efforts to put together subscription services that were intended to challenge the preeminence of Napster and its successors by offering downloads on a restricted basis. "When the internet came along and Napster came along, people in the music business didn't know what to make of the changes. A lot of these folks didn't use computers, weren't on e-mail—didn't really know what Napster was," said Jobs.[13]

What the song owners sought, initially, was a parallel to cable television: a general audience paying a monthly subscription for limited, short-term downloads of songs. But why would anyone subscribe, when that audience could obtain these same songs without restrictions, and for free? Struggling with early efforts along these lines, the major corporations took nearly two years before launching the first subscription services, Pressplay and RealOneMusic, early in 2002. Both failed quickly. In December 2003 the firm Roxio revived the Napster name for a pay-per-download service. Within a few months it too was failing.[14] There were other such attempts, but in 2004 the combined services had approximately fifty thousand subscribers, compared to millions of participants in unauthorized song sharing. Said Jobs: "The subscription model of buying music is bankrupt. I think you could make available the Second Coming in a subscription model, and it might not be successful."[15]

While the RIAA and its associates were fighting Napster and its successors, other corporations—and in some instances, other divisions of those same recording associates—were producing handheld MP3 players as successors to the transistor radio, the Sony Walkman cassette player, the Sony Walkman CD player, and all such related personalized radio, tape, and disc devices. In 2001 Jobs launched a beautifully designed MP3 player, the iPod. In April 2003, after finally breaking down fierce resistance from the recording industry, and with the bankruptcy of the subscription models becoming evident, Jobs launched a pay-per-song service, iTunes, with some limitations on and protections against copying built into the device. By 2006 iTunes had sold a billion downloads, and in May 2007 EMI began to allow iTunes to sell its catalog without the limitations on copying that the major labels had previously insisted upon. In 2009, unrestricted copying of downloaded songs became a general policy.[16]

Apart from the legitimacy that downloading from iTunes offered, and the question of whether the general public actually cared about that legitimacy, the service provided a reliability that the world of uncontrolled and unauthorized song sharing could not match. By their very nature, Napster and its successors allowed anything that was ostensibly a song file to be stored on and circulated through their networks. At their very best, these sites offered immediate access to songs in diverse genres that otherwise would not have been available for listening without extensive digging, and perhaps even a trip to a sound archives. At their mildly worst, unauthorized song-sharing sites collected files that might be inaudible, misidentified, incomplete, or altered, perhaps purposefully so. Indeed, in the course of its fight against Napster and its successors, the recording industry hired computer specialists to "spoof," distributing unplayable versions of desired titles on the song-sharing networks. At their very worst, unregulated sites of unrestricted files might host pornography, spyware, and computer viruses. By contrast, in exchange for its cost and limitations in repertory, iTunes provided a consistently high level of quality and reliability, with a low level of risk and annoyance. These are qualities that many people have been willing to pay for.

Because Jobs pretty well understood the situation, and the head of the recording corporations did not, Apple rose in the distribution of recorded songs to a position of power that made the major companies uncomfortable, and they continued to attempt to develop alternatives. In 2006 Universal introduced its SpiralFrog service, the survival of which would be based on advertising support, with free downloads of songs from the Universal catalogue offered in exchange for customers watching advertisements linked to those songs. In Britain in 2008, the world's leading cell phone maker, Nokia, instituted "Comes with Music," in which the purchase of certain phones enabled a buyer to have an unlimited number of downloads from a catalogue of some 5 million songs. That same year three of the major corporations—Universal, Warner, and Sony BMG Music Entertainment—agreed with the social networking company MySpace to create a music website on which they would attempt to sell digital versions of songs in their catalogues; the fourth major corporation, EMI, declined to participate. The excessively hopeful aim of the MySpace project was "to convert the existing social-networking audience into paying customers."[17]

**The RIAA versus disobedient individuals.** It is perhaps too late for that. Apple's iTunes dominates the legal market, but by 2008 its growth had begun to level off. Meanwhile, unauthorized song sharing has persisted through the decade. With the role of middlemen minimized through the incorporation of peer-to-peer networking designs, and with StreamCast and Grokster having been at least temporarily absolved of responsibility for policing the use of their networks for the purposes of unauthorized song sharing, the RIAA came up with a new tactic. In autumn 2003 the organization initiated what would become a long and bitterly received campaign designed to intimidate the general public, by filing civil suits against individuals who made large numbers of MP3 song files available for downloading.[18] In response, Ray Beckerman, a lawyer who represented a small number of the eventual thirty-five thousand defendants, established an exhaustively detailed archival website, "Recording

Industry vs. the People," to catalog the history of this process. Beckerman's documentation of this fight includes links to thousands of articles on the subject and thousands of relevant court documents.

The RIAA hired MediaSentry, a division of SafeNet, Inc., to collect data on illegal downloads and to identify participating individuals. Guided by these identifications, the RIAA then filed suits seeking large monetary awards for copyright infringement. The usual result, as it turned out, was either for a defendant to pay a several-thousand-dollar fine in an uncontested settlement, without trial, for fear of incurring substantial legal fees and perhaps much larger fines if the RIAA were taken to court, or alternatively, for the RIAA to drop the suit, without taking any responsibility for fees incurred, if it became apparent that MediaSentry had erred in its accusations of wrongdoing. Notable among the latter was a suit in September 2003 against Sarah Ward, a sixty-six-year-old Newbury, Massachusetts, resident whom the RIAA threatened with a liability of $150,000 per song for more than two thousand songs that she had allegedly downloaded through KaZaA. The charge was moot, as it turned out, not only because she had not done it, but because she had a Macintosh computer, and KaZaA only ran on Windows systems. In another notorious case, the RIAA mistakenly filed suit against a Gertrude Walton, who, apart from the question of never having participated in downloading, had died two years previously, at the age of eighty-three.

The RIAA clearly did not mind the outrage that this policy generated, and the organization pursued a brazenly aggressive legal path for another few years. The errors notwithstanding, collectively these suits brought settlements with some thousands of individuals, for a value of some millions of dollars. On a broad-based scale, however, the tactic was no more effective than the hard lines taken by the MPPA and RIAA and others in earlier decades. Despite the civil suits, illegal peer-to-peer downloading increased steadily throughout this period.[19]

In the latter part of the decade, a few victims of wrongful accusations or excessive fines endeavored to fight back. In a spectacular coincidence with the story of song-sheet bootlegging seven decades earlier, three of the most prominent individuals taking on the recording industry were named Santangelo (presumably no relation to John). In 2005 the RIAA sued Patti Santangelo, a mother of five, for illegal downloading. She denied any wrongdoing. In November 2006 the organization claimed that two of her children, Michelle, then age nineteen, and Robert, age fifteen, were the offenders, and the organization charged Patti with "secondary infringement" for allowing her children to take the alleged actions. Michelle, not responding to the lawsuit, was then hit with a $30,750 fine in absentia.

In January 2007 Robert denied the charges and demanded a trial by jury, arguing on a number of grounds. His lawyer claimed, among other things, that the major corporations were acting in collusion as a conspiracy to defraud American courts and as a cartel to prosecute individuals "in an identical manner and through common lawyers," and that the RIAA was seeking damages that were excessive, in violation of the Constitution.

In March 2007 Judge Colleen McMahon denied a motion from the RIAA's lawyers to dismiss the case against Patti Santangelo "without prejudice," that is to say, with neither side responsible for legal fees. The case had dragged on for two years, at considerable expense, and Judge McMahon instructed the RIAA that either Patti Santangelo should have the opportunity to seek vindication in a trial by jury or she should have the case dismissed "with prejudice." Judge McMahon stipulated the latter, making Santangelo the prevailing party and entitling her to file a motion to recover legal fees. Two years later, the Santangelo family and the RIAA reached a confidential settlement. So the outcome of this contest is unknown, but the substantial publicity that it received showed that there might be viable paths to opposing the institutional campaign.[20]

This path opened a bit further with the cases of two other wrongfully accused individuals, Debbie Foster and Tanya Anderson. Foster's case paralleled Patti Santangelo's closely. Its result was somewhat less ambiguous. Discovering an initial mistake in the charges against Debbie Foster, the RIAA shifted its accusations to her adult daughter, Amanda, but refused to drop the charges against Debbie, instead naming her a "secondary infringer." Like Michelle Santangelo, Amanda Foster failed to answer the suit and the RIAA was awarded a default judgment in her name. The RIAA then moved to drop its suit against Debbie, but she filed a counterclaim. In mid-2006 Judge Lee R. West dismissed both suits, while declaring Debbie Foster the prevailing party, with prejudice, and awarding her about $68,000 in attorneys' fees.[21]

Tanya Anderson was wrongly accused of downloading illicit copies of "gangsta rap." After the RIAA agreed to settle the suit in her favor, "with prejudice," Anderson filed a class action countersuit against MediaSentry and the RIAA Settlement Support Center, a Washington State phone solicitation company engaged in debt collection. She charged them with malicious prosecution, invasion of privacy, libel, slander, fraud, racketeering, and deceptive business practices. Here was another moment of irony, the tables turned in the public relations game, with some of these categories of crime having earlier provided vehicles for the prosecution of record and tape piracy, but now being thrown back in the face of the recording industry's own practices. The result for Anderson was the same as with Foster: a dismissal of both suits and a ruling in Anderson's favor, with prejudice, which obliged the RIAA to pay her approximately $108,000 in legal fees.[22]

During this same period, the RIAA charged Jammie Thomas with downloading twenty-four songs through KaZaA. Found guilty in a trial by jury, she was fined $222,000. This was initially a huge victory for the RIAA campaign. But in 2008, Federal District Judge Michael J. Davis reconsidered his ruling and ordered a new trial. Thinking along some of the lines that Robert Santangelo had raised in his countersuit, Judge Davis decided that he had been mistakenly convinced by arguments from lawyers for the RIAA that Jammie Thomas's actions constituted "making available" and an "offer to distribute" the songs that she downloaded. Without contesting that she had participated in infringement by downloading songs from KaZaA, the judge noted that she neither sought nor gained profit from that activity. Although the Copyright Act allowed for statutory damages well beyond the cost of purchasing the works in question, Judge Davis said that in this instance, with those damages magnified by a factor of some thousands, the award was excessive. As of mid-2010, the verdict in Thomas's second trial had been voided, and a third trial was scheduled for October, to reassess the amount of the award.[23]

But for the RIAA, the writing was evidently on the wall, that its legal strategy was failing. In December 2008 the RIAA ended its relationship with MediaSentry and announced that while continuing to pursue active individual suits in progress, it would cease to file new suits against individuals, except for those who were downloading five to six thousand songs per month.[24] Whether the cases of Santangelo, Foster, Andersen, and Thomas had caused the RIAA to rethink its policies, is unknown, but it seems likely. In any event, the organization said that it would turn its attention toward trying to compel Internet service providers to monitor their traffic in songs.

This path had already been re-enabled in 2005, when the U.S. Supreme Court overturned the Grokster and StreamCast decision. They had distributed technology that promoted copyright infringement, and therefore, the court ruled, they were liable for the resulting infringement, even if their products also had lawful uses. Grokster stopped distributing its software and maintaining its network late in 2005. StreamCast continued on. In a related case, Sharman Networks, the owners of KaZaA, reached a settlement in which it agreed to pay $115 million to the RIAA and unspecified further amounts to the Mo-

tion Picture Association of America and the software industry, while install-
ing filters on its networks that would somehow prevent users from sharing
copyrighted songs and movies.[25]

In Europe, French President Nicolas Sarkozy led the fight for the passage of
a bill based on the "three strikes and you're out" approach to criminality: any
individual who persisted in illegal downloading would receive a rising set of
penalties, culminating, upon the receipt of a third warning, in the discontinu-
ation of his or her Internet service. The French approach, which also attracted
considerable interest in the UK, did not provide for due process; accusers
would be presumed to be providing accurate information on the nature of
the downloading and the identification of the downloader, never mind the
experiences of Media Sentry in making mistaken accusations in the United
States. In the months that followed, negotiators for the European Parliament,
the European Commission, and the Council of Ministers overrode that French
bill, providing instead, as a component of a sweeping new European telecommunications law, that any such accusation must be subject to legal review.
The reporter Kevin O'Brien described the current situation as "a compromise
between national governments seeking to impose tough anti-piracy laws and
consumer representatives who wanted to enshrine internet access as an unas-
sailable right."[26]

Prominent among numerous other development in Europe, and with worldwide implications for song sharing, were the lawsuits and criminal charges
pursued against the organizers of the Pirate Bay, a Swedish-based "bit-torrent"
website. A bit-torrent enables individuals to download data files from other individuals. The function of the Pirate Bay was to index and thereby to facilitate
the sharing of copies of files throughout the world—not just songs, but also
games, videos, software applications, pornography, and anything else. In mid-
April 2009, Peter Sunde, Fredrik Neij, Gottfrid Svartholm, and Carl Lundstöm
received sentences of one year in prison for criminal copyright infringement
and a fine of 30 million Swedish kroner (about $3.6 million). At the time
of writing, these decisions were on appeal.[27] There was no reason to think,
however, that the grand result of the music industry's legal success would be
anything more than inconvenience. Yes, alternative bit-torrent sites were not
as handy as the Pirate Bay. Alternative sites offered less content, or less well-
organized content, than the Pirate Bay, or they were less benign, providing
heavy doses of pornography or greater risks of acquiring computer viruses. But
many such alternative bit-torrent sites were in place, hosted internationally.
Some had evidently "crawled" (i.e., copied by computerized robotic means)

the content of the Pirate Bay, whose offerings would thereby remain available even if the Pirate Bay were successfully shut down. Thus, whatever the prosecutorial outcome, this story will almost certainly provide yet another example, in the substantial history of music piracy, of a cat that was already far, far out of the bag.

Concurrently, Jammie Thomas's case resumed, and the results were a monetary roller-coaster ride. The verdict against Thomas was upped from $220,000 to $1.92 million, but the judge found that figure to be "so grossly excessive as to shock the conscience of the court." By January 2010, that fine had been reduced to $54,000. Opposing sides continued vehement arguments as to whether that amount was still far too high or now far too low, and the RIAA was considering whether to accept the verdict or initiate a third trial against Thomas. Concurrently, Joel Tenenbaum was engaged in a similar multiyear battle with SONY and the RIAA that had initially resulted in a $675,000 judgment against him. On the grounds that the judgment was unconstitutionally excessive, this figure was subsequently reduced by a factor of ten, to $67,500. As this book went to press, the legal maneuvering continued.[28]

What we seem to have going on is a gigantic negative lottery in which untold millions of people participate in downloading, legal or not, and a few individuals are the unlucky grand losers. Although legal victories clearly have helped the recording industry in its campaign of intimidation against unauthorized song sharing, particularly by striking the fear of litigation into the hearts of college and university corporate administrators, there has been no real-life connection to an alteration of behavior for the general public. People buy MP3 files from iTunes and from numerous other sites that have offered legitimate MP3 song sharing, including Rhapsody, Amazon MP3, and Lala.com, based in the United States; and Last.fm and Spotify, based in Europe.[29] And people secure MP3 files from illegal "bit-torrent" sites. Either way, individuals have come to expect the right to circulate information—including song files—on the Internet, without restraint. Transformative use trumps copyright in the operation of this wondrously effective and flexible song distribution system. So the legacy of Napster lives on, with no resolution in sight.[30]

# CONCLUSION

To some considerable extent we have been reliving the experiences of American music fans of earlier generations. Beginning in 1929, a cultural product, sheet music, in the course of its distribution in an authorized manner by the publishers who "owned" it, came to be challenged by a new commodity, the song sheet, which was distributed in an unauthorized manner by bootleggers. This unauthorized distribution caused great anguish to the song owners, who did battle against the unauthorized mode of distribution even while an authorized version of the new commodity had gotten underway, as legitimate song-lyric magazines. Seven decades later, another cultural product, the compact disc, in the course of its distribution in an authorized manner by the record companies who "owned" it, came to be challenged by a new commodity, the MP3 file, which was distributed in an unauthorized manner over uncontrolled digital networks. This unauthorized distribution caused great anguish to the song owners, who engaged the unauthorized mode of distribution in harsh confrontations, even while authorized versions of the new commodity got underway, as Apple's iTunes and its various rivals.

I would not go so far as to claim that song sheets and song sharing exemplify "history repeating itself." The historical contexts, then and now, are too drastically different from one another to exemplify repetition, and there is a substantial structural distinction between the respective distribution chains. In the song-sheet era, an identifiable set of "songlegging" middlemen—printers, distributors, peddlers, and store owners—took on the greatest legal risks. Today, with song sharing, Napster, Grokster, and other companies have been punished by litigation, but also—and this is new—individual listeners, the collectors of songs, have been hit hard via litigation, owing to the rise of peer-to-peer distribution systems that make middlemen hard to identify, if not cutting them out of the process altogether.

Nonetheless, the journey from song sheets to song sharing may well provoke a strong sense of the familiar, whereby patterns of human behavior, individual and corporate, have repeated themselves time and again. Someone comes along with a transformational song product. Legitimate companies try to suppress that product, for fear of the damage that it will do to profits from an existing song product. A "shadow" distribution chain comes into being, working around legitimate channels, to satisfy demand for whatever transformation happens to be at hand.

Bootleg song sheets and their legitimate successors functioned as a response to then-recent technological developments in the distribution system that was delivering Tin Pan Alley songs to audiences. This distribution system had been operating smoothly as a near-perfect monopoly during the 1920s. With the growing preeminence of records, radio, and musical film, one after the next, through the course of the 1920s, a sweeping change took place in the way that Americans related to popular songs. Increasingly people heard music, or made music, not by gathering around the piano and singing, but by listening passively to professional performances of songs in concerts, on stage, and in movie houses, or by actively singing along with music delivered directly into the home via mechanical, electric, and electronic means. As musical notation became less essential to the general listener, compilations of popular song lyrics without music were poised to become much more attractive than they would have been when the piano was preeminent. And if the general public did not need to convert notes into sound, if instead the music could be heard in film, musical theater, and vaudeville, or at home on records and via radio broadcasts, then a huge financial incentive emerged. Instead of paying the then-current price of thirty or thirty-five cents for a single piece of piano and vocal sheet music, listeners could get a bootleg sheet of lyrics to dozens, scores, or even hundreds of songs for only a nickel or a dime. Music publishers trembled, and this first contest, over song lyrics, was underway, extending from 1929 into the early 1940s: prohibition, failed containment, and then an ultimate assimilation into business as usual.

From the late 1940s into the 1970s, pop song fake books followed exactly the same path in principle, albeit under different circumstances and with a different purpose. Nightclub entertainers wanted handy volumes of popular songs to assist in fulfilling requests from patrons at the bar or from dancers. For fear of lost profit, legitimate music publishers refused to satisfy that need, a repackaging of individual sheet music into concise compilations of songs. So "gangsters" filled the gap. Once again it was prohibition, failed containment, and then an ultimate assimilation into business as usual.

Unauthorized music photocopying presented a thornier type of contest than did song sheets or fake books. This action was connected to, and indeed was subsidiary to, distribution fights extending far beyond the scope of music, and eventually it coalesced instead around the photocopying of educational course packets at colleges and universities. Within the sphere of music, the battle involved a tricky mixture of equivalency and transformational use, insofar as the act of photocopying copyrighted music might be done merely to save money, or alternatively to facilitate an array of possibilities in modifying printed music to suit diverse circumstances of musical performance. And the nature of the central participants in the music photocopying distribution chain—educators and clergymen—made it much more difficult for song owners to pursue the harsh paths that have been manifest elsewhere. This contest drags on.

Offshore broadcasting in northeastern Europe brought into play transnational relationships within the distribution chain, insofar as national control of the airwaves stood in conflict with international agreements on freedom of the seas. For decades, Europe was dominated by benevolent, noncommercial, national broadcasting monopolies that focused on the presentation of classical music, news, drama, and religious programming. Then, in the 1960s, rock music came along. When the existing national monopolists failed to understand its greatness and refused to broadcast it, defiant, commercially supported broadcasters stood their ships offshore, beyond territorial limits, and began to deliver popular music to eager land-based audiences.

In response, Scandinavian countries took a carrot-and-stick approach, commencing popular music programming on the national networks while cracking down on the offshore "pirates" via harsh new legislation. The Dutch averted their legal eyes, tolerating offshore stations for many years. The United Kingdom also tolerated its stations at first, but after a few years it tried the Scandinavian approach, combining suppression with assimilation. Unfortunately the BBC's version of popular-music broadcasting was so inept that the pirates continued onward. Finally, and only gradually over the course of the 1980s and 1990s, broadcasting monopolies lost some of their hold, and commercial, land-based, popular-music radio stations came into being throughout northwestern Europe. Yet again, in the big picture, it was prohibition, failed containment, and then an ultimate assimilation, albeit with a revised form of commercially based business, rather than the previous nationalized business as usual.

By contrast, the illegal copying of phonograph records, tapes, and compact discs has largely exemplified equivalency and scams, rather than transformational qualities and well-intended purposes. Many of its practitioners have clearly been in it just to make a buck, skimming profits from authorized manufacturers. And yet even here, as this story has moved through the decades from the 1940s to the present day, mitigating factors have emerged time and again, softening the venality. These factors have included a desire to issue recordings that had been long out of print; efforts of plant managers to keep record factories running when legitimate production was slow; an awareness among unauthorized manufacturers of an emerging market for party tapes and dance mixes that cut across the legitimate industry's normal lines and therefore precluded distribution through legitimate channels; the invention of hardware allowing individuals to copy songs with ever-greater ease and the consequent blurring of distinctions among rightful individual use, questionable individual use, and illegitimate mass distribution; and the emergence of a widespread, musically inspired interest in releasing "homemade" concert recordings, which from 1969 onward led to a new genre of recordings—album bootlegging—and consequent attempts at a strict semantic distinction between the act of pirating recordings and the act of creating bootleg albums, where previously these terms had been used interchangeably, without much care. From the 1970s onward, globalization has further complicated the picture, owing to contradictions among and between national and international agreements on copyright protection, and also owing to the emergence of cheap, unauthorized distribution chains suited to the realities of third-world economies.

Over the course of a half century, the illegal copying of recorded songs has done an uncertain amount of damage to recording corporations. In response to instances of piracy, laws have been enacted to protect recordings, and the penalties for violations have been raised substantially. Today, things seem to be at an impasse. A great deal of force may have been misapplied to small-time dealers who were bootlegging unauthorized new releases of rock music and songs in related genres, and recourses to legal action may not have had a meaningful effect on the distribution of mass-produced illegal copies of legitimate recordings, whatever their extent may be. But no one really knows. Meanwhile, formats have come and gone. If phonograph record and tape piracy eventually abated, the primary cause most likely was a falling out of fashion, as compact discs took over the market. If compact-disc piracy is currently abating, the primary cause most likely will be a falling out of fashion, as MP3 files continually gain favor. All the while, appeals against piracy have provided corporations with a powerful public relations tool for strengthening their control of songs (at least on paper, if not in actuality) via legislation.

Song sharing is the exclamation mark in the story, an utterly transformational song product that has operated through distribution networks that in some instances have been entirely independent of authorized channels. Song sharing redefines the meaning of the globalization of music distribution. Song sharing divorces recordings from physical objects. Song sharing subverts the concept of albums, splintering them into individual tracks. Song sharing hands over the control of the organization and presentation of those tracks from song owners to individual listeners, who may personalize and recontextualize their listening, however they see fit. Song sharing opens an unprecedented wide universe of possibilities for musical understanding and enjoyment to anyone who participates in Internet searching and downloading, legal or not.

The recording industry has received these possibilities as threats, rather than as a collective transformational wonder. Déjà vu, song sharing has become the new song sheet: the suppression of Napster, the failed containment of its successors, and a succession of meaningful but incomplete attempts at assimilation, through iTunes and other legitimized downloading services.

This category of contested distribution has now spilled out widely into other media, especially videos, software, and, increasingly in the past couple of years, electronic books. More generally, analogous contested structures can be found outside of these realms and in many different eras, any time a new and unauthorized transformational idea or product has appeared.[1]

The stories in this book still resonate. Several of them remain active today. LP piracy is done. Tape piracy is done, at least outside of the third world. Compact-disc piracy is perhaps less of an issue than it was a decade ago, but when Chinese authorities cracked down on pirated CDs in advance of the 2008 Beijing Olympics, in a gesture of conciliation toward Western mores, they needed bulldozers to get the job done.[2] So those illicit CDs haven't exactly gone away yet. Bootleg jazz fake books and pirate music radio continue to proliferate, but in nonthreatening small markets. Music photocopying, album bootlegging, and unauthorized song downloading are ongoing concerns. And the distant echo of John Santangelo's achievement of licensing agreements in the early 1940s was heard again in the spring of 2010, when Milun Tesovic negotiated an agreement with music publishers for the lyrics posted on his website, MetroLyrics.com, as the industry began to take steps toward assimilating a new era of the uncontrolled dissemination of song lyrics.[3] Corporate concerns notwithstanding, people will keep trying to sell songs they don't own or to acquire songs as cheaply as possible. More importantly, the music industry's persistent lagging behind in adopting innovative products will generate the very piracy it seeks to eliminate. The wholesale disobedient distribution of songs is going to continue so long as owners keep shouting "Equivalency!" while everyone else perceives transformational use.

# NOTES

INTRODUCTION

1. "5¢ Music Seller's Supply Source Told to Court," *Variety*, April 9, 1930, 73.

2. "Street Peddlers Termed 'Sharpers,'" *New York Times*, January 5, 1939.

3. For examples of the quashing of disk jockey disobedience in San Francisco's underground radio culture, see Krieger, *Hip Capitalism*, and the website jive95.com, in particular the latter's reproduction of a memo of June 20, 1974, from station manager Tom Donahue admonishing his staff for subverting the station's contracted advertisements, under the heading "Tom's Memos" at http://www.jive95.com/toms memos.htm.

4. The oft-quoted case on the question of whether a composition is "transformative," altering the original with new expression, meaning, or message in such a manner as to constitute "fair use," is Campbell v. Acuff-Rose Music, Inc., 510 U.S. 569 (1994), http://en.wikipedia.org/wiki/Campbell_v._Acuff-Rose_Music. Siva Vaidhyanathan provides a key survey of this subject in relation to pop music in his chapter "Hep Cats and Copy Cats: American Music Challenges the Copyright Tradition," in *Copyright and Copywrongs*, 117–48. In "Creativity and Culture in Copyright Theory," Julie E. Cohen places the concept of authorial transformative use within the context of a sweeping overview of copyright and cultural studies.

5. For a concise, reasoned, down-to-earth assessment of the relationship between song-sharing and criminality during the Napster era, see Shirky, *Cognitive Surplus*, 120–26.

6. Lev Grossman, "It's All Free," *Time*, May 5, 2003, 67.

7. Sparkman, "Tape Pirates"; Towe, "Record Piracy," Sanjek, *From Print to Plastic*; Sanjek, *American Popular Music and Its Business*; Frith, ed., *Music and Copyright*; Heylin, *Bootleg*; Douglas, "Copyright and Peer-to-Peer Music File Sharing"; Beckerman, "Recording Industry vs. the People"; Marshall, *Bootlegging*; Gillespie, *Wired Shut*; Rosen, *Music and Copyright*.

8. Vaidhyanathan, *The Anarchist in the Library*.

9. Johns, *Piracy*.

10. Ibid., 25.

11. Ibid., 156.

12. Ibid., 145.

13. Ibid., 357–58.

1. The survey in this chapter draws substantially from Tschmuck, *Creativity and Innovation in the Music Industry*, 1–90, while also incorporating aspects of overviews and interpretive comments by Hamm in relevant chapters of *Yesterdays*, and by Garofalo in the first chapter of *Rockin' Out*. In addition, this survey is informed by some expertise that I acquired in the course of editing articles on films, recording, and record companies for two editions of *The New Grove Dictionary of Jazz*. For lucid summaries of broadcasting and copyright in America, see H. Wiley Hitchcock and Stanley Sadie, eds., *The New Grove Dictionary of American Music*.

2. "First Survey of Sheet Music Market Puts Copy Sales at $30,000,000 Yearly," *Variety*, February 3, 1954, 49.

3. Russell Sanjek, *American Popular Music and Its Business* 2, 392–401.

4. Sanjek, *From Print to Plastic*, 6. For the full text of the Copyright Act of 1909, including the criminal infringement provisions (section 28), see E. Fulton Brylawski and Abe Goldman, eds. and comps., *Legislative History of the 1909 Copyright Act*.

5. For details on the American Society of Composers, Authors and Publishers (ASCAP) and the Music Publishers Protective Association (MPPA), see Sanjek, *American Popular Music and Its Business* 3, 32–44. Gilbert provides cynical, entertaining, and more anecdotal accounts of ASCAP and the MPPA in "Music for Profit" in his book *Lost Songs*, 336–44.

6. "Negotiations Open for Radio Music," *New York Times*, March 23, 1923.

CHAPTER 2

1. "America Singing: Nineteenth-Century Song Sheets," http://memory.loc.gov/ammem/amsshtml/amsshome.html.

2. Witmark, *The Story of the House of Witmark*, 119–22.

3. Johns, *Piracy*, 327–55.

4. "Publishers Complain of 5-cent Song Sheets," *New York Times*, September 24, 1929; "Bootleg Lyrics Sales Put Up to Government," *Variety*, January 22, 1930, 57.

5. For the source of this figure, see below, note 18. For a description of another early bootleg song sheet, see Lewis Nichols, "Tin Pan Alley Is Weaving Its Lyrics in New Ways," *New York Times*, June 6, 1930.

6. "Street Vendors Charged with Misrepresentation," *Variety*, October 30, 1929, 79.

7. "Bootleg Street Peddlers of Lyrics Hurt Trade," *Variety*, November 6, 1929, 65; "5¢ Song Racket Seems Serious," *Variety*, January 1, 1930, 57.

8. "Bootleg Lyrics Sales Put Up to Government," *Variety*, January 22, 1930, 57.

9. "'Song Racket' Charge Brings 2 into Court," *New York Times*, February 7, 1930, 13. The only other report of physical confrontations of this sort came in 1936, when the transient song-sheet vender Harold L. Berg decided to drop charges against police

officer Richard O. Bankert for striking him on the nose: "Street Vender Refuses to Prosecute Officer," *Washington Post*, November 12, 1936.

10. "Three Song Hawkers Plead Guilty, Go Free," *New York Times*, February 18, 1930; "Fight against Lyric Pirates," *Variety*, February 19, 1930, 61. See also United States of America vs. Samuel A. Cohen, vs. Morris Shapiro and Samuel A. Cohen, and vs. Harry B. Paul, *NARA—Northeast—NY*. These three files include indictments and bench warrants.

11. Edward A. Sargoy: "Rescinding the Supreme Court's Rules for Copyright Procedure under Sec. 101, Title 17," 355.

12. Uri Gneezy and Aldo Rustichini analyze responses to fines instituted at Israeli day-care centers in "A Fine Is a Price." The authors demonstrate how a financial penalty in a noncriminalized situation might actually serve to increase the occurrence of a behavior that the penalty was meant to deter. Applied retrospectively, seventy years earlier, and without regard to the question of criminality, their notion equally well describes the practices of song-sheet bootleggers.

13. On these events in Chicago, see "Threats, Losses Grow in 5 and 10c Lyric Sheet War," *Variety*, February 12, 1930, 65. Although the song-sheet battle was almost exclusively nonviolent (see above, note 9), there were evidently incidents of intimidation.

On events elsewhere during the early months of 1930, as covered in *Variety*, see "Fight against Lyric Pirates," February 19, 1930, 61; "Coast to Coast Slump in Music Sales for January Laid to Bootleg Lyric Racket," February 19, 1930, 62–63; "Lyric Racket Again," March 5, 1930, 65; "Fear Small Town Sheet Dealers May Go Bootleg," March 26, 1930, 73; "Raid Song Pirates; 3 Sellers Arrested," April 23, 1930, 72.

14. "Fight against Lyric Pirates," *Variety*, February 19, 1930, 61; "Senate Passes Music Bill," *New York Times*, March 19, 1930; "Roosevelt Signs Bill Outlawing 'Song Sheets'; Tells Composers Other States Should Copy Law," *New York Times*, March 27, 1930; "Song Hawker Arrested," *New York Times*, April 12, 1930.

15. "End 'Racketeering' by Song Peddlers," *New York Times*, May 5, 1930.

16. "Publishers Talk Printing Own Song Sheets to Eradicate Sheetleggers," *Variety*, March 15, 1932, 59. Other newspaper articles, all from *Variety* unless indicated otherwise, and court documents of May 1930 to August 1932 trace the ongoing battle against numerous individuals, including

Morris Cohen and G. A. Manteuffel: "Song Pirates Stiff Chi Rap," May 7, 1930, 73; United States of America vs. Morris Cohen and G. A. Manteuffel, *NARA— Great Lakes*.

Nat Tobin: "Sentence for Boy Selling 5c Music," May 7, 1930, 73.

Joseph Dawson: "Suspended Sentence for Pirated Song Seller," July 2, 1930, 72.

Salvatore Trelango: "New 5c Song Sheet Worrying Music Men," July 16, 1930, 58.

Joseph Tinit: "60 Days for Sheet Seller," July 16, 1930, 58; United States of America vs. Joseph Tinit, *NARA—Pacific*.

Frank and John Schumanski: "Song Pirates Get 30 Days," *New York Times*, October 21, 1930; "2 Pirate Song Sellers Given 30 Days in Jail," October 22, 1930, 75.

Joseph and Nathan Stein: "Indict Two 'Leggers," November 26, 1930, 66.

Irving Cohen: "Lyric 'Leggers Pinched," January 28, 1931, 77.

Victor Frediana: "Bootleg Song Pirate Raided," April 1, 1931, 59.

Abe Schrott and Joe Ansbetino: "Sale of Copyright Songs Brings Fine," *Washington Post*, April 3, 1931; "Society Convicts Gyp Lyric Peddler," April 8, 1931, 67; "Song Publishers Scored by Judge," *Washington Post*, May 27, 1931; United States vs. Joe Ansbetino, and United States vs. Abe Schrott, *NARA — Textual Archives*.

James Herron: "Song Seller Is Indicted," *New York Times*, July 23, 1931; United States of America vs. James Herron, *NARA — Northeast — NJ*.

For additional coverage of nationwide distributing and peddling (all in *Variety* unless indicated otherwise) see (all 1930) "Bootleg Song Sheets Again Being Vended," June 18, 81; "Bootleg Lyric Sheets Selling in Detroit," August 13, 65; "Newark Pirates," October 22, 75; "Song Bootleggers Pinched in West as Amer. Soc. Appeals to Law," October 29, 73; "Song Sheet Peddlers Pop Up Again on W.C.," November 26, 66; "Those Street Sellers!" December 24, 57; (all 1931) "Sheet 'Legger Nabbed," April 15, 75; "'Leggers Philly Jam," April 22, 66; "2 Lyric Sellers in Ptsbgh under Bail," April 22, 67; "Song Seller's Break," May 6, 66; "Police Parade Starts Field Day for Vendors; 600 Pushcart Men Reap Profit amid Crowds," *New York Times*, May 10; "Convict Lyric Sellers," May 13, 91; "L.A. 'Leggers Back," August 18, 60; "Sheetleggers Active Again," September 22, 59; "Song Sheet Merchant Held in $1,000 Bond," *Washington Post*, October 24; "Sheetleggers Fined," November 10, 61; "Back Again!" December 22, 53; "Musiclegger Jailed," December 29, 41; (both 1932) "Newsboys Fined on Song Sheet Charges," April 19, 61; "15 Song Sheet Peddlers Nabbed in N.Y.; $5 Fines," August 2, 51. See also "U.S. Investigates Street Hawkers of Sheet Music," *Chicago Tribune*, February 20, 1933, 12, in which the distinction between sheet music and song lyric sheets has gotten lost and the song sheets are referred to as "sheet music."

17. Assemblyman Milton M. Golden introduced a bill parallel to the New York state law into the California legislature; see "Hollywood, Feb. 3," *Variety*, February 4, 1931, 80.

On the use of parody as a ploy to avoid infringement, see, in *Variety*, "Those 5¢ Gyppers," August 27, 1930, 73; "Parodies with Hit Titles, New Sheet Gag," February 4, 1931, 80; "Coast Bootleg Music Peddlers Now Using Unheard of Lyrics," February 18, 1931, 71; "Sheetleggers Active Again," September 22, 1931, 59. The question of parody was later taken up in Robbins Music Corporation et al. v. Song Parodies, Inc., et al., 1942; see also "Parodies Ruled to be Infringement in N.Y. Decision Awarded MPPA after Long Fight for Clarification," *Variety*, March 22, 1944, 37.

For accounts of the attempts to prosecute through the Federal Trade Commission, see "Fed Commish Helps Soc. in Sheetleg Campaign," *Variety*, December 8, 1931, 61; "Trade Commish on Bootleg Song Sheets," *Variety*, September 6, 1932, 46; *Federal Trade Commission Decisions* 15 (1933), #915 and #916, 523–24; *Federal Trade Commission Decisions* 16 (1933), #936, 550–51.

18. Texts of the conspiracy laws may be found, respectively, in Sections 5440, 37, and 88 of *Revised Statues of the United States* 2, *The Statutes at Large of the United States of America*, 25, pt. 1, and *The Code of the Laws of the United States of America of a General and Permanent Character* 44, pt. 1. Section 88 remained in place through the years of song-sheet bootlegging; the text in the 1926 *Code* is the same as that found in *United States Code, 1940 Edition, Containing the General and Permanent Laws of the United States* 2. For a glimpse into the immensity of uses to which this law, now Section 371 of Title 18, has been put, see *United States Code Annotated: Title 18: Crimes and Criminal Procedure, §§ 331 to 400.*

Zickel's letter of June 29, 1932, to Zimmer, and Zimmer's undated letter of circa mid-November 1932 to Judge Hollzer, reside in United States of America vs. Al Friedman et al., Criminal Case 10910, *NARA—Pacific*. The file also includes an indictment of May 11, 1932, five song sheets captured as exhibits (among them, figure 2.1, *Songland Herald*), three pieces of sheet music illustrating the songs infringed upon ("By the Sycamore Tree," "'Leven Pounds of Heaven," and "All of Me"), and conditions of probation for the teenager Alexander Aggie, among many other documents.

A second conspiracy charge was brought as United States of America vs. Al Friedman et al., Criminal Case 11029, *NARA—Pacific*. Aggie was also separately charged with criminal copyright infringement in United States of America vs. Alexander Aggie, *NARA—Pacific*.

For coverage of these events, all in *Variety* in 1932, see "Dept. of Justice Indicts 7 in L.A. as Tune Leggers," June 7, 60; "Bootleg Song Sales Felony," July 12, 45; "L.A. Police Join Feds in Sheet Bootleg War," August 2, 51; "Five Song Sheet Sellers Convicted of Conspiracy," September 27, 59; "Song 'Leggers' Heavy Penalty," October 4, 53.

19. "Coast Songlegging," *Variety*, November 1, 1932, 53.

20. "Helpless Society on Song Sheets," *Variety*, June 15, 1933, 49.

For summaries of efforts to stop the bootlegging, see, in *Variety*, "50 Grand Already Spent on Fighting Illegal Music Vending; Will Be More," June 9, 1931, 55; "$65,000 Spent to Date in Bootleg Lyric Fight and No Results as Yet," October 6, 1931, 65; "Publishers Talk Printing Own Song Sheets to Eradicate Sheetleggers," March 15, 1932, 59; "Music Pubs Gumshoe on Their Own to Halt Bootleg Song Sheets," March 14, 1933, 49.

21. On Aaronson, see "Song Vendors Sought: Warrants Issued for Arrest of Four Broadway Sellers," *New York Times*, May 24, 1934; "Song Bootlegger Pinched 3d Time," *Variety*, October 21, 1936, 53; "2 Song Bootleggers Held in $100 Bail," *Variety*, October 28, 1936, 47; "N.Y. Song Bootlegger Gets 4 Mos. in Jail," *Variety*, November 11, 1936, 46.

Aaronson's court records reside in two files: United States of America vs. Theodore Aaronson, Criminal Case C96-263, *NARA—Northeast—NY*, including his indictment of June 22, 1934, and Judge Bondy's admonition at sentencing, June 25, 1934; United States of America vs. Theodore Aaronson, Criminal Case 99-217, *NARA—Northeast—NY*.

Occasional coverage on other song-sheet bootleggers of the mid-1930s includes "2 Held in Song-Sheet Raid," *New York Times*, August 14, 1934; "Seize 3 with Song Sheets," *New York Times*, January 6, 1935; "Nab Balto 'Leggers," *Variety*, February 20, 1935, 48; "Justice Dept. Joins Balto's 'Legger Drive," *Variety*, February 27, 1935, 53; "Convict Song 'Legger," *Variety*, December 9, 1936, 41. For further details of this last report, on Carmello Lapinto, alias Eddie Burke, see United States of America vs. E. Burke, *NARA—Northeast—NJ*. The case file includes orders to destroy the pirated material and the notice of its destruction by Deputy Marshall Pakozdi; Lapinto was fined, but eight years later, had not paid.

22. Notes on McCullagh's and Hoffman's activities derive from their obituaries in the *New York Times*, respectively, January 4, 1917, and November 4, 1954. References to Hoffman's positions with Feist and the MPPA appear in "Song Vendors Sought: Warrants Issued for Arrest of Four Broadway Sellers," *New York Times*, May 24, 1934; "2 Held in Song-Sheet Raid," *New York Times*, August 14, 1934.

23. "74-Year-Old Printer Nabbed in New Jersey Pirate Song Sheet Raid," *Variety*, September 25, 1935, 60.

24. "Song Sheeters Nabbed in D.C., Also N.Y.," *Variety*, March 31, 1937, 53.

25. The term "contraband folios" appears in "Song Bootlegger Pinched 3d Time," *Variety*, October 21, 1936, 53. Other terms for song-sheet magazine appear in U.S. vs. Aaronson, Criminal Case C96-245, within testimony in the Violation of Probation hearing of October 26, 1936, 2–3 and 6–9.

I acquired copies of a number of bootleg song-sheet magazines from newspaper and sheet-music dealers. In addition, a copy of *Paramount Book No. 17* resides as Exhibit B in Donaldson, Douglas & Gumble, et al. vs. United Magazine Supply, *NARA—Northeast—NY*; this case is reported in "3 Pubs Given Writs vs. Song Bootleggers," *Variety*, October 26, 1938, 39.

26. On John Santangelo's first appearance in *Variety*, see "Fed. Judge Holds Song 'Legger in $20,000 Bail," December 30, 1936, 41 (as John Angelo); "Song Sheet Peddlers Fined in Scranton, Pa.," March 17, 1937, 44 (as John Santangelo).

27. Santangelo's subsequent prosecutions were also covered in *Variety*: "Criminal and Civil Actions Beset John Santangelo of Derby, Conn., Wholesaler of Bootleg Songsheets," July 26, 1939, 41; "Four Hartford Retail Stores Sued for Damages on Copyright Songsheet Sales," August 16, 1939, 33; "Santangelo Sentenced," January 17, 1940, 39; "Conspiracy (Federal Pen Offense) Charged to 5 Bootleg Song Peddlers," January 24, 1940, 39; "Five Year Probation for Leaders of Bootleg Songsheet Racket," October 2, 1940, 49. Court documents include United States of America vs. Dominick

William Castaldo et al., Criminal Case 8801b, and United States of America vs. Dominick William Castaldo et al., Criminal Case 15c, both *NARA—Northeast—NJ.*

28. On Preziosa and Costello, see "Bootleg Music Plant Raided," *Variety,* December 11, 1940, 43; United States of America vs. James Preziosa and Tony Costello, *NARA—Northeast—NY.*

For ongoing reports of other activities, all in *Variety* unless indicated otherwise, see "Song Sheet Peddler Held," *New York Times,* March 26, 1937; "Song Peddlers Nabbed," April 14, 1937, 57; "Peddler Found Guilty," June 9, 1937, 42; "Merchants Fined: Bootleg Lyrics on Sheets Sold in Toronto Stores," August 4, 1937, 47; "Pressing Campaign against Bootleggers," October 13, 1937, 45; "Nab Music Sheet Peddlers," March 2, 1938, 39; "Bootleggers' $1,500 Bail All-Time High in N.Y.," September 21, 1938, 39; "Indict Song Peddler," November 2, 1938, 45; "Confiscate Bootleg Sheets," December 28, 1938, 33; "In Cleveland Area," April 3, 1940, 41; "ASCAP-Financed War on Bootleggers Protects BMI Copyright Infringements," February 12, 1941, 34; "Six Months in Jug for Song Bootlegger," April 23, 1941, 39; "Hold Song Bootlegger," August 26, 1942, 43; "B'klyn Song 'Legger Gets 60-Day Sentence," December 23, 1942, 41; "Songsheet Bootlegger Gets 6 Months in N.Y.," June 16, 1943, 41. At least two of these arrests made their way into federal prosecution, as United States of America vs. Morris Abrams, and United States of America vs. Philip Resnikoff, *NARA—Northeast—NJ.*

29. "Song Bootleggers Nearly Driven Out of Business," *Variety,* June 25, 1941, 35.

30. "Walgreen Stores Claim Clerks Peddled Pirate Songsheets sans Authority," *Variety,* September 29, 1937, 46. On the drive against retail chains, see also (all in *Variety*): "Warn Trade on Phoney Books," September 1, 1937, 48; "Infringers' Penance is 6G," October 6, 1937, 45; "Four Hartford Retail Stores Sued for Damages on Copyright Songsheet Sales," August 16, 1939, 33; "Druggists' Assn. Asking Members to Lay Off Bootleg Songsheets," September 30, 1939, 43; "MPPA Sues Two Philly Stores on 'Bootlegging,'" September 18, 1940, 33.

31. "Systematic Two-Way Drive by MPPA against Bootleg Music Song Sheets," *Variety,* January 10, 1940, 39. On the city-by-city, newstand-by-newstand, campaign, see (all in *Variety*) "Hartford Board Rules vs. MPPA on Bootlegging," August 30, 1939, 35; "Drive against Bootleg Folios in Drugstores Opens This Week," October 4, 1939, 33; "Sheetleggers," October 25, 1939, 37; "Tighten Lines of Piracy Fight as Santangelo Jailed for Eight Months," January 17, 1940, 45; "Bootleg-Chasers on Road," February 20, 1940, 34; "Sheet Sales Up as Pirates Lam," March 6, 1940, 41.

32. "Pirated Songsheets Are Pretty Thoroughly under Restraint, Morris Reports," *Variety,* November 19, 1941, 50.

33. A copy of *Popular Song Hits* 1, no. 1, is held at the John Hay Library at Brown University. Other references to song-lyric magazines are from my own collection.

34. "M.P.P.A. Remains Neutral on Question of Support for Legit Lyric Sheet," *Variety,* July 20, 1938, 39.

35. "More Pirate Sheets Raided," *Variety,* October 5, 1938, 45. On the subsequent

prosecution of the publishers of *Flash*, see "G-Men Score Again," *New York Times*, June 18, 1941; "Song Bootleggers Nearly Driven Out of Business," *Variety*, June 25, 1941, 35; "Indict 9 in N.Y. Song Sheet Racket," *Variety*, August 6, 1941, 43; "Pubs File Civil Suits against Song 'Leggers," *Variety*, September 10, 1941, 32; "Song Pirating Barred," *New York Times*, April 18, 1942. The case file is United States of America vs. Fernando Costa et al., *NARA—Northeast—NY*.

36. "Do You Love to Sing the Old Songs?" *Song Hits* 2, no. 10 (March 1939): 34. "WB in Song Sheet Market," *Variety*, September 13, 1939, 35. Advertisements for an issue of *Sing Session* and for the first issue of *Music Makers*, the latter including a description of contents and a picture of its cover, appear in *Song Hits* 3, no. 12 (May 1940). An illustrated ad for all three of the Song Lyrics, Inc., publications appears in *Song Hits* 4, no. 8 (January 1941): 26.

I have copies of the following issues of new song-lyrics magazines of the early 1940s: *Song Parade: America's Foremost Lyric Magazine* 1, no. 4 (August 1941), D. S. Publishing Company, Inc., at Rockefeller Plaza in New York; *Big Song Magazine* 1, no. 7 (September 1941), Charlton Publishing Corporation, 9–11 Barrow Street, New York; *Radio Hit Songs* 1, no. 2 (November 1941), also from Charlton; *Broadcast Song Hits* 1, no. 1 (October 1941), K. R. K. Publications, 280 Broadway, New York; and *Sing* 1, no. 3 (March 1942), also from K. R. K. Publications.

37. "Influx of Shady Characters into Song Sheet Biz Disturbs Music Publishers," *Variety*, September 9, 1942, 1.

38. "$275,000 Yearly Now Collected from Licensed Songsheets, M.P.P.A. Reports," *Variety*, November 25, 1942, 43.

39. Markstein, "Charlton Comics," http://www.toonpedia.com/charlton.htm (2003).

40. In advance of his new-found legitimacy, Santangelo's company Charlton probably published some of the main series of bootleg song-lyric magazines. In entering into evidence a description of a *Prosperity Big Book* of March 1941, Appellate Justice Bayes noted that "page 28 is entitled 'Charlton Choices' underneath which appear several items of a humorous or jocular nature"; see People v. Samuels et al., Court of Special Sessions, City of New York, Appellate Part, First Department, June 3, 1941, *New York Supplement Second Series* 28, 114.

41. Ralph H. Manard, "World's Largest Publisher of Song Magazines"; Mary Slezak, "The History of Charlton Press, Inc., and Its Song Lyric Periodicals." Further and in some cases alternative information on Santangelo appears in Jon B. Cooke and Christopher Irving, "The Charlton Empire: a Brief History of the Derby, Connecticut Publisher," http://www.twomorrows.com/comicbookartist/articles/09empire.html.

42. Among the many men found under the name John Santangelo in the Social Security Death Index at rootsweb.ancestry.com, this birth date, and a month and year of death of October 1979 are given for the John Santangelo whose last residence was Derby, Connecticut.

43. *Big Song Magazine* 1, no. 7 (September 1941): 9.

44. "Songsheet Mags in Legal Tiff on Format," *Variety*, February 3, 1943, 37.

45. United States of America vs. Dominick William Castaldo et al., *NARA—Northeast—NJ*, including Edgar Y. Dobbins's request for an Order Terminating Probation, September 5, 1947.

46. "Music Publishers Look to $750,000 Revenue This Year from Song Sheets," *Variety*, March 15, 1944, 54.

47. For a broader look at the give and play between prohibition and assimilation into legitimacy, with an argument for the virtual impossibility of prohibition, see Thornton, *The Economics of Prohibition*.

CHAPTER 3

1. On the decline of the piano, see "Mechanical Music Has Not Yet Won a Victory," *New York Times*, July 1, 1928.

2. "Bootleg Lyrics Sales Put Up to Government," *Variety*, January 22, 1930, 57.

3. "Whalen to Be Asked to War on Song Pirates; Publishers Say They Face $15,000,000 Loss," *New York Times*, March 17, 1930.

4. "A Curb on the Song Peddlers," *New York Times*, February 9, 1936.

5. "Foreword by the Editor," *Song Hits* 1, no. 1 (June 1937): 4.

6. For further thoughts and a different perspective on the interplay between technology and music, see Katz, *Capturing Sound*, 8–47. Katz sets up a structure of opposing concepts. He contrasts an established, nontechnological event, the concert—music that is fixed in place at a particular time—with a newer, technological invention, the recording—music that is portable and repeatable at any time, given the requisite equipment.

7. *Latest Songs*, the newspaper-sized sheet cited in chapter 1, was dated July 1933, but most of these bootleg publications did not provide a publication date. It seems safe to infer that the undated bootleg song-lyric magazines may be dated by the releases of the shows with which they are associated. I confirmed some release dates of musical films in the *Movie and Video Guide: 2008 Edition*, ed. Leonard Maltin (New York: Signet, 2007), but for most of the films and stage shows mentioned here, I simply used Google to search by title, and this yielded consistent, expected results for the release dates.

8. It was normal for a stage show or movie to come out in advance of the year in its title, as per *Gold Diggers of 1937* and *The Big Broadcast of 1937*. Among other contemporary examples, *The Big Broadcast of 1936* was released in 1935 and the *Hollywood Revels Revue 1937* was released in 1936, while *The Big Broadcast of 1938* actually came out that year, in 1938. *Hollywood Revels Revue 1937* was among the numerous other shows also excerpted in *Prosperity Book No. 36*.

9. *Prosperity Book No. 37* and *Prosperity Book No. 40* both gave a prominent place to the film *The Singing Marine*, released in 1937; hence a publication date of circa 1937 seems probable.

10. *Radio Hit Songs* 1, no. 2 (November 1941): 27.

11. *Radio Hit Songs* 1, no. 2 (November 1941): respectively, 16–19 and 28–29.

12. *Prosperity Book No. 36*, 30.

13. Hamm, *Yesterdays.*

14. *United Mine Workers Journal* 25 (December 3, 1914): 4.

15. Resolution no. R-221, *Proceedings of the Thirty-Third Constitutional Convention of the United Mine Workers of America* (1934), 466.

16. *Paramount Book No. 17* was exhibit B in Donaldson, Douglas & Gumble et. al vs. United Magazine Supply, *NARA*—Northeast—*NY*.

17. *Broadcast Hit Songs* 1, no. 1 (October 1941): 30; *Big Song Magazine* 1, no. 7 (September 1941): 28.

18. *Song Hit Folio*, no. 9 (November 10, 1934): 4.

19. "Foreword by the Editor," *Song Hits* 1, no. 1 (June 1937): 4.

20. For examples of record reviews in song-lyric magazines, see "Playback" in Santangelo's *Hit Parader* 1, no. 3 (January 1943): 20.

21. *Song Hit Folio* 3, no. 3 (June 1935): 6.

22. *Song Hit Folio* 3, no. 3 (June 1935): "a woman proposes!" and "you want a lovely bust & form," 12; "the secrets of sex daringly revealed!" 14. *Popular Song Hits* 3, no. 8 (December 1936—January 1937): "would you be interested in finding a short cut to romance?" 8; "beautiful eyes with Maybelline," 10; "your marriage forecast," 11; "skin eruptions" and "why be flat-chested?" 12; "I reduced 70 lbs." 13.

23. *Song Hit Folio*, no. 9 (November 10, 1934): "be popular! learn to play piano by ear," 11. *Song Hit Folio* 3, no. 3 (June 1935): "it's fun to play by ear on the guitar, tenorguitar, banjo or uke," 12; "to those who think learning music is hard," 13. *Popular Song Hits* 3, no. 8 (December 1936—January 1937): "your voice," 9; "learn to dance" and "compose popular songs," 11; "become a radio star!" 12.

24. Ads for Remington typewriters and cheap novels appear, e.g., in *Song Hit Folio* 3, no. 3 (June 1935): respectively, 13 and 16.

25. *Hit Parader* 1, no. 3 (January 1943): 2.

CHAPTER 4

1. This section of the chapter summarizes my earlier work on the subject, published as *The Story of Fake Books.*

2. "Major Bootleg Operation Suspected in Chi[cago] Copyright Infringement Suit," *Variety*, August 2, 1950, 37; "FBI Taking Action vs. Tune-Dex Bootleggers," *Down Beat* 18 (June 15, 1951): 1; "FBI Launches Nationwide Search to Nab Infringement Racketeers," *Variety*, November 22, 1951, 43; "Chi Songleggers Change Pleas to Guilty in Fed. Ct." *Variety*, December 19, 1962, 55, 59; "Musician Indicted over 'Fake-Books,'" *New York Times*, January 14, 1966; "Musician Is Fined $5,000 for His Illegal Songbook," *New York Times*, June 3, 1966, 31; "Jury Convicts 'Fake Book' Ops," *Variety*, October 15,

1969, 55; "2 Fined $4,500 for Making 'Fake Books' of Music Hits," *New York Times*, December 4, 1969.

3. An impressionistic sense of an overall decline in sheet-music sales, with brief periods of short-term recovery, may be gleaned from the following trade articles, all in *Variety* unless otherwise indicated: Leonard Allen, "The Battle of Tin Pan Alley," *Harper's Magazine*, 131 (October 1940): 514–23, esp. 519; "Biggest Sheet Music Sales in 15 Yrs," November 11, 1942, 1; "Disc Ban Clips Sheet Music," February 3, 1943, 37; "Publishers at Odds on Disc Ban's Effect on Sheet Music Business," September 15, 1943, 50; "Sheet Music Biz at 15-Year Crest," October 4, 1944, 1; "Music Biz Plenty Forte in '44: ASCAP Coin Up, also Sheet Sales," December 13, 1944, 1; "Pianos Make Sheet Music Sales," *The Billboard*, April 14, 1945, 11; "Music Publishers Unworried by Longest Sales Slump in Years," July 17, 1946, 39; "Sheet Music Sales Take Decided Upturn, Coinciding with Disk Hike," August 24, 1949, 43; "Disk, Sheet Music Hit High C-for-Coin," January 18, 1950, 1; "Music Publishers Map Campaign to Revive Sheet Sale," May 17, 1950, 1; "Songsmiths Spark Sheet Spurt," May 24, 1950, 53; "Music Leaders Meet Next Week to Launch Drive for Sheet Sales," May 31, 1950, 35; "Pubs, Composers Parlay Ideas on Crucial Sheet Sale Problem" and "Await Fall for Key to Slump on Sheet Sales," both June 7, 1950, 41; "Pave Way for Sheet Sale Push" and "Bad Slump in Sheet Sales? Just Back to Pre-War Normal, Say Some," both June 14, 1950, 55. "SPA Doctors Suggest Cures for Ailing Sheet Music Sales," *The Billboard*, June 17, 1950, 15; "Sheet Sales Continue Marked Rise, Business Well Above Last Year," August 16, 1950, 41; "'Big Three' Probes Sheet Sales," *The Billboard*, August 26, 1950, 11; "Music Hits Highest Peaks; Record and Sheet Sales Zoom," *The Billboard*, January 27, 1951, 11, 37; "Sheet Slump Blamed on Gimmick Disks, Floods," *The Billboard*, May 31, 1952, 18; "Zooming Sheet Sales Reach 100% over Last Six Months' Averages," *The Billboard*, September 27, 1952, 21; "Only Handful of Sheet Music Clicks," March 18, 1953, 46; "Publishing Industry Alarmed by Pop Sheet Music Decline," *The Billboard*, November 21, 1953, 1, 16, 48; "Sheets: Critical Year Weathered, Pop $$ Down," *The Billboard*, January 2, 1954, 11, 13; "Piano Sales Up but Wha' Hoppen to Sheet Music," March 21, 1956, 49.

On the specific decline of sheet-music sales per hit song, see, for example (all in *Variety*), "First 'Rack' Order, Now 87,000 Copies, Almost Enuff to Get Off Nut," September 20, 1944, 47; "500,000 Sheet Sale Now Tops; Pubs Need a Smash to Show Profit," July 8, 1953, 49; "200,000 Copies Now a Big Song Hit; Must Bank on ASCAP, BMI Coin," April 21, 1954, 53.

4. "Sheet Music Sales at Rock Bottom; Even Disk Clicks Sell Only 15,000," *Variety*, April 10, 1957, 65.

5. Jon Hendricks interview for the Smithsonian Jazz Oral History Program, August 17–18, 1995.

6. "Music Schools Habitually Violate Copyright but Nat'l Music Council Is Out to

Discourage Practice," *Variety*, December 10, 1941, 39; "MPPA Fights Schools' Using Own Copy Work," *The Billboard*, January 27, 1951, 11.

7. "MPA to Investigate Copyright Violations," *The Billboard*, January 17, 1953, 28; "Standard Pubbers Urged to Stop Copyright Infringement," *The Billboard*, June 13, 1953, 14, 35 (the quotation is from 14).

8. "Music Biz Hits $30,000,000 in Publications," *The Billboard*, February 6, 1954, 14.

9. "Sheet Market Solid for 'Right' Numbers; Educational Biz in 20% Annual Boosts," *Variety*, April 17, 1957, 45.

10. Paul Ackerman, "Sheet Music Sales Outlook Brightens after Dark Years," *The Billboard*, July 1, 1957, 1, 27 (the quotation is from 27).

11. "MDS Stress on Education Field Cues Thinking Switch," *The Billboard*, September 7, 1959, 3, 12; "Music Dealers Service, Hit by Fade of Rack Biz, Files under Chapter XI," *Variety*, September 16, 1959, 47.

12. "Photocopier," http://en.wikipedia.org/wiki/Photocopier; "Xerox," http://en.wikipedia.org/wiki/Xerox.

13. "Sheet Music Sales Making Dramatic Comeback after Decades of Drought," *Variety*, July 2, 1969, 51, 54. On the continuation of this trend into the 1970s, see Claude Hall, "Sheet Music 'Hits' Help WB Publishing Boost $$," *Billboard*, June 9, 1973, 1, 10; "Sheet Music Sales Up, Survey Shows," *Variety*, March 20, 1974, 61; Frank Meyer, "Sheet Music Sales Rebounding and Still Keyed to Enduring Hits," *Variety*, November 6, 1974, 54; Is Horowitz, "Sheet Music Trailing as Folio Sales Spurt," *Billboard*, September 20, 1975, 1, 12; Horowitz and Jim Melanson, "Print Music Burgeoning with Stability Wished for in Records/Tapes," *Billboard*, March 27, 1976, 52, 63.

14. Joe Di Sabato, "Sheet Music: Rumors of Death Exaggerated," *Billboard*, January 17, 1970, M6, M8.

15. "Printed Music Sales Reach $200-mil Annually; See Doubling in 5 Years," *Variety*, July 14, 1971, 43.

16. "Music Print Sales at $91-mil: AMC," *Variety*, July 28, 1971, 35; Is Horowitz, "Sheet Music Income Soars: New Record Gross of $170-mil Projected for 1974," *Billboard*, November 16, 1974, 1, 10.

17. Horowitz and Melanson, "Print Music Burgeoning with Stability Wished for in Records/Tapes," 52, 63.

18. Ingrid Hannigan, "School Drive Spurs Sheet Music Volume," *Billboard*, June 30, 1973, 1, 10.

19. Ian Dove, "Educators Aid Sheet/Folio $$," *Billboard*, January 27, 1973, 1, 126.

20. "Broido Calls Copying Unit Biggest Pirate," *Billboard*, October 19, 1974, 32.

21. Mildred Hall, "Music Publishers Worried: Supreme Court Sidesteps Copying Issue," *Billboard*, March 8, 1975, 3, 12; Hall, "No Accord Seen in Hassle over Copying Music, Texts," *Billboard*, May 24, 1975, 4.

22. Is Horowitz, "Photocopying Spurs Pubs' New 'Fair Use' Standards," *Billboard*, August 30, 1975, 1, 14, 50.

23. "Illegal Copying Condemned," *ASCAP Today* 8 (Fall 1976): 24.

24. Donn Laurence Mills, "Dracula Would Be Proud of Us," *Instrumentalist* 33 (October 1978): 64, 66.

25. Walfrid Kujala, "Letter from the President," *Flutist Quarterly* 14, no. 2 (1989): 3. For a later discussion along these lines, see "Photocopying Music," *Percussive Notes* 42, no. 6 (December 2004): 4.

26. For copies of the longstanding guidelines to educational fair use, see, e.g., "Photocopying for Educational Purposes," http://www.vpul.upenn.edu/osl/photocpy .html, and "MLA: Copyright for Music Librarians," http://www.lib.jmu.edu/org/mla/ Guidelines/Accepted_Guidelines/Educational_Photocopying.aspx.

27. Irv Lichtman, "Publishers Unite to Stem Copying," *Billboard*, November 24, 1979, 1, 64; "'Get Tough' Policy for Illegal Photocopying," *School Musician* 51 (December 1979): 10 (quotations from Burtch are from both articles). A similarly strong stand, labeling unauthorized photocopying as not merely illegal, but immoral, appears in Michael Schulman, "Publishers Avoid the Villain Role with Schools, Churches," *Music Scene*, no. 279 (September–October 1974): 5, 17. A number of other periodicals printed the announcement of the "Get Tough" policy, including, e.g., *NATS Bulletin* 36, no. 3 (1980): 38–39, and *National School Orchestra Association Bulletin* 23, no. 1 (1980): 7.

28. "Sue College for Alleged Photocopies," *Billboard*, June 14, 1980, 26; "Music Publishers Accuse College in Copyright Suits," *New York Times,* June 15, 1980.

29. "University of Texas at Austin Agrees to Stop Illegal Photocopying of Music," *ITG Journal* 9 (February 1985): 5.

30. "Appeals Court Sez Music Copying by Churches Is Illegal," *Variety,* April 14, 1982, 2, 96 (the quotation is from 2).

31. "Church Is Guilty in Copyright Case," *New York Times,* April 20, 1984.

32. F.E.L. Publications, Ltd., v. Catholic Bishop of Chicago, http://cases.justia.com/ us-court-of-appeals/F2/754/216/319020/.

33. Dennis J. Fitzpatrick, doing business as F.E.L. Publications, v. Catholic Bishop of Chicago, http://cases.justia.cm/us-court-of-appeals/F2/916/1254/208102.

34. "Feist Calls for Pubbery Conference on Copying; Rerun of Jukebox Push," *Variety,* March 23, 1983, 78; "Pubberies to Consider Issue of Illegal Copying by Schools, Churches," *Variety,* November 16, 1983, 65, 68.

35. "NMPA: Sheet Music Sales Up, Only in Line with Inflation; Piracy Blamed," *Variety,* October 18–24, 1989, 85.

36. "Xerox Commercial Advocates Lawlessness," *Music Trades* 139 (February 1991) 51.

37. "RPMDA Program Fights to Stop Illegal Copying," *Music Trades* 140 (Septem-

ber 1992): 36; Marjorie Gloyd, "Copying Printed Music: 'To Do or Not To Do,'" *Music Clubs Magazine* 72, no. 2 (Winter 1992): 11; Irv Lichtman, "Anti-Photocopying Campaign Launched: MPA Aims to Raise Copyright Awareness with Educators, Others," *Billboard*, September 12, 1998, 49.

38. James S. Heller, "Copyright, Fair Use, and the For-Profit Sector"; "Key Court Case Summaries on Fair Use"; "Q&A Concerning Copyright Compliance for Print and Software," http://www.wsubooks.com/store1/wichita/copyright.htm.

39. "The Internet . . . Xerox Machine of the '90s?" *Music Trades* 144 (May 1996): 67–68.

CHAPTER 5

1. Yoder, *Pirate Radio Stations.*

2. Street, *A Concise History of British Radio,* 22, 24; "Negotiations Open for Radio Music," *New York Times,* March 23, 1923.

3. Coase, *British Broadcasting,* 1–65 (the quotation is from 46–47); Johns, *Piracy,* 357–99.

4. Paulu, *Radio and Television Broadcasting on the European Continent,* 80; Karl Erik Gustafsson, "Sweden," in *Electronic Media and Politics in Western Europe,* ed. Kleinsteuber et al., 273–79.

5. Karen Siune, "Denmark," in *Electronic Media and Politics in Western Europe,* 30–31; Ib Poulsen and Henrik Søndergaard, "Denmark," in *Western Broadcasting at the Dawn of the 21st Century,* ed. d'Haenens and Saeys, 237.

6. Emery, "Five European Broadcasting Systems"; Browne, *Electronic Media and Industrialized Nations,* 160–62; Kees van der Haak and Leo van Snippenburg, "The Netherlands," in *Western Broadcasting at the Dawn of the 21st Century,* 209–11.

7. Paulu, *Radio and Television Broadcasting on the European Continent,* 85–86; Mario Hirsch, "Luxembourg," in *Electronic Media and Politics in Western Europe,* 191–94; Frédéric Antoine, "Luxembourg," in *Western Broadcasting at the Dawn of the 21st Century,* 193–95.

8. Coase, *British Broadcasting,* 101–53; Street, *A Concise History of British Radio,* 41–56, 87–104.

9. On the international division of the radio spectrum among the many parties and modes of transmission seeking to utilize it, see Paulu, *Radio and Television Broadcasting on the European Continent,* 11–15.

10. Coase, *British Broadcasting,* 110–16; Paulu, *Radio and Television Broadcasting on the European Continent,* 9–15.

11. Fisher, *Something in the Air,* 12.

12. Ibid., 1–28.

13. On the first and most contentious ban, see "J. Petrillo Issues Ultimatum: Will Shut Down on All Waxing after August 1: Battle Is On," *The Billboard,* July 4, 1942, 20; Gladys Chasins, "Record Ban Grows Tighter: Vocalists Agree to Stop Recording until

AFM Lifts Ban; Musicraft Deal Nixed," *The Billboard,* July 3, 1943, 23; "Ban Background and Effects," *The Billboard 1944 Music Year Book,* 1944, 145–47; "Chronological Chart of Events in the A.F.M. Ban," *The Billboard,* November 18, 1944, 13.

14. Fisher, *Something in the Air,* 1–28; Partridge, "Rock and the BBC" (the quotation is from 14).

15. Ray Coleman, "The Pop Power of 208," *Melody Maker,* May 2, 1964, 8–9; Don Wedge, "Luxembourg Going to Pirates' Format," *Billboard,* September 10, 1966, 1, 26; Street, *A Concise History of British Radio,* 91–92.

16. "Live at the BBC (The Beatles Album)," http://en.wikipedia.org/wiki/Live_at _the_BBC_(The_Beatles_album).

17. Leonard, *From International Waters,* 14–16 (the quotation is from 15).

18. Coase, *British Broadcasting,* 109.

19. Paulu, *Radio and Television Broadcasting on the European Continent,* 23, 120.

20. Andrew Rosenthal, "Reagan Extends Territorial Waters to 12 Miles," *New York Times,* December 29, 1988.

21. Leonard, *From International Waters,* 9–12.

22. Woodworth, "Hackers, Users, and Suits."

23. Gustafsson, "Sweden," in *Electronic Media and Politics in Western Europe,* 279.

24. Fisher, *Something in the Air,* 25–28.

25. Paulu, *Radio and Television Broadcasting on the European Continent,* 22–23.

26. On these developments in Scandinavia, see Leonard, *From International Waters,* 19–40, 96–97, 125, 195–96; Gustafsson, "Sweden," in *Electronic Media and Politics in Western Europe,* 279; Poulsen and Søndergaard, "Denmark," in *Western Broadcasting at the Dawn of the 21st Century,* 235–38.

27. On the willingness of record companies to supply disks to Radio Veronica, see "Dutch Diskeries Fall Overboard over 'Pirate,'" *Billboard,* July 17, 1965, 22. More generally, on events in the Netherlands, see van der Haak and van Snippenburg, "The Netherlands," in *Western Broadcasting at the Dawn of the 21st Century,* 224–26; Leonard, *From International Waters,* 41–47, 97, 194, 197–216, 241–84, 315–16, 323–76, 405–50, 461–94, 532–37, including details of expansion of Dutch-based offshore broadcasting into Belgium in the 1970s and 1980s; James Stappers, Frank Olderaan, and Pieter de Wit, "The Netherlands: Emergence of a New Medium," in *The People's Voice,* ed. Jankowski et al., 91.

28. In *Death of a Pirate,* Adrian Johns confirms my reason for including a chapter on pirate radio in the present book, namely, that this story bears considerably upon current-day battles over piracy. Johns's main concerns are political and social, rather than musical. He argues that the 1966 murder of Calvert, the head of Radio City, was the pivotal event in a near-century-long set of developments in which notions of liberty, freedom of speech, and engaged citizenship challenged centralized public service institutions in European broadcasting, particularly in the United Kingdom.

29. On events in the UK, see "BBC Needle Time Upped to [*sic:* from] 28 Hrs. a

Week to Compete with Pirates," *Variety*, July 1, 1964, 43; "Mystery of Those Pirate Pop Discs," *Melody Maker*, March 6, 1965, 12, including Mike Stone's quotation on the supply of phonograph records; Chris Hutchins, "Britain Plans Action vs. Pirates through Licensing Requirement," *Billboard*, December 25, 1965, 26, 28; "Scuttling of Pirates Not on Horizon," *Billboard*, May 14, 1966, 4, 24; Partridge, "Rock and the BBC" (Partridge's quotation on talking parrots is from 14); Peter Jones, "Pirate Ship 'Caroline' to Return Off U.K. on April 19 with 50 KW.," *Billboard*, March 7, 1981, 26, 69; "Radio Caroline Sails Back on Air," *Melody Maker*, September 3, 1983, 4; P. Strange, "Pirates of the Airwaves," *Melody Maker*, December 24, 1983, 46–47, 52; Chapman, *Selling the Sixties*; Leonard, *From International Waters*, 51–95, 103–94, 250–84, 315–76, 387–450, 461–504 (the quotation on Radio 390 is from 111); Jim Parkes, "The Laser Story."

30. Kees Brants, Martine Huizenga, and Denis McQuail, "The Netherlands," in *Electronic Media and Politics in Western Europe*, 202–7 (the quotation is from 207).

31. Richard Barbrook, "Melodies or Rhythms? The Competition for the Greater London FM Radio Licence"; Dave Jennings, "Stone Free," *Melody Maker*, September 1, 1990, 13; Peter Gray and Peter Lewis, "Great Britain: Community Broadcasting Revisited," in *The People's Voice*, ed. Jankowski et al., 156–69.

32. For an illustration of the game, see Leonard, *From International Waters*, 337.

CHAPTER 6

1. An example of significant non-American record bootlegging derived from an American wartime recording project, V-disks. The Special Services Division of the U.S. Armed Services established the V-disk label to distribute popular songs to the forces overseas. This nonprofit program emerged in the midst of a recording ban organized by the American Federation of Musicians, who were watching their opportunities for live performances increasingly being supplanted by the utilization of recordings. Consequently this exception to the ban, for the sake of entertaining Allied soldiers, sailors, and marines, was made with the express provision that recordings on V-disks would not be issued commercially and that the master recordings would eventually be destroyed. Of course, a situation developed that was somewhat akin to that of file-sharing in our own digital era: as soon as thousands of copies were put into circulation internationally, the cat was out of the bag. The prospect of subsequently suppressing all existing copies was not a viable idea. Owing to the nature of the original agreement, there was not a sanctioned program of reissues of V-disks, but unauthorized reissues of jazz and popular music on V-disks began to circulate in the early 1950s. In later decades ambitious programs were undertaken nonetheless, mainly in Europe, where the danger of prosecution by the American song owners was greatly reduced, and in Japan, where it was nonexistent. See "Disk-Pirating Spreads Abroad," *Variety*, November 28, 1951, 43, 48; Sears, *V-disks: A History and Discography*; Howard Rye, "V-disk," *The New Grove Dictionary of Jazz*, 2.

For reports on global phonograph-record piracy in the 1960s, see, for example,

"Disk Piracy Increasing in Far East; Formosa Counterfeiters Hit Hong Kong," *Variety,* August 9, 1961, 45; "Far East Disk Pirates Make U.S. Music Biz Walk Plank; WB's Weiss," *Variety,* September 26, 1962, 53; Luis Ma, "End of Pirate Decade," *Billboard,* January 5, 1963, 39 (the Philippines); "Castro Pirating U.S. Disks to Aid Ailing Economy," *Variety,* January 16, 1963, 1, 84 (Cuba); "Italo Labels Launch Drive vs. Rampant Piracy," *Variety,* January 1, 1969, 39 (Italy); "Lebanon Plagued by Pirates—Dealers Offer Copy Service," *Billboard,* May 9, 1970, 85.

2. Gordon Mumma, "Recording," *The New Grove Dictionary of Jazz,* 1.

3. The slang term "lacquer-legging" appears in "'Happiness' Disk Bootlegging Cues Appeal to FBI," *Variety,* August 4, 1948, 35; for "disklegging," see below, note 6.

4. The present discussion of copyright and recordings relies heavily upon Sparkman, "Tape Pirates"; Sparkman reproduces the record executive's quotation from *Newsweek,* October 5, 1970, 71, on 106.

5. "Many Firms Rent in Midtown Area," *New York Times,* April 17, 1935; Obituary, *New York Times,* May 6, 1953; "About HFA," http://www.harryfox.com/public/HFA Home.jsp.

6. "Diskleggers' $20,000,000 Biz," *Variety,* October 12, 1960, 57, 60; Art Talmadge, "Talmadge Points to ARMADA's Results in War against Counterfeit Racketeers," *Billboard Music Week,* June 26, 1961, 6; "2 Trade Assns. Pledge Full Support to Fox-Abeles' Drive vs. Disklegging," *Variety,* October 31, 1962, 41, 44.

7. "'Hit' Disks Hike via Black Market," *Variety,* February 20, 1946, 42.

8. "Indie Cos.' 'Silent' Partners," *Variety,* December 3, 1947, 39.

9. "Major Diskers Crack Down on Coast Bootlegging of Hit Recordings," *Variety,* April 7, 1948, 42; ; "L.A. Cracks Down," *Variety,* August 10, 1948, 37.

10. "Possible 350,000,000 Pressed in 1946 to Put Biz Near Top of Amus. Industry," *Variety,* January 8, 1947, 218; "Disk Sales Hit $230,520,000 in '59 for Manufacturers; 16½% over '58," *Variety,* May 25, 1960, 56.

11. "D.C. Bill Would Make Bootlegging Disks a Crime," *Variety,* August 10, 1948, 37, 42.

12. "Disk Bootleggers Are Waxing Fat on Stolen Goods," *Down Beat* 17 (June 16, 1950): 10; "RCA Gangs Up on 'Bootleggers,'" *Variety,* July 5, 1950, 23; "RCA Acts to Halt Bootleg Sale of Disks," *Down Beat* 17 (August 11, 1950): 1.

13. "Disk Pirates Now Dare Service DJ's," *The Billboard,* December 8, 1951, 1, 18.

14. "Big Push vs. Disk Bootleggers: N.Y. Co. Target of the Industry," *Variety,* November 21, 1951, 39; "Record Piracy Charged in Suit," *New York Times,* January 31, 1952; "Columbia Files Suit against 'Jolly Roger': Louis Armstrong Co-Plaintiff in Action; Fox-Abeles and Disk Ass'n May Also Act," *The Billboard,* February 9, 1952, 21, 50; "Injunction on Records: Columbia and Armstrong Win Suit against Paradox Industries," *New York Times,* February 10, 1952, 41; "Disk Pirates Scuttling Operations in Wake of Columbia Crackdown," *Variety,* February 20, 1952; "Nothing 'Jolly' in Disk Piracy, 4 Music Pubs Sue," *Variety,* April 16, 1952, 47; "Case Bolsters Pubs vs. Sharp Diskeries,"

*The Billboard*, June 14, 1952, 44, 71; "Pubs Win Legal Precedent vs. Pirates with 5G Award on $276 Royalty Claim," *Variety*, June 11, 1952, 39, 41; see also Johns, *Piracy*, 431–41. Devoted to music, Julian T. Abeles, "could not play or read a note but had a phenomenal memory for tunes": obituary, *New York Times*, March 7, 1973.

15. The four ten-inch LPs comprising *The Louis Armstrong Story* first appear, listed individually rather than as a package, in W. Schwann, *Long Playing Record Catalog* 3, no. 5 (May 1951): 61: *Louis Armstrong and His Hot Five*, ML-54383: *Louis Armstrong and His Hot Seven*, ML-54384; *Louis Armstrong and Earl Hines*, ML-54385; *Louis Armstrong Favorites*, ML-54386.

16. Joe Martin, "Piracy: 'Disklegger' Is Plague to Record Mfrs.," *The Billboard*, September 1, 1951, 1, 11 (the quotation is from 11).

17. "Col Records Warns. N.Y. Dealers on Peddling of Counterfeit Disks," *Variety*, January 9, 1952, 45.

18. "Points on Piracy," *Variety*, February 12, 1958, 55.

19. "Chi Makes Disk Pirates Walk Plank, Nabbing Pair for Phony Pressings," *Variety*, February 12, 1958, 55; Bernie Asbell, "Lid Off Chi Disk Bootleg Operation; Juke Ops Muscled," *The Billboard*, February 17, 1958, 1, 18, 84, 87; "Disk Piracy & Chi Mobsters," *Variety*, February 19, 1958, 43, 48; Bernie Asbell, "Chi Disk Racket Explosions May Be Traced to One Fuse," *The Billboard*, February 24, 1958, 3, 63.

20. Bernie Asbell, "Negligence Charged to Disk Industry in Piracy Issue: Review of Hilger Bootleg Case Amazes Racket Investigators," *The Billboard*, March 2, 1959, 1, 12 (the quotation is from 1).

21. "Bootlegging Singles Burgeon; N.Y. Area Latest Sufferer," *The Billboard*, November 9, 1959, 3, 14 (the quotation is from 14). For additional general accounts during this period, see (all in *The Billboard*) Mildred Hall, "Solons Told Disk Piracy Rampant: Abeles Charges Third of Total Output Bootlegged; Asks Law Change Relief," June 15, 1959, 3, 9; Bob Rolontz, "Disk Counterfeiting Major Thorn in Industry Side," December 14, 1959, 3, 140; Ren Grevatt, "Bootleg Platters Flood New York," May 30, 1960, 2, 44; "Anti-Disk Bootleg Battle Lines Dig In," June 27, 1960, 2; June Bundy, "Am-Par Distribs Hear Plans for War on Bootleggers," June 27, 1960, 3, 18.

22. Ren Grevatt, "Disk Bootlegging, Thievery Current Industry Topics," *The Billboard*, May 23, 1960, 1, 9 (the quotation is from 9).

23. "2 Dealers Charged in Disk Bootlegging," *New York Times*, June 11, 1960.

24. "8 Suspects Nabbed in Bootleg Raids," *The Billboard*, October 10, 1960, 3, 22; "Diskleggers' $20,000,000 Biz," *Variety*, October 12, 1960, 57, 60.

25. John Houser, "Upcoming Disk Forgery Trial in L.A. May Revise Distrib, Mfg. Patterns," *Variety*, October 26, 1960, 55, 57; "Indict Seven on Disk Bootlegging Charges," *The Billboard*, November 7, 1960, 4, 24; "Bootleg Disk Front Breaks Wide Open in Gotham, East," *Billboard Music Week*, May 8, 1961, 2, 169; "Disk Counterfeiters Throw in Sponge with No-Defense Plea in Jersey Court," *Variety*, May 17, 1961, 61; "Three Disk

Executives Sentenced in Plot," *New York Times*, June 3, 1961; "Diskleggers Get Fines, Probation from L.A. Court," *Variety*, December 13, 1961, 47.

26. "Extend Probe of Disk Bootleg Ring to 'Entertainment Field,'" *The Billboard*, December 12, 1960, 3, 14. For further arrests and prosecutions along these lines, see "Publishers Hem in Disk Pirates by Legal Clamp on Pressing Plants," *Variety*, July 1, 1959, 47, 50; "U.S. Court of Appeals Affirms Decision Widening Liability for Illegal Platters," *Variety*, December 21, 1960, 37, 44; "Bootleg Disk Front Breaks Wide Open in Gotham, East," *Billboard*, May 8, 1961, 2, 169; "Step Up War vs. Bogus Diskers," *Variety*, May 10, 1961, 75–76.

27. "N.Y. Legislature Gets Bill Making Disk-Pirating a Criminal Offense," *Variety*, February 27, 1952, 39; "Outlawing of Record Piracy Proposed in N.Y. State Bill," *The Billboard*, March 1, 1952, 1, 16; "Efforts to Wipe Out Diskleggers Snagged as Dewey Nixes Bennett Bill," *Variety*, April 23, 1952, 35.

28. "Anti-Piracy Bill Opposed: Diskery Charges Proposed Act Ignores Culture Side," *The Billboard*, February 28, 1953, 16, 20. For further details of classical-music bootlegging, see Johns, *Piracy*, 441–43.

29. "Pubs Challenge 'Miracle' Decision in War on Pirates," *Variety*, June 25, 1952, 41.

30. "Diskers Crack Down on Bootleggers; Piracy Charges to Be Filed Shortly," *Variety*, March 2, 1955, 49; "Diskeries Look for Piracy Bill Passage," *The Billboard*, April 2, 1955, 13.

31. "Celler's Proposed New Federal Act (Stiff Fine and Jail) Designed to Curb Disklegging Mfrs. & Distribs.," *Variety*, April 19, 1961, 57, 60; "Music Industry Sees 'Clear Sailing' for Celler Bill to Curb Disklegging," *Variety*, May 3, 1961, 65, 69; "House Passes Copyright Extension; Also Stiffer Disklegging Measure," *Variety*, June 20, 1962, 1, 50; "RIAA Beef to Senate Appropriations Committee Hits Taiwan Disk Pirates," *Variety*, November 27, 1963, 45.

32. "Disk Retailers May Come under Fire, for 1st Time, in Miller Piracy Claim," *Variety*, April 7, 1954, 44; "Unique Legal Move by Miller Estate vs. Disk Retailers to Scuttle Pirates," *Variety*, May 26, 1954, 67, 74; "Disk Pirates Again Roaming Market; Miller, Goodman Platters Plundered," *Variety*, January 26, 1955, 43; "Joe Krug's Arrest Marks Precedent in Drive vs. Piracy by Major Pubs," *Variety*, March 9, 1955, 51, 56; "Courts Nix Attempt to Pin Piracy Rap on Retailers in Suit vs. Sam Goody," *Variety*, March 21, 1956, 43–44; Is Horowitz, "Dealer Held Not Liable in Sale of Pirated Recordings: Decision in Miller-AFN Case Probes Flaws in Copyright Laws," *The Billboard*, March 24, 1956, 17, 20; "Harry Fox Suits Would Make Pressing Plants Liable in Disk Piracy Actions," *Variety*, May 29, 1957, 51, 60; "Distribs-Dealers Just as Liable as Record Mfrs. on Pirated Tunes, U.S. Appeals Ct. Rules in Reversal," *Variety*, October 9, 1957, 49, 55; "Disk Pirates Walk Plank: Dealers Want Pub-Disk Talks," *Variety*, October 9, 1957, 49; "High Court Bars Appeal by Goody," *New York Times*, March 4, 1958; "Supreme Ct.

Okay of 'Goody Decision' Sparking Broad Action vs. Piracy (Dealers and Distributors of Bootleg Disks Equally Liable for Damages)," *Variety*, March 5, 1958, 57.

33. "Hounds Bay on Disk Bootleggers' Trail," *The Billboard*, June 20, 1960, 4, 52.

34. "Harry Fox & J. T. Abeles Blow Whistle for N.J. Police Raid on Disk Pirates," *Variety*, October 5, 1960, 57, 63.

35. "Retailers Sued in Goody Case Sequel: Warner Group Charges Big Chains with Selling Disks by Unlicensed Makers," *The Billboard*, March 24, 1958, 3, 35; "15 Pubberies Sue H. L. Green Stores as 'Disk Mfr.'; Ask 2¢ Cut and Damages," *Variety*, May 28, 1958, 57; Ren Grevatt, "Disk Bootlegging, Thievery Current Industry Topics," *The Billboard*, May 23, 1960, 1, 9; "Retailers of Bootleg Disks Share Rap with Mfr. under N.Y. Ct.'s Precedental Decision; See Important Piracy Curb," *Variety*, August 8, 1962, 43–44; "Precedental Decision Holds Retailers also Liable in 'Bootleg' Disk Sales," *Variety*, April 24, 1963, 51, 56.

36. Shapiro, Bernstein & Co., Inc., et. al, v. H. L. Green Company, Inc., and Jalen Amusement Company, Inc., http://cases.justia.com/us-court-of-appeals/F2/316/304/187450/.

CHAPTER 7

1. "FBI Smashes Major Bootleg Ring in New York; RIAA Blows Whistle," *Variety*, December 16, 1970, 51; "FBI Raid Nets Man, 'Counterfeit' Set-Up," *Billboard*, December 19, 1970, 3; "Booty Worth More than $8-Mil Recovered from N.Y.-Area Pirates," *Variety*, March 26, 1980, 87.

2. "Modern Tape in Cassette Set-Up," *Billboard*, March 2, 1968, 45; Howard Rye, "Modern," *The New Grove Dictionary of Jazz*, 2.

3. John Sippel, "Police & FBI Raid Firm," *Billboard*, February 3, 1973, 3, 34 (the quotation is from 34).

4. "Labels Win Lengthy Court Battle with Conviction of Tape Pirates," *Variety*, December 23, 1981, 61.

5. "RIAA Documents Scope of 1982–1983 Counterfeit Fight," *Variety*, November 16, 1983, 65, 68.

6. Henry Schipper, "Disk Biz Hit Record Sales in '87; $5-Bil Mark Passed; CDs Soared," *Variety*, May 4, 1988, 547.

7. Begun, *Magnetic Recording*; chapter 1 of this book, a historical survey of magnetic recording, is posted at http://history.sandiego.edu/GEN/recording/begun1.html. See also "The History of Magnetic Recording," http://www.bbc.co.uk/dna/h2g2/A3224936; Gordon Mumma, "Recording," *The New Grove Dictionary of Jazz*, 1.

8. "Armour's Wire Recorder Seen Blow to Disc Cos. and Headache to Surveyors," *Variety*, October 11, 1944, 35.

9. "Possible 350,000,000 Pressed in 1946 to Put Biz Near Top of Amus. Industry," *Variety*, January 8, 1947, 218.

10. "Disk Sales Hit $230,520,000 in '59 for Manufacturers; 16 1/2% over '58," *Variety*, May 25, 1960, 56.

11. "Vintage Audio History," http://www.videointerchange.com/audio_history.htm.

12. "The History of Magnetic Recording"; Mumma, "Recording." For a detailed article on a later manifestation of the production of magnetic tapes, see Bert Whyte, "Behind the Scenes," *Audio* 57 (July 1973): 10, 12, 14.

13. Tschmuck, *Creativity and Innovation in the Music Industry*, 92–93; A. L. Seligson, "Radio Taping, Illegal but Fun," *New York Times*, June 3, 1962; Sherwin D. Smith, "All Wound Up in Tape," *New York Times*, April 12, 1964.

14. Harold S. Schonberg, "R.C.A. Introduces a Tape Cartridge: Stereophonic Unit Ending Need for Threading Works with Ease of LP Disk," *New York Times*, June 2, 1958; Herbert Reid, "Stereo's Impact on Tape," *New York Times*, November 16, 1958; R. S. Lanier, "Hi-Fi: The Battle of the Stereo Tapes," *New York Times*, July 5, 1959; Schonberg, "Hi-Fi: Cartridge," *New York Times*, October 4, 1959; "RCA Tape Cartridge," http://en.wikipedia.org/wiki/RCA_tape_cartridge; "Vintage Audio History."

15. "Cartridge," http://en.wikipedia.org/wiki/Cartridge; "Stereo 8," http://en.wikipedia.org/wiki/Stereo_8.

16. "Fidelipac," http://en.wikipedia.org/wiki/Fidelipac; "Vintage Audio History."

17. "Cartridge"; "Stereo 8"; "Stereo-Pak," http://en.wikipedia.org/wiki/Stereo-Pak. For some details of the manufacturing process, see Eliot Tiegel, "Streamlining Automation of CARtridge Assembly Studied," *Billboard*, June 14, 1969, 14.

18. Gene Smith, "Booming Tape-Cartridge Industry Faces Problems," *New York Times*, July 24, 1966.

19. "A Stereo System Devised for Cars," *New York Times*, April 16, 1965.

20. Jan Syrjala, "A Clear Road Ahead for Car Tape," *New York Times*, March 6, 1966; "Stereo 8"; "Vintage Audio History."

21. Syrjala, "Automobile Tapes: Going into High," *New York Times*, November 28, 1965; Marshall E. Newton, "New Stereo Cartridges Turn an Auto into Philharmonic Hall," *New York Times*, April 10, 1966; George Rood, "Tape Recorders Take to the Road," *New York Times*, April 11, 1966; "Cadillac in Gear, Too," *Billboard*, May 18, 1968, 55; "Stereo 8."

22. Syrjala, "A Clear Road Ahead for Car Tape."

23. "AM Debuts Blank Line," *Billboard*, June 13, 1970, 12.

24. "Stereo 8"; "Vintage Audio History."

25. Smith, "Booming Tape-Cartridge Industry Faces Problems."

26. "Compact Cassette," http://en.wikipedia.org/wiki/Compact_Cassette (including extensive bibliography); "Vintage Audio History."

27. "Toshiba Striving for More Car Player Units," *Billboard*, October 30, 1971, 29.

28. "A Case vs. Pirates," *Billboard*, December 14, 1968, 18; Hank Fox, "Fox Acts vs. Case Mfrs.," *Billboard*, December 21, 1968, 1, 10.

29. I have not found an illustration of cartridge or cassette duplication. For photographs of reel-to-reel tape recorders from this same period, taken at the Ampex plants in Chicago and Hackensack, New Jersey, both showing lines of slaves linked to a master, see Ed Zdobinski, "Tape Duplication at Ampex," *Audio* 49 (December 1965): 22; Ivan Berger, "The New Trend in Hi-Fi Is No Trend at All," *New York Times*, September 25, 1966.

30. Sippel, "Police & FBI Raid Firm."

31. "Col. Sues 2 Firms as Illegal Duplicators," *Billboard*, June 18, 1966, 8.

32. "Tape Duplications: A Hot New Process?" *High Fidelity and Musical America* 21 (July 1971): 32, 34 (the quotation is from 34).

33. Paul Ackerman, "Fox Agency Presses Piracy War in Suit," *Billboard*, November 14, 1970, 1, 16, 62; "Fox Agency Sues Top Tape Piracy Operation in U.S.; Has Own Catalog," *Variety*, December 23, 1970, 41, 44.

34. For example, as testimony to the proliferation of mass actions against tape piracy in the years 1969 to 1970, see (in *Billboard* unless indicated otherwise) "13 Pubs Sue Duping Firms on W. Coast," March 2, 1968, 45; "Cap Wins More Suits in Pirate Crackdown," March 7, 1970, 18; Paul Ackerman, "Fox Names 51 in Giant Piracy Suit on Coast," March 21, 1970, 1, 78; "Bootlegging Defendants in Fox's Coast Action Listed," March 21, 1970, 78; Fred Kirby, "Fox Springs Piracy Suit in New York; Dealer Is Joined," May 9, 1970, 1, 6; "CBS Charges 49 on Coast with Piracy," May 9, 1970, 3–4; Eliot Teigel, "Top Court Upholds Cap in Pirate Suit; Landmark Seen," July 4, 1970, 1, 8; "Capitol, RCA Enjoin Illegal Tapers as NARM Prepares Bootleg Symposium," *Variety*, August 26, 1970, 41.

35. Sparkman, "Tape Pirates," 109–19; "13 Pubs Sue Duping Firms on W. Coast"; "Courts Scuttle Pirates on 2 Coasts; A&M to Push Crackdown on Tapes," *Variety*, April 24, 1968, 57; "Tape Pirates Get Scuttled," *Billboard*, May 18, 1968, 1, 55.

36. Bruce Weber, "15 Pubs Slap Pirate Suit on 2 Coast Firms," *Billboard*, January 4, 1969, 1, 14; Eliot Teigel, "Top Court Upholds Cap in Pirate Suit; Landmark Seen," *Billboard*, July 4, 1970, 1, 8; Towe, "Record Piracy" (the quotation is from 259).

37. Kirby, "Fox Springs Piracy Suit in New York; Dealer Is Joined." For an account of party-tape manufacturing in Tennessee, see "Injunctions Seen Routing Piracy in Nashville," *Billboard*, December 26, 1970, 37.

38. Heylin, *Bootleg*, 236–42, 262; Johns, *Piracy*, 444–47.

39. Towe, "Record Piracy," 262–65.

40. "N.Y. Disk Piracy Bills Stir Industry," *Variety*, March 30, 1966, 1, 94; Sparkman, "Tape Pirates," 119–23 (the quotation is on 119); Towe, "Record Piracy," 259–60.

41. "Courts Scuttle Pirates on 2 Coasts."

42. "Three Fined $1,400 in 1st California Piracy Case," *Billboard*, July 10, 1971, 10; "Convict 3 Individual Defendants on Coast Tape Piracy Charges," *Variety*, July 14, 1971, 46; "2nd Piracy Guilty Verdict," *Billboard*, December 11, 1971, 3, 59; "Supreme Court Upholds State Laws vs. Piracy," *Variety*, June 20, 1973, 49; "Diskers Win Supreme Court

Battle but War vs. Pirates Still Not Over," *Variety*, June 27, 1973, 63; M. Hall, "5–4 Supreme Court OK's State Piracy Laws," *Billboard*, June 30, 1973, 1, 70.

43. "Disk, Tape Pirates Find Bonanza on Georgia Bways," *Variety*, May 23, 1973, 61.

44. Edwin McDowell, "Record Pirates: Industry Sings the Blues," *New York Times*, June 30, 1978. For examples of investigations into violations of new state copyright laws, see "8 Arrested in 1st Texas Tape Law Crackdown," *Billboard*, October 30, 1971, 29; "Tennessee in Pirate Raids," *Billboard*, November 6, 1971, 27; "First Fed. Indictment on Piracy Entered against Outfit in New Mex.," *Variety*, May 2, 1973, 57; "Tennessee Cops Nab Pirate in C&W Groove," *Variety*, May 23, 1973, 61; John Rockwell, "Pirates Now a Big Thorn Hurting Record Industry," *New York Times*, December 7, 1978.

45. "Pact Will Prohibit Piracy of Records," *New York Times*, October 29, 1971; "First Fed. Indictment on Piracy Entered against Outfit in New Mex"; Sparkman, "Tape Pirates," 122–23; Robert Sobel, "Justice Orders FBI Arrest of Pirates of Pre-1972 Titles," *Billboard*, March 8, 1975, 1, 10; Towe, "Record Piracy," 259–62; McDowell: "Record Pirates."

46. Towe, "Record Piracy," 246–58 (the quotations are, respectively, from 255, 256, and 257); "Federal Judge Fines Unlicensed Duplicator $1 per Infringement; Spies Must Pay $176,592 to 37," *Billboard*, February 10, 1973, 3, 74.

47. Towe, "Record Piracy," 260–62 (the quotations are from 260 and 261, respectively)

48. "Drive Continues vs. Tape Pirates," *Variety*, June 13, 1973, 45.

49. Is Horowitz and Maurie Orodenker, "U.S. Appeals Court Slaps Reversal on Tape Pirates," *Billboard*, January 11, 1975, 1, 6, 42 (the quotation from Judge Weis in on 6).

50. "Diskeries Win Round in $75,000,000 Piracy Suit; Indict Jersey Repeater," *Variety*, October 1, 1975, 107.

51. "Atlantic, A&M, WB & Col Records File Piracy Suits vs. 52 Tape, Disk Outlets," *Variety*, November 17, 1971, 77.

52. Sippel, "Police & FBI Raid Firm."

53. "Tape Pirates Make Copyright Bid: Doctor Original Hits into 'New Works,'" *Variety*, June 20, 1973, 49; Sippel, "Novel Marketing for $2.49 Tapes," *Billboard*, January 12, 1974, 1, 6; Sippel, "Sellers' Antipiracy Involvement Grows," *Billboard*, February 9, 1974, 1, 15 ; Sippel, "Govt. Wins Duplicator Case 1st Round against Taxe," *Billboard*, June 15, 1974, 3, 14; Sippel, "Jury Votes Taxe Guilty of Piracy," *Billboard*, August 3, 1974, 1, 10; Sippel, "Taxe Named in 2 Suits," *Billboard*, August 24, 1974, 3; "Taxe, 3 Others Land Jail Terms," *Billboard*, August 24, 1974, 3, 6.

54. "9 Diskeries Awarded over $4-Mil in Heilman, E-C Tape Piracy Case," *Variety*, January 2, 1980, 41, 43; "$4-Mil Judgment against Heilman to Bring Appeal," *Billboard*, January 5, 1980, 3, 78; "Ruling in E-C Tape, Heilman Piracy Suit Increases $ Award," *Variety*, March 26, 1980, 83; "High Court Denies Heilman's Petition for Review of Case," *Variety*, July 2, 1980, 53; "Wisconsin Appeals Bench Upholds $6.7-Mil Judgment vs. Heilman," *Variety*, November 4, 1981, 65, 74.

55. "Fla. Court Upholds Pirate's Conviction; Rule Sets Precedent," *Variety*, December 3, 1980, 91; "Stiffest Sentence Ever for Record Piracy Meted Out," *Variety*, April 29, 1981, 1, 98; "Pirates to Prison in 'Turntable' Case," *Billboard*, May 9, 1981, 6, 67.

56. Robert D. McFadden, "U.S. Indicts Jerseyan and His Concern in the Pirating of Hit Recordings Worth Millions," *New York Times*, January 28, 1979; John Sippel, "Polygram Distribution Discovery: Huge Haul of Illicit LPs in Goody Return," *Billboard*, February 9, 1980, 1, 55; "Sam Goody Prez, V.P. Indicted in Corruption Scam," *Variety*, March 5, 1980, 1, 73; Pamela G. Hollie, "Piracy Costly Plague in Record Industry," *New York Times*, March 10, 1980; Richard M. Nusser, "Sam Goody Attorneys Slap RIAA," *Billboard*, May 3, 1980, 1, 62; Fred Kirby, "Tucker, Goody Court Dates Slated; Retailer to See RIAA Document," *Variety*, July 30, 1980, 71, 73; "Verner Testifies at Tucker Trial; Says He Paid $100,000 for LPs," *Variety*, September 3, 1980, 69; Kirby, "Goody Trial Put Off Indefinitely; RIAA in Contempt for Failing to Surrender Its Field Reports," *Variety*, September 3, 1980, 65, 69; Kirby, "N.Y. Pirate's Fate in Jury's Hands; Recantation Cited by Defense," *Variety*, September 10, 1980, 73, 77; Nusser, "Convicted Buccaneer; Will Tucker, Who Faces 16 Jail Years, Cooperate Now?" *Billboard*, September 20, 1980, 3, 78; Kirby, "Tucker Jail-Bound for 5 Years, Fined 25G in Fed Piracy Case," *Variety*, October 1, 1980, 103, 105; "Judge Given Confidential RIAA Papers," *Billboard*, December 6, 1980, 6, 48; Kirby, "Judge Thinks Most of Material from RIAA Can Go to Defense Attorneys in Sam Goody Case," *Variety*, December 10, 1980, 95, 100; Nusser, "Goody Trial Nears: Court Upholds RIAA," *Billboard*, December 27, 1980, 4; Joseph P. Fried, "Sam Goody Company Accused as 'Pirate,'" *New York Times*, March 1, 1981; Joseph B. Treaster, "Sam Goody Sister Company Subpoenaed in Tape Inquiry," *New York Times*, March 3, 1981; Fried, "Judge Told Goody Co. Had Knowingly Dealt in Counterfeit Tapes; Witnesses' Motives Assailed," *New York Times*, March 6, 1981; "One Acquittal Ordered at Goody Music Trial over Lack of Evidence," *New York Times*, March 31, 1981; Fried, "Goody Company and an Executive Convicted in Bogus Tape Scheme," *New York Times*, April 10, 1981; Treaster, "F.B.I. Getting New Help from Abscam Informer," *New York Times*, July 31, 1981; Fried, "Prosecution in Goody Case Denies Misconduct," *New York Times*, October 25, 1981; "1981 Dismissal of Goody Case Survives Appeal," *New York Times*, March 16, 1982; Ralph Blumenthal, "Goody Chain and Ex-Official Are Sentenced in Tapes Case," *New York Times*, November 6, 1982; "Sentence Is Reduced in Goody Tapes Case," *New York Times*, April 7, 1983.

57. For example, see Sam Sutherland, "FBI Nabs 10 in Tape Sweep," *Billboard*, October 23, 1982, 1, 78; L. Sacks, "Larceny Charged in Piracy Case; Indictment of N.Y. Manufacturer Called 'Significant,'" *Billboard*, February 19, 1983, 3, 63.

CHAPTER 8

1. Heylin, *Bootleg*, 42–49.

2. Michael Cuscuna, liner notes, *John Coltrane and Johnny Hartman* (Impulse! 40, 1995); for further details, see Kernfeld, "John Coltrane in Rudy van Gelder's Studio."

3. Heylin, *Bootleg*, 410.

4. See, for example, Grace Lichtenstein, "Tape 'Bootleggers' Still Active," *New York Times*, June 5, 1971; Edwin McDowell, "Record Pirates: Industry Sings the Blues," *New York Times*, June 30, 1978; Pamela G. Hollie, "Piracy Costly Plague in Record Industry," *New York Times*, March 10, 1980; Joseph B. Treaster, "Counterfeit Albums Seized in a Raid at L.I. Factory," *New York Times*, March 19, 1980.

5. Towe, in "Record Piracy," contrasts "record piracy" with "performance piracy," rather than using the term "album bootlegging" for the latter practice; see 245–46. Sparkman, in "Tape Piracy," analyzes legal difficulties of defining these terms; see 103–4.

6. Heylin, *Bootleg*, 59–65.

7. Ibid., 72–76; "Royal Albert Hall," http://en.wikipedia.org/wiki/Royal_Albert_Hall.

8. Heylin, *Bootleg*, 76–84.

9. Ibid., 86–88.

10. Ibid., 149–50.

11. Ibid., 151.

12. Ibid., 195–97.

13. Ibid., 130.

14. Ibid., 134–35, 179, 189–90.

15. Ibid., 163–77.

16. Ibid., 135–39.

17. Ibid., 181.

18. Ibid., 302–5.

CHAPTER 9

1. Lynette Holloway, "Arrests Illustrate a Growing Concern over Bootlegged Recordings," *New York Times*, December 2, 2002.

2. Bill Holland, "Long Island Bootleg Seizure Is Largest in RIAA History," *Billboard*, July 6, 1996, 100.

3. Holland, "RIAA Releases '95 Piracy Statistics," *Billboard*, March 23, 1996, 6, 95.

4. Gillespie, *Wired Shut*, 137–65, 168 (the quotation is from 6).

5. Ken Terry, "Diskeries '86 Dollar Volume Up, but Unit Shipments Decline Again," *Variety*, April 15, 1987, 209, 213; Henry Schipper, "Disk Biz Hit Record Sales in '87; $5-Bil Mark Passed; CDs Soared," *Variety*, May 4, 1988, 547; Irv Lichtman, "Music Shipments Hit New Mark," *Billboard*, March 18, 1989, 1, 82; Susan Nunziata, "'90 Label Tally: Units Up 7.3%, $ Jump 14.6%," *Billboard*, April 6, 1991, 1, 80; Chris Morris, "RIAA '92 Figures Show a Major Rebound for U.S. Music Business," *Billboard*, March 20, 1993, 6, 96; Don Jeffrey, "U.S. Music Business Jumps 20% to $12-Billion in 1994," *Billboard*, February 25, 1995, 1, 144; Don Jeffrey, "Multiple Formats Boost U.S.," *Billboard*, February 25, 1995, 1, 76; Holland, "U.S. Music Growth 'Modest' in '95 1st-Half RIAA Figures,"

*Billboard*, August 19, 1995, 3, 96; Holland, "RIAA Reports Flat '96; Teams with NARM in Industry Study," *Billboard*, February 22, 1997, 3, 101; Ed Christman, "Hit-Driven Album Sales Lead in '99 Report," *Billboard*, January 15, 2000, 5, 76; Tschmuck, *Creativity and Innovation in the Music Industry*, 149, 152, 168; "U.S. Industry Profile: Phonograph Records and Prerecorded Audio Tapes and Disks (SIC 3652)," http://www.answers.com/topic/phonograph-records-and-prerecorded-audio-tapes-and-disks.

6. "How the CD Was Developed," http://news.bbc.co.uk/2/hi/technology/6950933.stm; "Compact Disc," http://en.wikipedia.org/wiki/Compact_disc; "Compact Disc Manufacturing," http://en.wikipedia.org/wiki/Compact_disc_manufacturing.

7. Heylin, *Bootleg*, 340.

8. Ibid., 292–302.

9. J. Clark-Meads, "$2-Million in Bulgarian Pirate CDs Seized: Amsterdam Bust Adds to Plea for Better EU Control," *Billboard*, April 5, 1997, 6, 93.

10. Heylin, *Bootleg*, 295, 334–61.

11. "Everybody's," "Jazz Society (ii)," in *The New Grove Dictionary of Jazz*, 2.

12. These descriptions come from pamphlets in my personal collection: "Official Records and Associated Labels" (undated) and "Document Records Catalogue" (undated [circa 1999]).

13. Heylin, *Bootleg*, 266–76, 325–26, 344–47 (the quotations are from 326 and 347, respectively).

14. Holloway, "Arrests Illustrate a Growing Concern over Bootlegged Recordings."

15. Tschmuck, *Creativity and Innovation in the Music Industry*, 150–51.

16. "Tapes Are Seized in Florida," *Billboard*, January 29, 1972, 3.

17. Heylin, *Bootleg*, 409.

18. Pamela G. Hollie, "Piracy Costly Plague in Record Industry," *New York Times*, March 10, 1980.

19. Grace Lichtenstein, "Tape 'Bootleggers' Still Active," *New York Times*, June 5, 1971.

20. Morris Kaplan, "Smut and Pirated Tapes Seized in Brooklyn Raids," *New York Times*, December 12, 1972.

21. Edwin McDowell, "Record Pirates: Industry Sings the Blues," *New York Times*, June 30, 1978; John Rockwell, "Pirates Now a Big Thorn Hurting Record Industry," *New York Times*, December 7, 1978.

22. Hollie, "Piracy Costly Plague in Record Industry."

23. Joseph B. Treaster, "Counterfeit Albums Seized in a Raid at L.I. Factory," *New York Times*, March 19, 1980.

24. "RIAA Documents Scope of 1982–1983 Counterfeit Fight," *Variety*, November 16, 1983, 65, 68.

25. Henry Schipper, "Counterfeiting Arrests & Seizures Rose in '85, According to RIAA," *Variety*, February 19, 1986, 429.

26. Growth charts for the recording industry in the United States for the years 1945 through 2003 appear in Tschmuck, *Creativity and Innovation in the Music Industry*, respectively, on 91, 115, 136, 149, and 168. See also "Disk, Tape Sales Rose Some 10 Percent in 1972, to $1,924,000,000," *Variety*, May 16, 1973, 1, 117; "Disk Biz Hits $2.36-Bil High, Undiscounted," *Variety*, June 2, 1976, 2, 70; "U.S. Disk-Tape Sales Up 15% to List-Price Peak of $2.7-Bil; Cassettes in Sharp Comeback," *Variety*, May 18, 1977, 1, 125; "U.S Disks Up 28% to Record $3.5-Bil; Sharpest Sales Jump since '56," *Variety*, July 12, 1978, 55–56; "Disk-Tape Sales Top $4-Bil in U.S. Market," *Variety*, June 20, 1979, 2.

27. "Industry's 1980 Unit Shipments Decline 5%, Dollar Sales Steady; LP and Tape Unit Volume Rises," *Variety*, April 1, 1981, 71; "U.S. Diskery Biz 1981 Dollar Volume Showed No Growth," *Variety*, March 31, 1982, 94; Ken Terry, "Disk Biz Basking in Sales Glow," *Variety*, August 29, 1984, 1, 92; Terry, "U.S. Record Sales Still Upward Bound," *Variety*, April 10, 1985, 87; Hollie, "Piracy Costly Plague in Record Industry"; Tschmuck, *Creativity and Innovation in the Music Industry*, 135, 149–52.

28. Schipper, "RIAA Anti-Piracy Crackdown Hits Record 1987 Proportions," *Variety*, February 17, 1988, 169; Jean Rosenbluth, "RIAA Anti-Piracy Campaign Pays Off in 1st Half of '89," *Variety*, August 30–September 5, 1989, 90; Kevin Zimmerman, "Piracy War Continues in N.Y., U.K.," *Variety*, April 29, 1991, 105. For further industry statistics from this era, see above, note 5. For a consideration of these statistical questions in later years, see Susan Butler, "Piracy Losses: New Report on U.S. Economic Toll May Not Add Up," *Billboard*, September 8, 2007, 18. For speculations on the specific economic impact of album bootlegging and industry growth, see Marshall, *Bootlegging*, 132–39.

29. Mike Hennessey, "CD Burning the Chief Cause of a $3.3-Billion Downturn in World Record Sales Last Year," *Crescendo and Jazz Music* 39 (August–September 2002): 14–15.

CHAPTER 10

1. For a history of this era from the point of view of an informed insider sympathetic to unrestricted downloading, see Kot, *Ripped*.

2. Fred Goodman, "The Future Is Now: How the Internet Is Reshaping the Record Industry," *Rolling Stone*, no. 844–845 (July 6–20, 2000): 41–42, 45 (the quotation is from 42); Edna Gundersen, "Any Way You Spin It, the Music Biz Is in Trouble: Fans, Artists and Industry: Nobody's Rocking," *USA Today*, June 5, 2002. Along these same lines, see Jack Bishop, "Forum: Who Are the Pirates?"

3. Katz, *Capturing Sound*, 158–87. Writing about the potential of tape recorders in automobiles, George Rood had this to say in 1966: "They make possible the private selection of music and provide freedom from what [an unnamed spokesman for the industry] termed 'too many commercials, too much disc-jockey chatter, [and] static and dim-outs in poor reception areas.'" Rood, "Tape Recorders Take to the Road," *New York Times*, April 11, 1966.

4. Woodworth, "Hackers, Users, and Suits," 173. For a broad perspective on the issue of personal versus corporate control in the digital age, see Shapiro, *The Control Revolution*.

5. Katz, *Capturing Sound*, 166–67.

6. Ibid., 8–47.

7. Jonathan Sterne analyzes technical and psychoacoustic aspects of MP3 listening in "The mp3 as Cultural Artifact." The extent of audible loss of sound quality generated through this technology seems to be a matter of permanent dispute. Some audiophiles have argued that digital files are inherently inferior to a well-made analogue of sound as captured in the groove of a high-quality phonograph record. Some audiophiles have complained that when a CD audio files is compressed via Chiariglione's method, significant degradation occurs. Also, by comparison with home stereo equipment, many computer systems have speakers of only moderate quality that cannot bring out great distinction between CD audio quality and MP3 quality. Most people evidently do not care.

The contrast between tapes, which degrade in quality when dubbed from one copy to the next, and audio CDs, which reproduce a digital code exactly from one copy to the next, can apply to different categories of MP3 files. If one selects, for reasons of storage, the most compact type of MP3 files, the sound degrades to an extent that many listeners might find objectionable: the lower the sampling rate, the smaller the files, the lower the fidelity. Conversely, the higher the sampling rate, the more closely the fidelity of sound would approach to CD audio quality, but the larger and more unwieldy the resulting digital file.

8. For accounts of the development of MP3 files and Napster, see "Napster Closes 300,00 Music Accounts," *New York Times*, May 12, 2000; Alec Foege, "The Future of Digital Music," *Spin* 16 (September 2000): 164; Mann, "The Heavenly Jukebox"; Rob Sheffield, "The Most Dangerous Man in the Music Biz," *Rolling Stone*, no. 844–845 (July 6–20, 2000): 42, 45; "Call and Response: A Discussion about Napster"; Tim Race, "New Economy: Beyond File-Sharing Software, the Music Industry Faces Business Challenges That May Be Even More Daunting," *New York Times*, March 19, 2001; Matt Diehl, "The 50th Anniversary of Rock: The Hit Moments—Hit 1998: Napster's Free-for-All," *Rolling Stone*, no. 951 (June 24, 2004): 158; Woodworth, "Hackers, Users, and Suits," 161–84; Gillespie, *Wired Shut*, 40–50.

9. For an in-depth analysis of the lawsuit against Napster, see Douglas, "Copyright and Peer-to-Peer Music File Sharing."

10. Matt Richtel, "With Napster Down, Its Audience Fans Out," *New York Times*, July 20, 2001; Richard Abowitz, "Napster: The Next Generation—New Sites Offering Free Downloads Continue to Flourish on the Web," *Rolling Stone*, no. 876 (August 30, 2001): 29, 32; Gary Andrew Poole, "Music World Can Mine Internet," *USA Today*, June 5, 2002; "Music-Swapping Site Kazaa Forges a Deal with Tiscali," *International Herald Tribune*, September 24, 2002; Lev Grossman, "It's All Free," *Time*, May 5, 2003,

60–67; Damien Cave, "Downloading Special: Legal or Not, Digital Music Thrives: How to Get It Online," *Rolling Stone*, no. 941 (February 5, 2004): 16.

11. Richtel, "Entertainment Industry Loses in New Case," *New York Times*, April 26, 2003.

12. Metro-Goldwyn-Mayer v. Grokster, United States Court of Appeals for the Ninth Circuit, no. 03-55894, D.C. No. CV-01-08541-SVW (200), 11746-22747, reproduced at http://www.groklaw.net/pdf/Grokster.pdf.

13. Jeff Goodell, "The Rolling Stone Interview: Steve Jobs," *Rolling Stone*, no. 938–939 (December 25, 2003—January 8, 2004): 31.

14. Goodman, "The Future Is Now"; Goodman, "Will Fans Pay for Music Online? Labels Launch Fee Services," *Rolling Stone*, no. 888 (January 31, 2002): 17–18; Damien Cave, "Napster Troubles Grow," *Rolling Stone*, no. 945 (April 1, 2004): 30.

15. Goodell, "The Rolling Stone Interview: Steve Jobs." Bill Werde summarizes the recording industry's long-term resistance to authorized song sharing in "A Decade in Relief: What the Oughts Wrought," *Billboard*, December 19, 2009, 6.

16. Evan Serpick, "iTunes: 1 Billion Downloads Strong," *Rolling Stone*, no. 996 (March 23, 2006): 12; Brian Hiatt, "The Record Industry Hits Slow Fade," *Rolling Stone*, no. 1029 (June 28, 2007): 13–14.

17. Eric Pfanner, "'Free' Music Downloads, Complete with a Hook," *International Herald Tribune*, August 30, 2006; Evan Serpick, "Digital: Get Music for Free, Legally," *Rolling Stone*, no. 1032 (August 9, 2007): 34; Jeff Leeds and Brad Stone, "Three Record Companies Team Up with MySpace for Music Web Site," *New York Times*, April 4, 2008; Eric Pfanner, "Digital Music Embraces the 'Freebie,'" *International Herald Tribune*, January 19, 2009, 14. On tensions between Jobs and the recording "majors" on the question of the pricing of music downloads, see Johnnie L. Roberts, "Selling Songs for a Song," *Newsweek*, October 17, 2005, 45.

18. Bill Holland, "Piracy Suits: Shock and Awe": (1) "Courts: A Powerful Boost"; (2) "RIAA: Amnesty Nets Calls"; (3) "Congress: Support Grows," all *Billboard*, September 20, 2003, 1, 78.

19. Chris Gaither, "Recording Industry Withdraws Suit; Mistaken Identity Raises Questions on Legal Strategy," *Boston Globe*, September 24, 2003; Eric Bangeman, "I Sue Dead People . . . ," *Ars Technica*, February 4, 2005, http://arstechnica.com/old/content/2005/02/4587.ars; Bangeman, "RIAA Drops File Sharing Case," *Ars Technica*, October 15, 2006, http://arstechnica.com/tech-policy/news/2006/10/7990.ars; Hiatt, "The Record Industry Hits Slow Fade"; Bangeman, "RIAA versus Grandma, Part II: The Showdown That Wasn't," *Ars Technica*, December 16, 2007, http://arstechnica.com/tech-policy/news/2007/12/riaa-versus-grandma-part-ii-the-showdown-that-wasnt.ars; Sarah McBride, "Changing Tack, RIAA Ditches MediaSentry," *Wall Street Journal*, January 5, 2009.

20. David Scharfenberg, "Defying a Music Industry Crackdown," *New York Times*, January 15, 2006; Bangeman, "Son of File-Sharing Defendant Fights Back

against RIAA," *Ars Technica,* January 31, 2007, http://arstechnica.com/tech-policy/news/2007/01/8740.ars; Bangeman, "Judge's Decision Leaves RIAA with Lose-Lose Situation in Elektra v. Santangelo," *Ars Technica,* March 21, 2007, http://arstechnica.com/tech-policy/news/2007/03/judges-decision-leaves-riaa-with-lose-lose-situation-in-elektra-v-santangelo.ars; "Patti Santangelo v. RIAA: The Path of Courage," http://www.p2pnet.net/story/18656; "Santangelo v. RIAA," http://en.wikipedia.org/wiki/Santangelo_v._RIAA.

21. "Capitol Records v. Deborah Foster," http://en.wikipedia.org/wiki/Capitol_Records_v._Deborah_Foster; Bangeman, "Victim of RIAA 'Driftnet' Awarded Attorneys' Fees," *Ars Technica,* February 7, 2007, http://arstechnica.com/old/content/2007/02/8786.ars; Bangeman, "RIAA Appeals Attorneys' Fees Award," *Ars Technica,* February 22, 2007, http://arstechnica.com/old/content/2007/02/8902.ars; "Judge Says RIAA 'Disingenuous,' Decision Stands," *Slashdot,* April 24, 2007, http://yro.slashdot.org/article.pl?sid=07/04/24/177255.

22. Beckerman, "Oregon RIAA Victim Fights Back; Sues RIAA for Electronic Trespass, Violations of Computer Fraud & Abuse, Invasion of Privacy, RICO, Fraud," *Recording Industry vs. the People,* October 3, 2005, http://recordingindustryvspeople.blogspot.com/; Bangeman, "Why the RIAA Doesn't Want Defendants Exonerated," *Ars Technica,* March 29, 2007, http://arstechnica.com/tech-policy/news/2007/03/why-the-riaa-doesnt-want-defendants-exonerated.ars; Bangeman, "Exonerated Defendant Sues RIAA for Malicious Prosecution," *Ars Technica,* March 21, 2007, http://arstechnica.com/tech-policy/news/2007/06/exonerated-defendant-sues-riaa-for-malicious-prosecution.ars; "RIAA Beaten in Court by Tanya Andersen Yet Again," January 17, 2008, http://www.afterdawn.com/news/archive/12599.cfm; Eliot Van Buskirk, "Lawsuit Could Force RIAA to Reveal Secrets," *Listening Post,* March 6, 2008, http://blog.wired.com/music/2008/03/andersen-might.html; Mike Masnick, "Once Again (with Feeling): RIAA Told to Pay Tanya Andersen's Legal Fees," July 28, 2008, http://techdirt.com/articles/20080728/1844461819.shtml.

23. Bangeman, "RIAA Trial Verdict Is In: Jury Finds Thomas Liable for Infringement," *Ars Technica,* October 4, 2007, http://arstechnica.com/tech-policy/news/2007/10/verdict-is-in.ars; Beckerman, "RIAA's $222,000 Verdict in *Capitol v. Thomas* Set Aside; Judge Rejects 'Making Available'; Attacks Excessive Damages," *Recording Industry vs. the People,* September 24, 2008, http://recordingindustryvspeople.blogspot.com/; "Capitol v Thomas Round 3 Scheduled for October," March 5, 2010, http://recordingindustryvspeople.blogspot.com/.

24. Brennon Slattery, "RIAA Stops Suing Individuals: Are We Home Free?" *PC World,* December 19, 2008; Nate Anderson, "No More Lawsuits: ISPs to Work with RIAA, Cut Off P2P Users," *Ars Technica,* December 19, 2008, http://arstechnica.com/tech-policy/news/2008/12/no-more-lawsuits-isps-to-work-with-riaa-cut-off-p2p-users.ars; Sarah McBride, "Changing Tack, RIAA Ditches MediaSentry," *Wall Street Journal,* January 5, 2009.

25. David Chartier, "ISP Tell RIAA Piracy Protection Doesn't Come Free," *Ars Technica*, December 22, 2008, http://arstechnica.com/business/news/2008/12/isp-to-riaa-outsourced-piracy-protection-isnt-free.ars; Linda Greenhouse, "Justices Agree to Hear Case on File Sharing," *New York Times*, December 11, 2004; Jeff Leeds and Steve Lohr, "No Pot of Gold in Court Ruling for the Studios," *New York Times*, June 28, 2005; Leeds, "Grokster Calls It Quits on Sharing Music Files," *New York Times*, November 8, 2005; Bangeman, "Sharman Networks Settles KaZaA File-Sharing Lawsuits," July 27, 2006, *Recording Industry vs. the People*, http://recordingindustryvspeople.blogspot.com/. Rosen presents a legal survey of Napster, Grokster, and other file sharing cases in *Music and Copyright*, 547–74.

26. Kevin J. O'Brien, "E.U. Bolsters Protection for Web Access," *International Herald Tribune*, November 6, 2009.

27. "The Pirate Bay," http://en.wikipedia.org/wiki/The_Pirate_Bay; "The Pirate Bay Trial," http://en.wikipedia.org/wiki/The_Pirate_Bay_trial.

28. "Jammie Thomas Verdict Reduced from $1.92M to $54,000," January 22, 2010; "RIAA Asks for Extensions of Time in Tenenbaum & in Thomas-Rasset Cases," January 28, 2010; "Reported That RIAA Will Ask for a 3rd Trial in Capitol Records v. Thomas," January 29, 2010; "$675,000 Verdict Reduced to $67,500 in Sony v. Tenenbaum," July 9, 2010, all in *Recording Industry vs. the People*, http://recordingindustryvspeople.blogspot.com/.

29. "Rhapsody (Online Music Service)," http://en.wikipedia.org/wiki/Rhapsody_(online_music_service); "Amazon MP3," http://en.wikipedia.org/wiki/Amazon_MP3; "Lala (Website)," http://en.wikipedia.org/wiki/Lala_(website); "Last.fm," http://en.wikipedia.org/wiki/Last.fm; "Spotify," http://en.wikipedia.org/wiki/Spotify.

30. Tom Zeller, Jr., "The Imps of File Sharing May Lose in Court, but They Are Winning in the Marketplace," *New York Times*, July 4, 2005.

CONCLUSION

1. In *Piracy*, Johns fleshes out this big picture. See also a brief essay posted on the Internet, "100 years of Big Content Fearing Technology—in Its Own Words," in which Nate Anderson links together, through a series of quotations, battles over the Gramophone, photocopiers, videocassette recorders, audiocassettes, MP3 players, Napster, digital video recorders, and digital radio and television (October 11, 2009), http://arstechnica.com/tech-policy/news/2009/10/100-years-of-big-content-fearing-technology-in-its-own-words.ars.

2. John Hillery and Niccolo Pantucci, "The U.S. Escalates Its WTO Complaint against China," *CSIS Commentary*, August 31, 2007, http://csis.org/files/media/csis/pubs/070831_chinawto.pdf.

3. Joseph Plambeck, "Lyric Sites at Center of Fight Over Royalties," *International Herald Tribune*, May 9, 2010.

# BIBLIOGRAPHY

*The bibliography is arranged as follows:*

## PRIMARY SOURCES

### Court Records and Government Publications

CASES AT THE NATIONAL ARCHIVES AND RECORDS ADMINISTRATION

*NARA—Great Lakes.* Records of the U.S. District Court, Northern District, Eastern Division (Chicago), Record Group 21, Records of U.S. District and Circuit Courts, the National Archives and Records Administration—Great Lakes Region (Chicago).

United States of America vs. Morris Cohen and G. A. Manteuffel, indictment, March 1930, Criminal Case 21267.

*NARA—Northeast—NJ.* U.S. District Court for the District of New Jersey. Record Group 21, Records of U.S. District and Circuit Courts, National Archives and Records Administration—Northeast Region (New York City).

United States of America vs. James Herron, 1931, Criminal Case 3178b.

United States of America vs. E. Burke, 1936, Criminal Case 7645b.

United States of America vs. Morris Abrams, alias Morris Abromovitz, 1938, Criminal Case 8545b.

United States of America vs. Dominick William Castaldo, Dominick Mancini, John Santangelo (with aliases), 1939, Criminal Case 8801b.

United States of America vs. Dominick William Castaldo; Dominick Mancini, alias Frank DePetre, etc.; John Santangelo, alias John Amoretti, etc; John Pomyanicki, alias Joey Pomyanicki; John Iannini, 1940, Criminal Case 15c.

United States of America vs. Philip Resnikoff, Defendant, 1941, Criminal Case C109-228.

*NARA—Northeast—NY.* U.S. District Court for the Southern District of New York. Record Group 21, Records of U.S. District and Circuit Courts, National Archives and Records Administration—Northeast Region (New York City).

United States of America vs. Samuel A. Cohen, vs. Morris Shapiro and Samuel A. Cohen, and vs. Harry B. Paul, all 1930, respectively, Criminal Cases C68-519, C68-520, and C68-521.

United States of America vs. Theodore Aaronson alias "Puggy," 1934, Criminal Case C96-263.

United States of America, Plaintiff, vs. Theodore Aaronson, alias Puggy, alias Joe Davis, 1936, Criminal Case 99-217.

Donaldson, Douglas & Gumble, Inc., Schuster & Miller, Inc., Southern Music Pub. Co. Inc., Plaintiffs, vs. United Magazine Supply, Inc., Defendant, 1937–38, Civil Action E-85-82.

United States of America vs. James Preziosa and Tony Costello, Defendants, 1941, Criminal Case C-109-151.

United States of America vs. Fernando Costa, Alexander Aliani, John Doe, alias Sammy, alias Flash, Thomas Bruce, Ciro Salerno, Matthew S. Peters, Frank Kane, George Dacyenski, Walter Kynsky, and Benjamin Miller, Defendants, 1941–44, Criminal Case C110-237.

*NARA—Pacific.* Records of the U.S. District Court, Southern District of California, Central Division (Los Angeles), Record Group 21, Records of U.S. District and Circuit Courts, the National Archives and Records Administration—Pacific Region (Laguna Niguel)

United States of America vs. Joseph Tinit, alias Joe Tint, alias Joe Mann, alias Joe Kini, July 1930, Criminal Case 10079.

United States of America vs. Al Friedman (alias Ellis Friedman, alias Frank Miller), William Zimmer (alias William Zimmerman), Alexander Aggie, Al Barbour (alias Bert Barbour), Jimmie Jackson, James Gilligan, and George Liebercranz (alias George W. Lieber, alias George Roxey), 1932, Criminal Case 10910.

United States of America vs. Al Friedman (alias Alex Freedman), William M. Zimmer, Leo Zickel, and Al Barber (alias Bert Barber, alias George Barbee), 1932, Criminal Case 11029.

United States of America vs. Alexander Aggie, 1932, Criminal Case 11019.

NARA—*Textual Archives.* Records of the Supreme Court of the District of Columbia (Washington), Record Group 21, Records of U.S. District and Circuit Courts, the National Archives and Records Administration—Textual Archives Services Division, Old Military and Civil Records (Washington).

United States vs. Joe Ansbetino, alias Joe Dagostino, 1931, Criminal Case file number 50600.

United States vs. Abe Schrott, 1931, Criminal Case file number 50601.

### NINETEENTH-CENTURY SONG SHEETS

"America Singing: Nineteenth-Century Song Sheets" is an archival collection in the "American Memory" section of the Rare Book and Special Collections Division of the Library of Congress. For the Internet guide to this collection, see http://memory.loc.gov/ammem/amsshtml/amsshome.html.

### DESCRIPTION OF A BOOTLEG SONG SHEET

People v. Samuels et al., Court of Special Sessions, City of New York, Appellate Part, First Department, June 3, 1941, *New York Supplement Second Series* 28, N.Y.S.2d, 114. St. Paul, Minn.: West, 1941.

### STIPULATIONS AGAINST SONG SHEETS

*Federal Trade Commission Decisions* 15. Washington, D.C.: Government Printing Office, 1933. #915 and #916, 523–24.

*Federal Trade Commission Decisions* 16. Washington, D.C.: Government Printing Office, 1933. #936, 550–51.

### TEXTS OF U.S. CONSPIRACY LAWS

*Revised Statues of the United States, §5440.* 2nd. ed., 1055. Washington, D.C.: Government Printing Office, 1878.

*The Statutes at Large of the United States of America, §37* 25, pt. 1, 1096. Washington, D.C.: Government Printing Office, 1909.

*The Code of the Laws of the United States of America of a General and Permanent Character, §88* 44, pt. 1, 465. Washington, D.C.: Government Printing Office, 1926.

*United States Code, 1940 Edition, Containing the General and Permanent Laws of the United States, §88* 2, 1533. Washington, D.C.: Government Printing Office, 1941..

*United States Code Annotated: Title 18: Crimes and Criminal Procedure, §§331 to 400* 41. St. Paul, Minn.: West, 1987.

### PARODY AND SONGS

Robbins Music Corporation et al. v. Song Parodies, Inc., et al. Supreme Court. Special Term. New York County. October 27, 1942. *New York Supplement Second Series* 38, N.Y.S.2d, 223–24. St. Paul, Minn.: West, 1943.

F.E.L. Publications, Ltd., v. Catholic Bishop of Chicago, 754 F.2d 216, 225 U.S.P.Q. 278, *Decisions of the United States Courts Involving Copyright, 1985*. Washington, D.C.: Copyright Office, 1985. http://cases.justia.com/us-court-of-appeals/F2/754/216/319020/.

Dennis J. Fitzpatrick, doing business as F.E.L. Publications, v. Catholic Bishop of Chicago, 916 F.2d 1254, *Decisions of the United States Courts Involving Copyright, 1990*. Washington, D.C.: Copyright Office, 1990. http://cases.justia.com/us-court-of-appeals/F2/916/1254/208102.

PHONOGRAPH RECORD PIRACY

Shapiro, Bernstein & Co., Inc., et. al, v. H. L. Green Company, Inc., and Jalen Amusement Company, Inc., no. 294, Docket 27979, U.S. Court of Appeals Second Circuit, 1963. http://cases.justia.com/us-court-of-appeals/F2/316/304/187450/.

### Bootleg Song Sheets

Newspaper-sized bootleg song sheets, including the *Songland Herald*, were entered into evidence in United States of America vs. Al Friedman et. al., Criminal Case 10910 (see above, Court Documents, *NARA—Pacific*).

The bootleg song-sheet magazine *Paramount Book No. 17* is preserved from Donaldson, Douglas & Gumble et. al. vs. United Magazine Supply (see above, Court Documents, *NARA—Northeast—NY*).

Otherwise the bootleg and quasi-bootleg publications cited below are from my own collection, acquired in the course of writing this book. I will be donating these periodicals to the Sibley Library, Eastman School of Music, at the conclusion of the project. They appeared under the following titles between the years 1932 and 1941:

*American*
*Big Song Magazine* (New York)
*Broadcast Song Hits* (New York)
*Continental*
*Latest Songs*
*Prosperity*

### Newspapers, Trade Papers, and Entertainment and Music Magazines

*ARS Technica* (http://arstechnica.com)
*ASCAP Today* (New York)
*Audio* (New York)
*The Billboard* (New York); from January 9, 1961, *Billboard: the International Music-Record Newsweekly*; from June 7, 1969, *Billboard: The International Music-Record-Tape Newsweekly*

Boston Globe

*CSIS Commentary* (Center for Strategic and International Studies; Washington, D.C.)

*Crescendo and Jazz Music* (London)

*Down Beat* (Chicago)

*The Flutist Quarterly: The Official Magazine of the National Flute Association* (Royal Oak, Mich.)

*Harper's Magazine* (New York)

*High Fidelity and Musical America* (Great Barrington, Mass.)

*Hit Parader* (Derby, Conn.)

*The Instrumentalist* (Glen Ellyn, Ill.)

*International Herald Tribune* (Paris)

*ITG Journal* (International Trumpet Guild; Nashville, Tenn.)

*Listening Post* (http://blog.wired.com/music)

*Melody Maker* (London)

*Music Clubs Magazine* (Indianapolis, Ind.)

*The Music Scene* (Don Mills, Ontario, Canada)

*Music Trades* (Englewood, N.J.)

*The NATS Bulletin* (National Association of Teachers of Singing; Oberlin, Ohio)

*Newsweek* (New York)

*New York Times*

*NSOA Bulletin* (National School Orchestra Association; Terre Haute, Indiana)

*PC World* (San Francisco)

*Percussive Notes* (Urbana, Ill.)

*Popular Song Hits* (Evanston, Ill.)

*Radio Hit Songs* (Derby, Conn.)

*Rolling Stone* (San Francisco)

*The School Musician, Director & Teacher* (Joliet, Ill.)

*Slashdot* (http://yro.slashdot.org)

*Song Hit Folio* (Dunellen, N.J.)

*Song Hits* (Dunellen, N.J.)

*Song Parade: America's Foremost Lyric Magazine* (New York)

*Spin* (New York)

*Techdirt* (http://techdirt.com)

*Time* (New York)

*United Mine Workers Journal* (Indianapolis)

*USA Today* (Arlington, Va.)

*Variety* (New York)

*Wall Street Journal*

*Washington Post*

## Oral Histories

Golson, Benny. Interviewed by Anthony Brown. September 23–24, 2008. Smithsonian Jazz Oral History Program. Repository: Archives Center, National Museum of American History.

Hendricks, Jon. Interviewed by James Zimmerman. August 17–18, 1995. Smithsonian Jazz Oral History Program. Repository: Archives Center, National Museum of American History.

## SECONDARY SOURCES

"About HFA" (the Harry Fox Agency). http://www.harryfox.com/public/HFAHome.jsp.

Barbrook, Richard. "Melodies or Rhythms? The Competition for the Greater London FM Radio Licence." *Popular Music* 9, no. 2 (April 1990): 203–19.

Beckerman, Ray. "Recording Industry vs. the People" (2004– ). http://recordingindustryvspeople.blogspot.com/.

Begun, Semi J. *Magnetic Recording*. New York: McGraw Hill, 1949.

Bishop, Jack. "Forum: Who Are the Pirates? The Politics of Piracy, Poverty, and Greed in a Globalized Music Market." *Popular Music and Society* 27 (February 2004): 101–6.

Browne, Donald R. *Electronic Media and Industrialized Nations: A Comparative Study.* Ames: Iowa State University Press, 1999.

Brylawski, E. Fulton, and Abe Goldman, eds. and comps. *Legislative History of the 1909 Copyright Act.* South Hackensack, N.J.: Fred B. Rothman & Co., 1976.

"Call and Response: A Discussion about Napster." *Journal of Popular Music Studies* 13 (2001): 93–102.

Chapman, Robert. *Selling the Sixties: The Pirates and Pop Music Radio.* London: Routledge, 1992.

Coase, R. H. *British Broadcasting: A Study in Monopoly.* London, New York, and Toronto: London School of Economics and Political Science, 1950.

Cohen, Julie E. "Creativity and Culture in Copyright Theory." *UC Davis Law Review* 40 (2007): 1151–1205.

Cooke, Jon B., and Christopher Irving. "The Charlton Empire: A Brief History of the Derby, Connecticut Publisher." http://www.twomorrows.com/comicbookartist/articles/09empire.html.

d'Haenens, Leen, and Frieda Saeys, eds. *Western Broadcasting at the Dawn of the 21st Century.* Berlin and New York: Mouton de Gruyter, 2001.

Douglas, Guy. "Copyright and Peer-to-Peer Music File Sharing: The Napster Case and the Argument against Legislative Reform." *Murdoch University Electronic Journal of Law.* http://www.murdoch.edu.au/elaw/issues/v11n1/douglas111_text.html.

Emery, Walter B. "Five European Broadcasting Systems." *Journalism Monographs* 1 (August 1966): 21–38.

Fisher, Marc. *Something in the Air: Radio, Rock, and the Revolution That Shaped a Generation*. New York: Random House, 2007.

Frith, Simon, ed., *Music and Copyright*. Edinburgh: University of Edinburgh Press, 1993.

Foege, Alec. "The Future of Digital Music: Free Music and the Death of the Album." *Spin* 16 (September 2000): 164.

Garofalo, Reebee. *Rockin' Out: Popular Music in the USA*. 3rd. ed. Upper Saddle River, N.J.: Prentice Hall, 2004.

Gilbert, Douglas. *Lost Songs: The Diverting Story of American Popular Songs*. Garden City, N.Y.: Doubleday, Doran and Co., 1942.

Gillespie, Tarleton. *Wired Shut: Copyright and the Shape of Digital Culture*. Cambridge, Mass., and London: MIT, 2007.

Gneezy, Uri, and Aldo Rustichini. "A Fine Is a Price." *Journal of Legal Studies* 29 (January 2000): 1–17.

Hamm, Charles. *Yesterdays: Popular Song in America*. New York and London: Norton, 1979.

Heller, James S. "Copyright, Fair Use, and the For-Profit Sector." *Information Outlook* (May 2002). Reproduced at http://findarticles.com/p/articles/mi_m0FWE/is_5 _6/ai_85880884.

Heylin, Clinton. *Bootleg: The Secret History of the Other Recording Industry*. New York: St. Martin's, 1994.

"The History of Magnetic Recording." http://www.bbc.co.uk/dna/h2g2/A3224936.

Hitchcock, H. Wiley, and Stanley Sadie, eds. *The New Grove Dictionary of American Music*. London: Macmillan, 1986.

"How the CD Was Developed." http://news.bbc.co.uk/2/hi/technology/6950933.stm.

Jankowski, Nick, Ole Prehn, and James Stappers, eds. *The People's Voice: Local Radio and Television in Europe*. London: John Libby, 1992.

Johns, Adrian. *Death of a Pirate: British Radio and the Making of the Information Age*. New York and London: W. W. Norton, 2010.

———. *Piracy: The Intellectual Property Wars from Gutenberg to Gates*. Chicago and London: University of Chicago Press, 2009.

Katz, Mark. *Capturing Sound: How Technology Has Changed Music*. Berkeley, Los Angeles, and London: University of California Press, 2004.

Kernfeld, Barry. "John Coltrane in Rudy van Gelder's Studio." *Names and Numbers*, no. 33 (April 2005): 2–7; no. 34 (July 2005): 3–9, 14–15.

———, ed. *The New Grove Dictionary of Jazz*. London: Macmillan, 1988; 2nd. ed. 2001.

———. *The Story of Fake Books: Bootlegging Songs to Musicians*. Lanham, Md., Toronto, and Oxford: Scarecrow, 2006.

"Key Court Case Summaries on Fair Use." http://www.copyright.iupui.edu/FU
summaries.htm.

Kleinsteuber, Hans J., Denis McQuail, and Karen Siune, eds. *Electronic Media and Politics in Western Europe.* Frankfurt and New York: Campus Verlag, 1986.

Kot, Greg. *Ripped: How the Wired Generation Revolutionized Music.* New York: Scribner, 2009.

Krieger, Susan. *Hip Capitalism.* Beverly Hills, Calif., and London: Sage, 1979.

Leonard, Mike. *From International Waters: Sixty Years of Offshore Broadcasting.* Heswal, U.K.: Forest, 1996.

Manard, Ralph H. "World's Largest Publisher of Song Magazines." *New England Printer and Lithographer,* November 1954, 49–53, 56.

Mann, Charles C. "The Heavenly Jukebox." *Atlantic Monthly* 286 (September 2000): 39–42, 44–46, 48–50, 52–54, 56–59.

Marshall, Lee. *Bootlegging: Romanticism and Copyright in the Music Industry.* London, Thousand Oaks, Calif., and New Delhi: Sage, 2005.

Markstein, Donald M. "Charlton Comics." http://www.toonpedia.com/charlton.htm. 2003.

"MLA: Copyright for Music Librarians." http://www.lib.jmu.edu/org/mla/Guidelines/Accepted_Guidelines/Educational_Photocopying.aspx.

Parkes, Jim. "The Laser Story." *Offshore Echo's Magazine,* comp. Chris Story. Reprint, http://www.cwgsy.net/rivate/offshorepirateradio/laser1.html.

Partridge, Robert. "Rock and the BBC." *Melody Maker.* June 23, 1973, 14; June 30, 1973, 10.

Paulu, Burton. *Radio and Television Broadcasting on the European Continent.* Minneapolis: University of Minnesota Press, 1967.

"Photocopying for Educational Purposes." http://www.vpul.upenn.edu/osl/photocpy.html.

"Q&A Concerning Copyright Compliance for Print and Software." http://www.wsubooks.com/store1/wichita/copyright.htm.

Rosen, Ronald S. *Music and Copyright.* Oxford and New York: Oxford University Press, 2008.

Sanjek, Russell. *From Print to Plastic: Publishing and Promoting America's Popular Music (1900–1980).* Brooklyn, N.Y.: Institute for Studies in American Music, 1983.

———. *American Popular Music and Its Business: The First Four Hundred Years.* New York, and Oxford: Oxford University Press, 1988.

Sargoy, Edward A. "Rescinding the Supreme Court's Rules for Copyright Procedure under Sec. 101, Title 17." *Bulletin of the Copyright Society of the U.S.A.* 9 (1962): 355.

Sears, Richard S. *V-disks: A History and Discography.* Westport, Conn., and London: Greenwood, 1980.

Shapiro, Andrew L. *The Control Revolution: How the Internet Is Putting Individuals in Charge and Changing the World We Know.* New York: Century Foundation, 1999.

Shirky, Clay. *Cognitive Surplus: Creativity and Generosity in a Connected Age.* New York: Penguin, 2010.

Slezak, Mary. "The History of Charlton Press, Inc., and Its Song Lyric Periodicals." *Journal of American Culture* 3 (1980): 184–94.

Sparkman, Steven L. "Tape Pirates: The New 'Buck'-aneer\$." *Copyright Law Symposium,* vol. 21, 98–123. New York and London: Columbia University Press, 1974.

Sterne, Jonathan. "The mp3 as Cultural Artifact." *New Media & Society* 8 (2006): 825–42.

Street, Seán. *A Concise History of British Radio, 1922–2002.* Tiverton, U.K.: Kelly Publications, 2002.

Thornton, Mark. *The Economics of Prohibition.* Salt Lake City: University of Utah, 1991.

Towe, Teri Noel. "Record Piracy." *Copyright Law Symposium,* vol. 22, 243–77. New York and London: Columbia University Press, 1977.

Tschmuck, Peter. *Creativity and Innovation in the Music Industry.* English trans. by Marco Abel. Dordrecht: Springer, 2006.

"U.S. Industry Profile: Phonograph Records and Prerecorded Audio Tapes and Disks (SIC 3652)." http://www.answers.com/topic/phonograph-records-and-prerecorded-audio-tapes-and-disks.

Vaidhyanathan, Siva. *The Anarchist in the Library: How the Clash between Freedom and Control Is Hacking the Real World and Crashing the System.* New York: Basic Books, 2004.

———. *Copyright and Copywrongs: The Rise of Intellectual Property and How It Threatens Creativity.* New York: New York University Press, 2001.

"Vintage Audio History." http://www.videointerchange.com/audio_history.htm.

"Welcome, Mighty KSAN, the Jive 95!" http://www.jive95.com.

Witmark, Isadore, with Isaac Goldberg. *The Story of the House of Witmark: From Ragtime to Swingtime.* New York: L. Furman, 1939.

Woodworth, Griffin Mead. "Hackers, Users, and Suits: Napster and Representations of Identity." *Popular Music and Society* 27 (June 2004): 161–84.

Yoder, Andrew. *Pirate Radio Stations.* 3rd ed. New York: McGraw-Hill, 2002.

# INDEX

—parodies of copyrighted songs, 34
—protection of "live" recordings vs. studio recordings, 179, 181–82
—provisions for licensing recordings and radio broadcasts, 21, 23, 37, 45, 48–49, 73–74, 88–89, 97–101, 103–4, 107–9, 112, 114, 116, 121, 129–32, 152, 159–61, 164–65, 183, 188–89
—public domain, 20, 138, 159, 180–81, 188
—scholarship, 9–12
—"similar use" clause, 163–65
—vs. transformative use, 5–8, 223n4
*Cotton Club Parade*, 58
counterfeiting, terminological distinctions in usage of the term, 163–64, 174, 191–95. *See also under* audiocassettes; cartridge tapes; compact discs; phonograph records and players
Cousino, Bernard, 151, 153
Craig, Francis, 132
Crawford, Allen, 113, 115
Creedence Clearwater Revival, 158
"Cry," 134

dance mix. *See* equivalency vs. transformational use: unauthorized anthologies and compilations
Danmarks Radio (DR), 100–101, 108, 111
*Dark Side of the Moo, The*, 177
*Dark Side of the Moon, The*, 177
Decca, 106, 134, 154
Deep Purple, 166
"Ding-a-Ling," 136
Dion and the Belmonts, 136
disobedience and criminality, 8–9
*Divine Miss M, The*, 165
DJ mix. *See* equivalency vs. transformational use: unauthorized anthologies and compilations
DR (Danmarks Radio), 100–101, 108, 111
Dub, 171, 175–77
"Duelin' Banjos," 84

Dutch Marine Offenses Act, 113, 119
Dylan, Bob, 158, 167, 171, 175–76, 189

Eglise (English), Charles, 135
EMI, 188, 208, 210–11
Engel, Lyle, 49, 51
Engel–van Wiseman, Incorporated, 41
equivalency vs. transformational use: album bootlegging, in, 171–74; artistic control, 142, 172–74, 201–2, 205–6, 249n3; audiocassettes, in uses of, 142, 150, 155–57; cartridges, in uses of, 142, 151–54; compact discs, in uses of, 182–83; copyright, relationship to, 6–8; fake books, in uses of, 73–76, 78; functionality, 53–54, 56–57, 85–87, 156–57, 182–83, 201; general characteristics of, 4–8, 217–21; interpersonal use, 56–57; vs. legal conception of "transformative use," 7–8; mobility, 56–57, 142, 150, 249n3; musical exploration, 202–3; organization, 73–76; personalization (or "singles listening" and "solitary listening"), 201–2, 249n3; photocopying, in uses of, 81, 85–87; portability, 56–57, 75–76, 148–49, 203, 231n6; recordings, in duplicating, 125–27, 133–34, 138; sheet music, in uses of, 26; song sharing, in uses of, 201–5; song sheets, in uses of, 53–57; unauthorized anthologies and compilations, 5, 9, 142, 160–62, 167, 178, 180–81, 201
European ethnicity and song sheets, 63–68

fake books: bootlegging and piracy, 76–80; jazz, 79–80; pop music, 73–79; transformational use of, 73–76, 78
Fanning, Shawn, 183, 205–6
FBI. *See* Federal Bureau of Investigation (FBI)